Islam, Nationalism and Democracy

A Political Biography of Mohammad Natsir

Mohammad Natsir.

Islam, Nationalism and Democracy

A Political Biography of Mohammad Natsir

Audrey R. Kahin

NUS PRESS
SINGAPORE

Published by:

NUS Press
National University of Singapore
AS3-01-02, 3 Arts Link
Singapore 117569

Fax: (65) 6774-0652
E-mail: nusbooks@nus.edu.sg
Website: http://www.nus.edu.sg/nuspress

ISBN 978-9971-69-571-2 (Paper)

National Library Board, Singapore Cataloguing-in-Publication Data

Kahin, Audrey.
    Islam, nationalism and democracy: a political biography of Mohammad Natsir / Audrey R. Kahin. – Singapore: NUS Press, c2012.
    p. cm.
    Includes bibliographical references and index.
    ISBN: 978-9971-69-571-2 (pbk.)

    1. Natsir, M.,1908–1993. 2. Ex-prime ministers – Indonesia – Biography. 3. Politicians – Indonesia – Biography. 4. Muslim scholars – Indonesia – Biography. 5. Islam and politics – Indonesia. 6. Islam and state – Indonesia. 7. Indonesia – Politics and government – 20th century. I. Title.

DS644.1
959.803092 -- dc22   OCN742519241

Typeset by: Forum, Kuala Lumpur, Malaysia

Contents

Maps

Illustrations

Acknowledgements

I am grateful to the many people who have helped me over the years I have been working on this biography. Above all, I would like to thank Mohammad Natsir's children (Fauzie Natsir, Sitti Moechliesah [Lies], Asma Faridah [Ida] and Hasnah Faizah [Has]), who gave freely of their time and made materials in their possession available to me, including the photographs in this book. (I regret I was unable to meet with Aisyatu Asri.). Their generosity and patience are greatly appreciated.

I would also like to thank Prof. Burhan Magenda and his wife Janti for providing me with a home and warm hospitality during my time in Jakarta, and Dr. Azmi and Dr. Buchari Nurdin who were, as always, of invaluable assistance when I visited West Sumatra. I also owe a great debt to the late Dr. Deliar Noer, who shared with me over the years his deep understanding of political developments in the Indonesian Muslim community and many memories of his long association with Mohammad Natsir. Also in Indonesia I would like to thank the many people who spoke to me of Natsir and were willing to share their recollections of him. Their names appear in the footnotes to the text.

Thanks also go to Benedict Anderson, who read first drafts of the early chapters and gave me valuable advice, and especially to Greg Fealy who alerted me to important materials on Islamic movements in Indonesia and whose constructive criticisms helped make this a better book. Among other people who helped me in different ways in preparing this book for publication, I would like to thank Ben Abel, Merle Ricklefs, William Tuchrello, Arifin Pramono, Paul Kratoska and Lena Qua.

Any errors of fact or interpretation are, of course, completely my responsibility.

Introduction

In late September 1961, Mohammad Natsir crouched on a hillside in the interior of Sumatra accompanied by fewer than ten followers. The man who a decade earlier had served as Indonesia's prime minister and head of its largest political party knew that all his options had now vanished. He had just learned that his long-time friend Dahlan Djambek, the last military commander to stay on to protect him, was dead — gunned down on September 13 in a nearby village as he prepared to be arrested by government troops. Several weeks previously Natsir had sent his own family back to Bukittinggi, and his other military and civilian companions in the anti-Soekarno rebellion had already taken advantage of the president's promise of amnesty to "return to the motherland (*ibu pertiwi*)." At that time Natsir had warned Djambek not to surrender, as he knew that Communist activists among the government troops wanted to kill them both — the rebels' two strongest Muslim leaders, who over the past months had intensified their verbal attacks on the Communists in an effort to alienate more Muslims from the Soekarno government. But Djambek disregarded Natsir's advice and was now dead. Nearly four years before, Natsir had fled Indonesia's capital city of Jakarta to join with the regional rebels. He had lost the gamble he made at that time and was now faced, if not with death, then with imprisonment and humiliation.

That was probably the nadir of his life. But Natsir's whole history, both before and after his years as a rebel, was marked perhaps more by disappointments and failures than by triumphs. And contradictions.

Tracing the course of Natsir's career raises questions concerning not only his personality and beliefs but also the history of the country and the religion that formed the center of his life. Principal among the disputes that have arisen over the eighteen years since his death has been: how did a man who in the 1940s and 1950s was perceived as one of the most broad-minded and pro-Western Muslim thinkers and politicians come to be viewed forty years later as leading Islam's most rigid and narrow faction? Robert Hefner has written that toward the end of his life Natsir headed the ultra conservative stream of the former Masjumi political party, adding: "the Natsir group came to emphasize not merely the shariah-mindedness of Masyumi conservatives but the strict anti-cosmopolitan Islamism of the urban poor and lumpen-middle class."[1] Had Natsir changed, or merely the society around him? Or did he encompass within himself characteristics that combine these apparently contradictory assessments? Alternatively, were perceptions of him incorrect either when he led the Indonesian government in its first year of complete independence or when in his old age he was a thorn in the side of the Suharto regime and of those middle-class and intellectual Muslims who tried to accommodate with it and with the Indonesian society of the late 20th century? In forging ties with, and gaining immense prestige in the Muslim world of the Middle East, did Natsir perceive the shortcomings of the societies of that region and the dangers for Indonesia in the introduction of their ideas?

Inherent in these questions is another more current dispute: how far was the *da'wah* organization that Natsir founded and headed after the Suharto regime forbade his re-entry into politics in 1967 a breeding ground for radical Islamist movements that developed in Indonesia and are seen as responsible for the acts of terror that plagued the country in the early years of the 21st century?[2]

In tracing the course of Natsir's life, I will attempt to address, if not answer, these questions, some of which are also applicable to many members of the modernist Islamic movement that greatly influenced political thinkers in colonial countries in the first half of the 20th century. Seen as narrow and radical and the source of Islamic terrorism in the early 21st century, modernist or reformist Islam had earlier been viewed as the major stream adapting Muslim thought to the modern technological age and was thus often disparaged as too accommodative to Western ideas and practices. And it should be remembered that, though Natsir was one of the leading Islamic leaders in Indonesia of the second half of the 20th century, his formal education was almost purely in Western-stream institutions and his religious learning, though deep and widespread, was largely informal.

Any biography of Natsir must also assess his responses to the major political and social upheavals in Indonesia that occurred during his lifetime:

---

[1] See Robert W. Hefner, *Civil Islam* (Princeton: Princeton University Press, 2000), pp. 103, 105.

[2] See, for example, ICG Asia Report No. 63, *Jemaah Islamiyah in South East Asia: Damaged but Still Dangerous* (August 26, 2003), pp. 2–4. There are also writers who charge that one of the Masjumi's successor parties, the Partai Keadilan Sejahtera (PKS, Justice Prosperity Party), is also far more radical than it appears, and accuse it of ties to Osama bin Laden's El Qaeda. See Sadanand Dhume, "Radicals March on Indonesia's Future," *Far Eastern Economic Review* 168, 5 (May 2005): 11–26.

born and educated under Dutch colonial rule he was already a recognized intellectual and teacher at the time of the Japanese occupation and the anti-Dutch Revolution; almost by chance he became a politician, rising to head the newly independent government and to lead Indonesia's largest Islamic party throughout the period of parliamentary democracy; under Soekarno's Guided Democracy of the late 1950s Natsir joined anti-government rebels in a regional rebellion that encompassed large parts of the islands of Sumatra and Sulawesi, spending nearly four years in the Sumatran jungle and the following six in jail; while initially welcoming the advent of the military regime known as the "New Order," he became, in the 1970s and 1980s, one of the most prominent critics of the increasingly autocratic dictatorship of General Suharto. He died five years before the overthrow of that regime.

Before attempting to relate this history, I should outline the background to my interest in writing this biography. On my first visit to Indonesia in 1967 I accompanied my husband, George Kahin, who had been a good friend of Natsir since they first met in Yogyakarta nearly twenty years earlier, during the Revolution for Indonesian independence. Natsir struck me as an unusual leader at the time, displaying integrity, modesty, warmth and kindness, as well as clearly attracting deep devotion from his many followers. My husband had long been planning to publish a collection of Natsir's writings in translation, a project that had been postponed because of Natsir's period in the jungle and then in detention. In preparing an introduction for the proposed volume of his writings, and also for early research on a book George and I were contemplating on American involvement in the regional rebellion,[3] I accompanied my husband for a series of eight long interviews with Natsir at his house in Jakarta in the first half of 1971. I took verbatim notes of these interviews, and much of my understanding of Natsir's thinking is based on them. In addition, I have drawn from earlier interviews we conducted in 1967, and some I myself had with Natsir in 1976 in connection with my research on the 20th-century history of West Sumatra. (I have also consulted my husband's interviews with Natsir in the 1940s and early 1950s.)

My interest in writing on Natsir is also grounded in my own research on the Minangkabau region of West Sumatra, where Natsir was born and brought up and which affected his thinking and attitudes throughout his life. As I carried out research for my dissertation on the history of the independence

---

[3] This was eventually published as *Subversion as Foreign Policy: The Secret Eisenhower and Dulles Debacle in Indonesia* (New York: The New Press, 1995). The volume of translations of Natsir's collected writings was never completed.

struggle in the Minangkabau, I became aware of the mingling of nationalist and religious thought in the local movements that sought to free Indonesia from Dutch colonial rule.[4] These are characteristics also seen in Natsir's own political development.

In writing this biography, however, I became conscious of the depth of Natsir's understanding of the history and philosophy of Islam, which was the center of his life, and a realization that I could not deal adequately with that aspect of his thinking. This, then, is a biography that started from interest in Natsir's position in Indonesian society in the early years of the Suharto regime and a fascination with the history of his home region. Its primary focus is not Natsir's philosophical and religious development, but rather the political questions that absorbed his public life, addressing religious matters only with reference to their influence upon his political history and that of Indonesia.

---

[4] See my *Rebellion to Integration: West Sumatra and the Indonesian Polity* (Amsterdam: University of Amsterdam Press, 1999), chapters 1–6.

N
South China Sea
PACIFIC OCEAN
Strait of Malacca
Banda Aceh
ACEH
Medan
MALAYSIA
SUMATRA
Minangkabau Region
RIAU
SINGAPORE
Padang
Jambi
Palembang
Bengkulu
KALIMANTAN
Amuntai
Menado
SULAWESI
MALUKU
Ambon
Banda Neira
Makassar
NEW GUINEA
WEST IRIAN/ PAPUA
Boven Digul
INDIAN OCEAN
Jakarta (Batavia)
Linggajati
Surabaya
Bandung
JAVA
Yogyakarta
Solo/Surakarta
Malang
Madiun
BALI
SUMBAWA
FLORES
TIMOR
0
400
800km

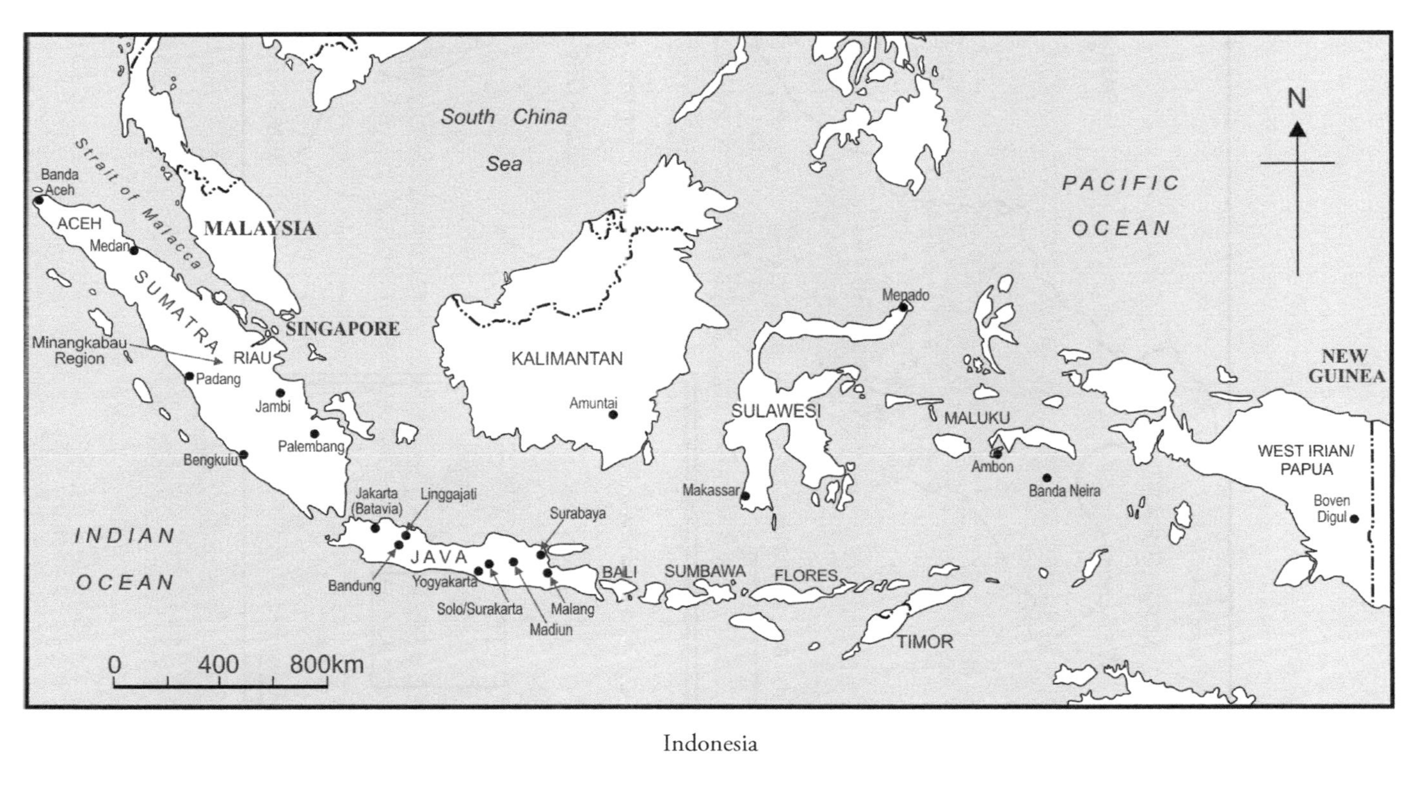

Indonesia

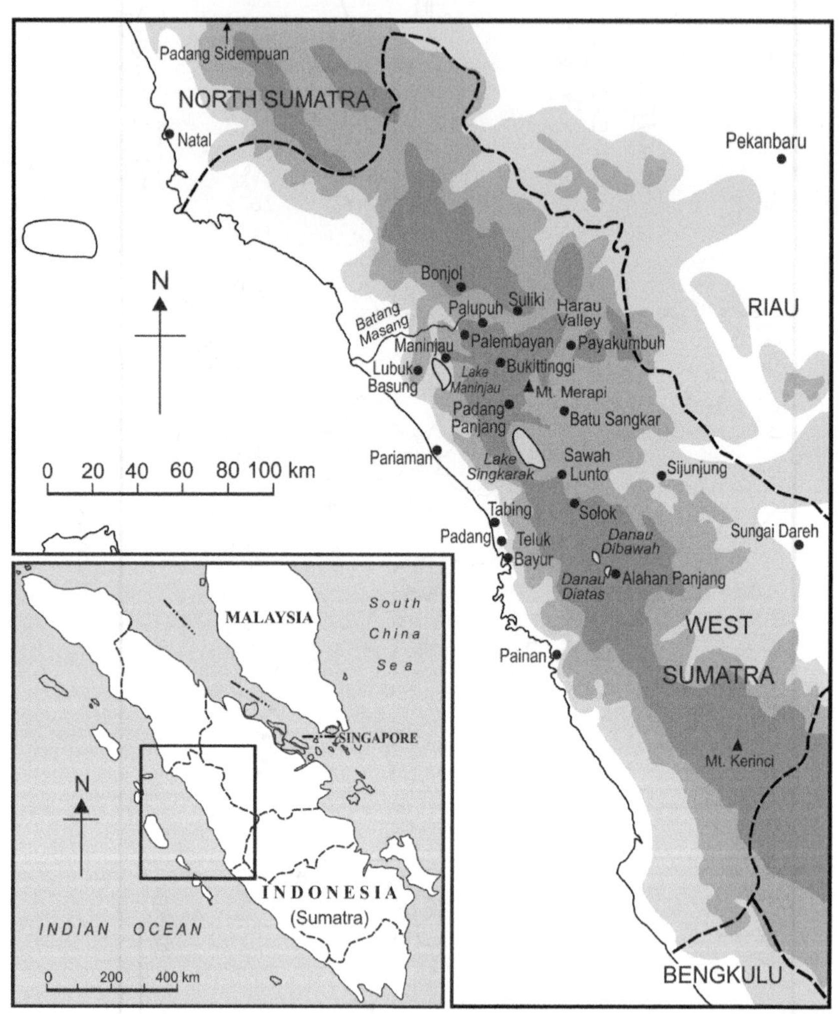

West Sumatra

1

Childhood, Education and Influence from his Minangkabau Homeland[1]

Mohammad Natsir was born on July 17, 1908, in the small town of Alahan Panjang, which lies in the foothills of Sumatra's highest mountain, Mt. Kerinci (3,805 meters), in the southern part of what was then the Dutch Governorship of Sumatra's West Coast. Stretching across the equator, West Sumatra is home to the Minangkabau people who term the region "the Minangkabau world" (*alam Minangkabau*). The heartland of this world lies in the fertile interior highlands of central Sumatra where the Minangkabau people traditionally lived in self-governing extended villages (*nagari*). From their ancestral home area they migrated both to the narrow plain that stretches down Sumatra's western coastline for some three hundred kilometers, and also to the cosmopolitan trading world of east Sumatra bordering on the Strait of Malacca. From these

---

[1] Much of the material in this chapter is drawn from the account of his childhood given by Natsir in letters sent to his own children in 1958, which they collected under the title *Kumpulan Surat-Surat Pribadi*. Most words within quotation marks in this chapter come from these letters and I am grateful to the Natsir family for letting me have a copy of them. The letters were later published in a book that Natsir's children brought out in 2008 in memory of their father, *Aba: M. Natsir sebagai Cahaya Keluarga*, ed. Raja Juli Antoni (Jakarta: Yayasan Capita Selecta, 2008). I have also drawn on Ajip Rosidi, *M. Natsir: Sebuah Biografi* 1 (Jakarta: PTGirimukti Pasaka, 1990), pp. 145ff, Mohammad Natsir, *Politik Melalui Jalur Dakwah* (Jakarta: Media Da'wah, 2008), and interviews with Natsir in the early 1970s and with his children in 2003 and 2009.

coastal regions they traveled further to trading and religious centers throughout the Indonesian archipelago and beyond.

More than fifty kilometers south of the region's heartland and in striking contrast to its prosperous irrigated rice-fields, the upland areas around Natsir's birthplace of Alahan Panjang were mainly devoted to the cultivation of coffee, vegetables, tea and cinnamon. Today the road to the town is still lined with the red cinnamon bark stretched out to dry in front of the houses. The small, rather scruffy town of Alahan Panjang is close to two of the most beautiful of the region's small lakes, known merely as Upper and Lower Lake (Danau Diatas and Danau Dibawah). The house where Natsir was born stood on the banks of a fast-flowing river on the outskirts of the town, near what is now the bus station, but the original house was burned down and the only reminder of Natsir is a photo of him on the wall of the new house, and a *pesantren* named after him in the town itself.[2] From the outskirts of Alahan Panjang, Mt. Kerinci looms in the distance, its peak clear through a gap in the mountains.

1908, the year of Natsir's birth, was a year of rebellion in West Sumatra. Many peasants, led first by their traditional heads and then by their Muslim teachers, revolted against the taxes that the colonial government had introduced in violation of a pledge made in 1837 when the Dutch first brought the highlands under their control at the end of the Bonjol war.[3]

The 1908 tax rebellion was bloody. But neither Natsir's birthplace nor his family was involved in the struggle. Natsir was the third of four children born to his father, Idris Sutan Saripado, who was at the time a minor clerk (*juru tulis*) in a government office in Alahan Panjang. Idris had only graduated from a local primary school and could not speak Dutch, nor could his wife Khalida, who had not gone to school but had nevertheless learned to read.[4] Shortly after his wife gave birth to their first son, Mohammad, Idris was sent north to Bonjol — the center of the earlier anti-colonial war — as a government official (assistant *demang*). He remained there with his family for several years before being again transferred, this time to the small town of Maninjau, on the shores of the spectacular lake of the same name, where he served as a clerk in the Assistant Resident (*Controleur*)'s office.

---

[2] I visited the town at the end of 2003, and it is possible that more memorials were built to Natsir when the centennial of his birth was celebrated in 2008.

[3] The best and fullest description of the 1908 rebellion can be found in Ken Young's *Islamic Peasants and the State: The 1908 Anti-Tax Rebellion in West Sumatra* (New Haven: Yale Southeast Asia Studies, 1994). For the Bonjol war, see Christine Dobbin, *Islamic Revivalism in a Changing Peasant Economy: Central Sumatra, 1784–1847* (London: Curzon Press, 1983).

[4] Mohammad Natsir, interview, Jakarta, May 31, 1971.

Writing to his own children forty years later, Natsir recalled that it was at this time, when he was seven or eight years old, that he first heard the word "struggle." But in using the word he was not referring to the anti-colonial struggle or to the political rebellions that wracked his home region but to his own strenuous efforts to gain an education. By this age, young boys in the Minangkabau region no longer slept at their family's house, but were expected to leave their homes every evening to spend the night in the local *surau* (prayer-house). During the day Natsir at first only attended the Indonesian-language village school. His father, Idris, although a government employee, lacked the money to send his son to the Dutch Native School (HIS, Hollandse Inlandsche School), the seven-year primary school with Dutch as the medium of instruction that was the key to advancing in the colonial society. However, perhaps recognizing the young boy's precocity, the head teacher at the local HIS did permit him to attend classes there so long as he absented himself whenever the school inspector appeared.

In the early decades of the 20th century both coastal and upland regions of West Sumatra were home to a large number of private educational institutions sponsored by the local merchants and taught by Islamic scholars. Resentful of what they perceived as Dutch efforts to restrict advanced education to students who were expected to enter government service, and suspicious that the authorities were using Western education to bring Christianity to the region, Muslim scholars and entrepreneurs had come together to found schools where the teaching quality would rival that offered in Dutch government schools.[5] In Padang a leading reformist scholar, Abdullah Ahmad, had established an independent school, the HIS Adabiyah, offering quality education to local children unable to afford entry to a government school.

When his father was reassigned to Makassar, Natsir came under the care of his elder sister Rabiah, who brought him to Padang, hoping to enroll him in the government HIS there, but when she failed to do so, he began to take classes in the Adabiyah school every evening, after attending public school during the day. He later recalled walking past the imposing cement building that housed the government school on his way to the wooden building where local "struggle leaders" (*orang-orang perjuangan*) offered classes to the less privileged Padang children. But although their buildings were poor the Muslim teachers at the Adabiyah school gave Natsir an education of sufficiently high quality for him

---

[5] The best account of the development of these private schools can be found in Taufik Abdullah, *Schools and Politics: The Kaum Muda Movement in West Sumatra* (Ithaca: Cornell Modern Indonesia Project, 1971). See also my *Rebellion to Integration: West Sumatra and the Indonesian Polity* (Amsterdam: Amsterdam University Press, 1999), chapters 1–3.

to pass entry exams for a government HIS when one was opened in the interior town of Solok.

By then his father had been transferred again, this time back to Natsir's birthplace of Alahan Panjang. With no relatives in Solok, Natsir was taken into the house of a prosperous merchant, Haji Musa, in Solok's market district, and for the next three years he and Haji Musa's own son were educated together. They went to the HIS during the day while attending a Diniyyah school — part of another educational network run by local Muslim scholars[6] — in the evening and studying the Qur'an at night. After three years Natsir was hired as an assistant teacher at the Diniyyah school and was able to begin to contribute toward the cost of his board. But his teaching career only lasted a few months before he finally earned a place at the Dutch Native School (HIS) in Padang.

Natsir then returned to the coastal town. While waiting to move in with his grandmother, he stayed with his aunt, Macik Rahim, who earned her living sorting coffee in a warehouse at the water's edge. Rahim shared her meager wages (70–80 cents a day), with Natsir, who helped in running the household. Despite the fact that in Padang life was harder than when he boarded with the rich Solok merchant, Natsir later wrote about his happiness during these months. He felt he had scored a victory in being admitted to the school that had previously rejected him, and at the age of eleven he was now standing on his own feet. Acting as the household cook and walking along the seashore every evening to collect firewood, he felt "free from … the emotional stress of being deeply in debt (*tekanan perasaan 'berhutang budi'*)." He recalled a saying of the Prophet Mohammad: "take a length of rope, go to the jungle to gather firewood, sell the firewood for your family's needs, this is better than begging." The lesson he later drew for his own children from these experiences was that happiness was not derived from wealth and ease, but from a heart that was free from oppression. He admonished his children to trust in the strength that lay within them, and to prize freedom of spirit over life's luxuries.[7]

---

[6] For a biography of the brother and sister who established the Diniyyah schools, see *H. Rahmah el Yunusiyyah dan Zainuddin Labay el Yunusy: Dua Bersaudara Tokoh Pembaharu Sistem Pendidikan di Indonesia* (Jakarta: Pengurus Perguruan Diniyyah Puteri Padang Panjang, 1991).

[7] It should be noted that these admonishments were written during the regional rebellion when not only Natsir, but also his wife and children were living in the jungle. Even in the urban settings of Jakarta and Bandung, Natsir had seen to it that his family lived very modestly, but when they accompanied him to the jungle they must have been faced with a level of deprivation and hardship that they had never previously experienced. In writing his children Natsir adapted the lesson he had learned in his childhood to the situation existing in Indonesia at that time: "That our country and society now have become so confused that

At the end of his years at the HIS Natsir emerged at the top of his class and in 1923 was awarded a scholarship to the MULO (Meer Uitgebreid Lager Onderwijs), the advanced elementary school in Padang, where for the first time his fellow pupils included Dutch children. Previously he had thought that Europeans surpassed Indonesians in all fields and he was now surprised to find that their skin color did not guarantee academic superiority. The Dutch children subjected their Indonesian classmates to harassment and name-calling, and the battles of words frequently escalated into physical fights. Some of the teachers scolded the Dutch boys for insulting their fellow pupils, but others urged them on, sometimes joining them in taunting the Sumatran children. Such treatment spurred Natsir and his friends, both boys and girls, into joining the youth branches of local nationalist organizations — Sumatran Youth (Jong Sumatera) and the Islamic Youth League (Jong Islamieten Bond), where Natsir was a member of the scout movement.[8] From these associations they drew the courage and self respect to challenge their Dutch detractors.

Natsir enjoyed his classes and got good grades. Despite his membership in the nationalist youth organizations, he seems to have been largely untouched by the political turmoil that embroiled West Sumatra during his final year of schooling in Padang. Early in 1927, the year he graduated from MULO, a bloody Communist rebellion erupted first in the weaving town of Silungkang and the mining center of Sijunjung, and then spread through much of the region. It was brutally repressed by the Dutch authorities, with over a hundred killed and thousands arrested.[9] Natsir makes no mention of the rebellion in his recollections of the period, perhaps because, although anti-colonial, the revolt was mainly the work of Communist-affiliated associations and labor unions. In his letters to his children Natsir's attention is focused only on his own education.

After graduating from MULO he was now qualified for a job as a minor clerk. By this time his father had been pensioned and returned to West Sumatra, and was living in Batu Sangkar. Natsir realized that, if he went straight to work, the wages he earned could do much to make the lives of his parents easier, and he was willing to leave school and enter the work force. But to his relief his

---

they can be fooled [*dikutak katikkan*] by such as Sukarno is partly because too many of our leaders are willing to sell freedom of spirit for temporary ease of living.

[8] The Islamic National Scouts (Nationale Islamitische Padvindrij or Natipij). Natsir, "Politik," p. 7.

[9] On this rebellion, see for example, Harry J. Benda and Ruth T. McVey, eds. *The Communist Uprisings of 1926–1927 in Indonesia: Key Documents* (Ithaca: Cornell Modern Indonesia Project, 1960) and Kahin, *Rebellion to Integration,* chapter 1.

father made it clear that he wanted his son to continue his studies. Again Natsir was faced with finding funds for his education. But having attended the MULO on a scholarship (of 20 rp a month) and graduated satisfactorily, he found that this qualified him to continue with a government scholarship (of 30 rp a month) at the General Secondary School (AMS, Algemeene Middelbare School) in Bandung.[10] With great excitement he boarded the ship for Java.

It took three days for the ship to make the journey from Emmahaven (now Teluk Bayur), the port of Padang, to Tanjung Priok, the port for Batavia, the capital city of the Netherlands East Indies. On board Natsir met dozens of other young Sumatrans making their way to Java to pursue their education. As they approached the Javanese port, night was falling and he saw hundreds of small lights flickering in welcome, he thought, for the new arrivals.

In July 1927, just as he turned nineteen, Natsir entered the AMS in Bandung, the one school in the Indies at the time that offered indigenous students a classical education in Latin and Greek.[11] Immediately he was aware that his knowledge of Dutch, learned in the Padang MULO, was not nearly as advanced as that of his fellow students from Java. He also realized that Latin was fundamental to the education offered at his new school. But he found it so difficult that he had to spend hours of memorizing to force the classical language into his brain. Six days a week from morning till night he fought at his studies. Only on Saturday evening did he leave his room to eat *sate Madura* at a stall near the Homan Hotel in the center of town. Lingering outside the hotel to listen to the hotel orchestra he felt a longing for the violin that he had played in Padang, but had neglected when he started school in Bandung because he feared that the time spent practicing would distract him from his studies. These studies centered almost completely on the classics. He had his first reward after three months when he got a high grade (9, with some of his fellow pupils only getting a 3 or 4) in Latin. But his lack of fluency in Dutch still held him back and he was only able to get a grade of 5. Mocking his pronunciation, his teacher asked him: "You're from which MULO?" When Natsir replied, "MULO Padang," the teacher's rejoinder shamed the young man, "Ah yes, no wonder!"

Determined not to accept such an assessment of himself or his home region, Natsir set about improving his Dutch, enlisting the help of a fellow Minang student, Bachtiar Effendi, who was much more fluent and who was

---

[10] Natsir later stated that he was attracted to the Bandung AMS because it was the only one in Indonesia with a literature division where one could get Western classical training. Interview, Jakarta, May 31, 1971.

[11] At the time he was intending to follow a law career, for which he needed these languages.

already an able orator. He also hung around the shops in downtown Bandung to listen to the conversations of Dutch men and women there and devoted himself to reading as many Dutch books as he could get from the library.

At the end of the first academic year he entered a competition in Dutch oratory, choosing to recite a poem, "The Flood (De Banjir)" by Multatuli. Bachtiar coached him, training him to raise and lower his voice and use gestures to emphasize his points. Before appearing on stage he donned traditional Minangkabau dress, and as he began to speak he saw the teacher who had denigrated his Dutch standing in the audience. It took him about ten minutes to recite the poem, and there was a burst of applause when he finished. He noticed that the teacher also clapped, but with a mocking smile on his face (*ketawanya "galak sengeng" saja*). This didn't concern him, however, as the jury awarded him first prize, a book of works by L.C. Westenenk (who had been *Controleur* in West Sumatra), with the title "Where men and tigers live as neighbors (*Waar mensen tiyger beuren ziyn*)." Natsir was content, "not only because I had got first prize, but because the name of the Padang MULO, formerly ridiculed, had been vindicated."

This teacher, however, continued to plague Natsir's life. When he entered class 5 the same teacher was in charge of economic geography and took advantage of these classes to make fun of the growing Indonesian nationalist movement while at the same time not allowing his pupils to discuss politics. The teacher did, however, encourage them to discuss economic problems, selecting as a topic for discussion "the influence of sugar cane plantations and sugar factories on the people of Java." Natsir recalled that the teacher smiled on seeing that Natsir had entered his name as a discussant for this topic.

During the next two weeks Natsir collected all the nationalist magazines he could find and studied the Volksraad debates on the subject.[12] At the end of his preparation he was able to give a searing critique of the sugar industry in a 40-minute address. He argued that it wasn't true that the Javanese people had profited from the sugar factories in central and east Java. Those who had profited were the capitalists and the district heads (*bupati*), who had persuaded the people to lease their land to the factory at far too low a rent. The sugar factory system had transformed the peasants who had been poor but free into factory workers, tied to their wages and burdened with perpetual debt. As Natsir voiced these accusations the class was silent and he could see the

---

[12] The Volksraad (People's Council) had been set up in 1918 as an advisory council to the colonial government. In the 1930s it had a membership of 60, including 30 Indonesians, of whom 20 were elected by local councils.

teacher frowning at him from the corner of the room. He felt that the teacher was shocked at his ability to present such an indictment and in fluent Dutch: "Throughout my speech, I was thinking to myself: 'This is the product of the Padang MULO whose Dutch instruction you have been mocking all this time!'" The teacher said nothing at the end of the talk. "His face remained dark, the bell sounded, the class was dismissed. I felt content."

But in writing to his children so many years later, Natsir was able to express gratitude to the teacher who had goaded him to conduct research on the actual conditions under which his fellow Indonesians lived. In working out his analysis he had begun for the first time to realize the miseries they suffered under colonialism. Thus, through his personal and academic experience Natsir had moved from an early childhood where he seems to have been oblivious to the anti-colonial, religious and nationalist turmoil that embroiled his home region during the first three decades of the 20th century, to a consciousness of the political and economic injustices of Dutch colonial rule in the Netherlands East Indies. And he began to be drawn into active participation in the turmoil as parties and leaders representing competing streams of political and religious thought strove to represent the Indonesian people in confronting Dutch rule and seeking alternative roads to ultimate independence.

2

Nationalist and Religious Involvement, 1929–42

Secular and Religious Studies

In the late 1920s gifted or privileged young people from throughout the Netherlands East Indies congregated in the West Java city of Bandung where most of the advanced Western-education schools in the archipelago were concentrated. As a result, Bandung became the center of anti-colonial discussion and activity embracing all forms of the new Indonesian nationalism. In the same month that Natsir arrived there, July 1927, the foremost leader of the Indonesian nationalist movement, Soekarno, founded the party that "came to dominate nationalist politics not only in the city but throughout Java and beyond."[1] Initially known as the Indonesian National Association, it was soon renamed the Indonesian National Party (PNI, Partai Nasional Indonesia). Under Dutch pressure the PNI was dissolved in 1931, but it exerted an enduring influence over all subsequent political parties working for Indonesian independence. And although Soekarno was arrested in 1929, and in 1933 was sent into internal exile until the Japanese invasion, he continued to dominate nationalist politics and embody the Indonesian people's desire for freedom from Dutch rule.

After entering the turbulent student world in Bandung, Natsir was initially engrossed in his studies, but he was at the same time aware of the ferment of the nationalist movement around him. He later recalled attending talks by

---

[1] Rudolf Mrazek, *Sjahrir: Politics and Exile in Indonesia* (Ithaca, NY: Southeast Asia Program, 1994), p. 49.

9

prominent Indonesians of many political stripes from the soon-to-be-exiled Tjipto Mangoenkoesoemo of the PNI[2] to the controversial Islamic leader, Haji Agus Salim.[3] As he became more confident in his studies, Natsir began also to seek instruction from political and religious scholars outside the confines of his AMS school. Most influential among his early teachers was Ahmad Hassan, a major figure in the Islamic Union, Persis (Persatuan Islam), one of the strictest and most uncompromising Muslim groups of the time.[4]

Hassan had been born in Singapore in 1887, the son of a Tamil scholar and a Javanese mother, and had come to Bandung in the early 1920s, joining the Persis in 1924. Natsir was introduced to him by Fachroeddin Al-Khahiri, who had been a close friend since the two were classmates at the Padang MULO.[5] Natsir was immediately drawn to Hassan, struck by "his simplicity, his orderliness, his breadth and acuity in conversation — he was a scholar who was original — courageous in putting forward his ideas and opinions. Not caring

---

[2] Born in 1886, Tjipto Mangoenkoesoemo was one of the earliest nationalist leaders, being a founder of the Budi Utomo and the radical multiracial Indische Partij. He was appointed to the first Volksraad, but was exiled to Banda in 1928 accused of complicity in the 1926–7 Communist uprisings.

[3] Haji Agus Salim was born in Kota Gedang in West Sumatra in 1884, the son of a government official. He graduated from the Hogere Burger School in Jakarta, was employed as interpreter in the Dutch consulate in Jeddah 1906–9, and became a protégé of Adviser for Native Affairs, Snouck Hurgronje. He later worked in the Office of Public Works (1911–2) and then, in 1912, set up a HIS school in West Sumatra, where he taught until 1915 when, in addition to working as a translator for Balai Pustaka, he became a police informant. It was in this capacity that he first came into contact with the Sarekat Islam (SI). When he joined the organization he left the police force. With H.O.S. Tjokroaminoto, Salim was responsible for policies that led to the ousting of Communists from the Sarekat Islam in 1921. From then on he acted as spokesman for the anti-Communist group within the SI. See Deliar Noer, *The Modernist Muslim Movement in Indonesia 1900–1942* (Singapore: Oxford University Press, 1973), pp. 110–1, 124; Takashi Shiraishi, *An Age in Motion: Popular Radicalism in Java, 1912–1926* (Ithaca: Cornell University Press, 1990), p. 219; Michael Laffan, *Islamic Nationhood and Colonial Indonesia* (London/New York: RoutledgeCurzon, 2003), p. 185.

[4] Muslim entrepreneurs mostly from the Palembang region of Sumatra had founded the Persis with the aim of exploring the place of reformist ideas in the established religious system. Its members initially came from both the reformist and traditionalist streams of Islam, but the traditionalists split off from the organization in 1926. See Howard M. Federspiel, *Persatuan Islam: Islamic Reform in Twentieth Century Indonesia* (Ithaca: Modern Indonesia Project, 1970), pp. 12–5. On Hassan, see also Tamar Djaja, *Riwayat Hidup A. Hassan* (Jakarta: Mutiara, 1980), Ajip Rosidi, *M. Natsir: Sebuah Biografi* (Jakarta: Girimukti Pasaka, 1990), p. 27.

[5] See Rosidi, *M. Natsir*, p. 159.

if most people agreed or not, not caring whether he caused offense or not."[6] But clearly what impressed Natsir the most was that whenever he dropped in at his teacher's house, Hassan would put aside his work, however important, and focus his attention on the young man. Their discussions ranged from religion to politics to the problems of the nationalist movement and independence.

As he came under Hassan's influence, Natsir entered one of the major areas of conflict within the early Indonesian nationalist movement. He was again being influenced by the point of view that had spurred the Islamic scholars in West Sumatra to establish their private schools: the fear that the Dutch were using Western education to draw Indonesians away from Islam and into the purview of Christianity. This feeling intensified on one occasion in 1929 when an AMS teacher took his whole class to church to hear a series of three lectures by a Protestant minister, Dr. A.C. Christoffels, who contrasted the teachings in the Qur'an with those of Christianity. Dr. Christoffels did not attack Islam directly, but, in Natsir's view, while pretending to praise Mohammad, the minister was at the same time attempting to prove that the real Prophet was Jesus Christ. When Christoffels' talk was published in the newspaper the next day, Natsir determined to counter the arguments put forward there and sought Hassan's help in finding the necessary source material, eventually persuading the newspaper to publish his rebuttal.[7]

Natsir's admiration of Hassan was to last throughout his life. In recent years there has been a tendency to see the narrowness of the Islamic Union (Persis) and Hassan's strict adherence to its views as a thread in Natsir's religious thinking that became dominant especially in the 1970s and 1980s when he founded and headed the Dewan Da'wah Islamiyah Indonesia (DDII). There is certainly an element of truth in this view, but Natsir's religious faith was always broader and less dogmatic than that of his mentor or of the Persis, the movement with which both men were identified, or even of many of his later followers in the Dewan Da'wah. And in the 1930s Haji Agus Salim, a much less rigid and more broad-minded scholar, provided a balancing influence to Hassan.

Natsir had joined the Jong Islamieten Bond (JIB, Union of Young Muslims) while still in West Sumatra and in 1928 was appointed head of its

---

[6] *Kumpulan Surat-Surat; Aba: M. Natsir, sebagai Cahaya Keluarga* (Jakarta: Yayasan Capita Selecta, 1908), p. 146; also Mohammad Natsir, "Membina Kader Bertanggung Jawab," in Djaja, *Riwayat Hidup*, pp. 54–6.

[7] According to Natsir, in an interview January 30, 1971, this article appeared in *Preanger Bode* sometime in 1929. In his memorial article for Hassan, Natsir states that he first tried to persuade Hassan to write the rebuttal, but because he did not know Dutch, Hassan encouraged Natsir to do it himself. It appeared under the title *Muhammad als Profeet*. Natsir, "Membina Kader," pp. 54–5. I have been unable to obtain a copy of the article.

Mohammad Natsir and Haji Agus Salim.

Bandung branch. In his view, the JIB's goal was "to study Islam in a critical way"[8] and to recall Muslim young people receiving a Western education to their religion. It had been founded in 1925 by Haji Agus Salim, who "served as a shield" for the organization because of his good relations with the Dutch.[9] It was in the JIB that Natsir first met some of the friends and colleagues he would remain closest to throughout his life, including Mohamad Roem, Prawoto Mangkusasmito, and Kasman Singodimejo. These friends formed part of a small group within the JIB that would meet frequently in the Batavia home of Haji Agus Salim. Natsir would travel from Bandung to attend these meetings, which he would later characterize as a form of cadre training.[10] Salim soon joined Hassan as one of Natsir's most influential mentors.

By the time Natsir graduated from the AMS, in 1930, he was already giving religious instruction to pupils in the local MULO school and in the HIK Gunung Sri in Lembang,[11] and was also making speeches at JIB meetings and debating the organization's opponents. He soon met other prominent Muslim

---

⁸ Natsir interview, Jakarta, May 31, 1971.

⁹ On Haji Agus Salim, see above, n. 3.

¹⁰ Mohammad Natsir, "Insya Allah: Roem tetap Roem," in *Mohamad Roem 70 Tahun: Pejuang Perunding* (Jakarta: Bulan Bintang, 1978), p. 209.

¹¹ Rosidi, *M. Natsir*, p. 158

leaders and became friendly with Ummi Nur-Nahar, who was also from West Sumatra and had been a member of the JIB's women's branch in Padang, though the two met for the first time in Bandung.[12]

When Natsir completed his studies at AMS, the Rector informed him that he had done well enough to qualify for a scholarship to the Law Faculty in Batavia, or possibly the Economics Faculty in Rotterdam. But by now Natsir realized that he no longer wished to pursue his projected career in law. He therefore rejected these openings in favor of remaining in Bandung to continue studying, writing and teaching on Islam. He later acknowledged how much Hassan influenced him in reaching this decision, for in the years between leaving the Diniyyah school in Solok and coming under Hassan's influence — years when his education had been totally Western — Natsir had largely abandoned his study of Islam.

But though he now rejected a career in law or economics in favor of pursuing his religious studies, the Western secular education that he had acquired at the AMS in Bandung would temper his political stance throughout his career. This was especially noteworthy when he accepted a position in the independent Indonesian government and was able to find a basis for cooperating with politicians of different or no religious affiliation in reaching mutually acceptable goals for the good of the Indonesian people as a whole.

Nationalist Involvement

His decision to focus on teaching and studying religion meant that Natsir had to relinquish the scholarship that had previously supported him and learn to live on the Rp. 20 a month he received from Hassan for help in publishing Persis's journal *Pembela Islam* (Defender of Islam).[13] In writing for the journal Natsir began to confront some basic problems regarding the place of Islam in the Indonesian nationalist movement. As a correspondent for the magazine, he attended the demonstrations mounted by the National Party (PNI) and reported on Soekarno's speeches but, though strongly attracted to the PNI's condemnation of Dutch colonialism and its demands for an independent

---

[12] Interview with Natsir family, Jakarta, October 28, 2008. Natsir and his family use various spellings for Ummi's name (e.g. Ummie, Umi) but Ummi seems to be the one most frequently used.

[13] *Pembela Islam* published 71 issues between 1929 and 1932, and engaged in many disputes with secular nationalist organizations, especially the PNI. It had a readership of about 2,000 throughout the archipelago, especially Java, Sulawesi, Kalimantan and West Sumatra, as well as Siam and Malaya. Deliar Noer, "Research Notes" (typescript [1956]).

Indonesia, he was worried by the growing criticisms voiced by its leaders against aspects of Islamic teachings.[14]

In articles written under the alias of "Is," Natsir attempted to rebut these criticisms. He later recalled defending polygamy and also criticizing the veteran nationalist leader in Surabaya, Dr. Sutomo, for a series of articles appearing in the journal he edited, *Swara Umum*, which compared the exile of nationalist leaders to Digul (the place of internal exile for political opponents of the Dutch) with the Muslim pilgrimage to Mecca. In these articles Dr. Sutomo arrived at the conclusion that "those who went to the internment camp deserved more praise than those who performed the haj."[15] In his response, Natsir queried whether the writer had been aware of how many Indonesians "with the title of Haji" had been exiled to Digul because they were considered dangerous by the Dutch authorities.[16]

Alienated by the PNI's criticisms of Islam, Natsir turned to the Partai Sarekat Islam Indonesia (PSII), the successor to the first nationalist association in Indonesia, the Sarekat Islam (SI). In its heyday in the late 1910s the SI had claimed a membership of nearly two and a half million throughout the archipelago,[17] but after its more radical members had resigned and formed the Communist Party of Indonesia (PKI), the rump SI was severely weakened. The party's decision in 1927 to purge all members of the respected Muslim social organization, the Muhammadiyah,[18] further undermined whatever appeal it exerted on the broader Islamic community.[19] Three years later the Sarekat Islam

---

[14] On his attitude toward Soekarno at this time, see his interview with a correspondent from *Editor* in *Pemimpin Pulang: Rekaman Peristiwa Wafatny M. Natsir*, ed. Lukman Hakiem (Jakarta: Yayasan Piranti Ilmu, 1993), p. 242.

[15] *Swara Umum*, I, no. 54 (June 27, 1930) and no. 66 (July 25, 1930) cited in Noer, *Modernist Muslim Movement*, p. 258. See also John Ingleson, *Road to Exile: The Indonesian Nationalist Movement 1927–1934* (Singapore: Heinemann, 1979), p. 130; Rosidi, *M. Natsir*, p. 116.

[16] *Pembela Islam*, no. 26 (May 1931): 9.

[17] George McTurnan Kahin, *Nationalism and Revolution in Indonesia* (Ithaca: Cornell University Press, 1952), p. 74.

[18] Muhammadiyah was formed on November 18, 1912, by the Yogyakarta *santri* Ahmad Dahlan (1868?–1923) to further Islamic propagation and education. Mitsuo Nakamura, "The Crescent arises over the Banyan Tree: A Study of the Muhammadijah Movement in a Central Javanese Town," Ph.D. dissertation, Cornell University, 1976, pp. 109–12.

[19] Leaders of the two organizations had quarreled throughout the 1920s, in part over the non-cooperation stance of the Sarekat Islam, which contrasted with the Muhammadiyah's willingness to accept funding from the colonial government, and in part because of dissatisfaction with the leadership of SI head Tjokroaminoto. See Noer, *Modernist Muslim Movement*, pp. 235–7.

reconstituted itself into the much narrower and less inclusive party, the Partai Sarekat Islam Indonesia, PSII. Though certainly conscious of its weaknesses, Natsir decided that, rather than belonging to a political party that lacked an Islamic foundation, he would ally with the PSII, viewing it as a basically Islamic party, led by men he admired, such as Haji Agus Salim and H.O.S. Tjokroaminoto. Nevertheless, he never actually joined the party.

In his writings Natsir began to draw a sharp line between a struggle for independence emphasizing nationalism, as was espoused by Soekarno, and a struggle for independence based on Islamic ideals. In *Pembela Islam*, still writing under the alias, Is, he grouped his arguments regarding the place Islam should occupy in the nationalist movement under the following six headings: (1) Islam is not merely a religion in the sense of only worshipping Allah; (2) Islam opposes colonialism; so it is the duty of the Islamic community to struggle for independence; (3) Islam offers an ideological basis for an independent state; (4) The Islamic community has the duty to organize that independent state on bases that are determined by Islam; (5) This aim cannot be achieved by the Islamic community if they struggle to achieve independence in a merely nationalist party, even more so if this party hates Islam; (6) Therefore the Islamic Community [should] from the beginning enter and strengthen a struggle for independence that is based on Islamic ideals.[20] Many nationalists reacted angrily to this position and accused *Pembela Islam* of splitting the unity of the independence movement.

But while arguing that an independence struggle should be based on religion, Natsir never condemned nationalist aspirations in the way his mentor Hassan did. He rather stressed the need to create a community or society, using whatever tie would help in establishing that unity, and noted Islam's acknowledgement that love of one's native area or land was a natural human characteristic. Twenty years later he spelled this out. Stating that people often said that Islam opposed the love of one's country (*kebangsaan*), he dismissed such a notion as incorrect:

> We can be obedient Muslims who with great joy can sing "Indonesia my Native Land [*Tanah Airku*]." How can we eliminate our Indonesian-ness [*ke-Indonesiaan kita*]? Because it is God who created the different peoples who now inhabit the earth. We must be glad and joyful in showing to the outside world that we are the Indonesian people, this is our language, this our culture, our batik, our carving, our music, and so on.[21]

---

[20] *Aba*, p. 159.
[21] Mohammad Natsir, "Revolusi Indonesia [1955]," in M. Natsir, *Agama dan Negara dalam Perspektif Islam* (Jakarta: Media Da'wah, 2001), p. 179.

Only when this natural affiliation was exaggerated into an ideology and assumed the character of racism or chauvinism did it become dangerous. Thus, while embracing patriotism, or love of country, he generally opposed nationalism in the sense of believing in the superiority of one's own nation. He later clarified the Islamic attitude, when he stated:

> Islam does not agree with racism and except for an anti-colonialist struggle, or struggle for political freedom, it opposes the concept of nationalism, i.e., xenophobia, or the idea of "my country right or wrong."[22]

Thus, in the view of Taufik Abdullah, Natsir emphasized a common nationality, such as portrayed in the Indonesian word *"kebangsaan"* rather than the concept embodied in the borrowed word *"nasionalisme"*:

> *Kebangsaan* had a respected place in Natsir's thought. But *nasionalisme* is a different matter. It appears that even though Pak Natsir continued to use the word *kebangsaan*, he strongly differentiated between *kebangsaan* and *nasionalisme*. *Nasionalisme* was an "ideologization" of the ideals of *kebangsaan*. Natsir was rather cool to the process of *nasionalisme*.[23]

Opposing the "ideologization" of *kebangsaan* while embracing its anti-colonial characteristics was an integral part of Natsir's attempt in the prewar period to harmonize his view of the need for an independent Indonesian state with his conviction that the movement toward that end had to be based on Islam. In a series of articles in *Pembela Islam* in 1932 he responded to accusations by members of the religiously neutral parties that Natsir and his fellows in the Persatuan Islam were splitting the nationalist movement.[24] In these articles Natsir strove to define what he thought was the essence of *kebangsaan* in Indonesia.

Recognizing that at that time the peoples of the Indonesian archipelago lacked many characteristics often used as criteria for defining national conscious-

---

[22] Natsir interview, Jakarta, February 24, 1971. He would have agreed with Jonathan Haidt, who has written: "Many social psychologists distinguish patriotism — a love of one's own country — from nationalism, which is the view that one's own country is superior to other countries and should therefore be dominant. Nationalism is generally found to be correlated with racism and with hostility toward other countries, but patriotism by itself is not." *New York Times*, May 8, 2011.

[23] Taufik Abdullah, "Natsir, Seorang Guru yang Perfeksionis Filosofis," in *Pemikiran dan Perjuangan Mohammad Natsir*, ed. Anwar Haryono, *et al.* (Jakarta: Firdaus, 2001), p. 53.

[24] Mohammad Natsir, [Is], "Kebangsaan Moeslimin, 1–5," *Pembela Islam*, nos. 41–5 (January–April 1932).

ness (i.e. shared language, physical characteristics, customs, etc.), he sought "the unifying tie" that could not be shattered by "the force of law, constitutions or military arms."[25] He focused on Ernest Renan's emphasis on "the sufferings that we have together experienced," that connect and unify a people more than their shared joys and happiness.[26] Natsir linked the sufferings of the Indonesian people to "an awareness of our current situation," and "the realization that our self-respect does not accord with that situation [*keinsjafan kepada harga diri sendiri jang tidak tjotjok dengan keadaan itoe*]."[27] In his view, the Sarekat Islam and other Islamic organizations, such as the Muhammadiyah, had restored the sense of dignity and unity among the peoples of the scattered islands of the archipelago, separated not only by the sea, but also by customs, language and the efforts of the colonial government. These Muslim organizations had raised the consciousness of the diverse peoples of the archipelago so that they "remain closely aligned spiritually [*tetap berbaris rapat dalam kebathinan*], linked by feelings of brotherhood and a yearning to live and die together."[28] Thus, "these joint ideals became a connection for a group [*kaoem*] spread out (dispersed), with different customs and behavior [*adat dan tabiat*], and differing in the color of their skin and in their languages."[29]

Over the next twenty years Natsir's concept of the position of Islam in the emerging nation of Indonesia embraced not only the diverse ethnicities that composed it but also the different religions. This religious tolerance, however, never extended to any acceptance of Christian missionary activities aimed at Muslim adherents.

* * *

In the late 1920s and early 1930s, leaders of nationalist organizations, both those belonging to specifically Islamic parties and those who defined themselves as religiously neutral, were attempting to work out the most viable basis for drawing the people of the Dutch East Indies into an overarching nationalist movement. Soekarno himself had been struggling to harmonize the major

---

[25] Ibid., 1, p. II.

[26] Ibid., 2, p. 2.

[27] Ibid., 3, p. 2.

[28] Ibid., p. 3.

[29] In his writings in the early 1930s, *kaoem Muslimin* [Muslim group or clan] was the term Natsir used most frequently in describing the Muslim community. He also often used *kaoem* to describe the people of a nation, occasionally as an alternative to *bangsa*. Less frequently he used *oemmat* to describe both the Muslim and national community. See Mohammad Natsir [Is], "Kebangsaan Moeslimin, 1–5," *Pembela Islam*, nos. 41–5 (January–April 1932), passim.

streams in the nationalist movement since writing his influential 1925 essay, "Nationalism, Islam and Marxism."[30]

With a few exceptions, most of the earliest nationalist organizations, other than the Sarekat Islam, had been primarily limited to a particular region or to one of the specific ethnic groups making up the Indies population.[31] Although some of these organizations, such as the Jong Sumatranen Bond to which Natsir himself belonged as a schoolboy, were based in the Outer Islands, the vast majority and strongest of them were Javanese and held little attraction for ethnic groups outside Java, other than among some intellectuals. A great leap forward in unifying the ethnically based nationalist groups had been taken at the second Youth Congress in October 1928 at which the Red and White (the *Merah Putih*), the future national flag, was raised and Indonesia Raya, the future Indonesian national anthem, was sung for the first time. All participants took an oath pledging allegiance to one people, the Indonesian People, one nation, the Indonesian Nation and one language, the Indonesian Language — a language based on Malay that was spoken as a lingua franca through most of the archipelago.[32]

But the momentum of the religiously neutral nationalists stalled when, fearful of the threat posed by their movement, the colonial government cracked down on their political activity. As early as 1929 the authorities arrested Soekarno, and the following year they tried him publicly in Bandung where he was sentenced to four years in jail. At that time the police were breaking up political meetings and arresting the speakers. Under the pressure of this persecution the National Party finally dissolved.

The nationalists would never retrieve the unity they apparently enjoyed in 1928, as in subsequent years their leaders diverged on the strategies to be employed in the face of the colonial repression. A permanent split developed

---

[30] See Soekarno, *Nationalism, Islam and Marxism*, trans. Karel H. Warouw and Peter D. Weldon, with an introduction by Ruth T. McVey (Ithaca: Cornell University Modern Indonesia Project, 1969).

[31] One notable exception was the Indische Partij (Indies Party) founded by the Eurasian E.F.E. Douwes Dekker which was one of the first political organizations which attempted to transcend ethnic, religious, and regional divisions within the Indies and called for the country's independence.

[32] Mitsuo Nakamura has noted that this language had also been a lingua franca for most of the Malay Muslim world prior to the development of modern nationalism, citing the observation of Snouck Hurgronje in the 1890s that "Mekka Malay was used as the medium of interethnic communication among the Jawah community consisting of 'all people[s] of Malay race in the fullest meaning of the term, the geographic boundary is perhaps from Siam and Malacca to New Guinea.'" Nakamura, "Crescent Arises," pp. 174–5, citing Snouck Hurgronje, *Mekka in the Latter Part of the 19th Century* (1931), pp. 215, 229.

between the Partindo, the successor organization to Soekarno's PNI, and a new party, the Pendidikan Nasional Indonesia (Indonesian National Education) or PNI Baru ("New PNI"), founded and led by two Minangkabau students then studying in the Netherlands — Mohammad Hatta and his younger colleague, Sutan Sjahrir. Seeking to avoid an open confrontation with the colonial government, Hatta and Sjahrir pursued the strategy of establishing a cadre party rather than attempting to form a movement based on mass action, such as Soekarno's original PNI. Nevertheless, they were still unable to avoid Dutch retribution, and within a couple of years of returning to Java both men were arrested in February 1934 and exiled first to Boven Digul and later to Banda Neira. Soekarno himself was rearrested in August 1933 and exiled to Flores and later to Bengkulu.

Natsir versus Soekarno

After his 1933 arrest Soekarno was initially held in Sukamiskin jail in Bandung, where Natsir's mentor, the Persis leader Ahmad Hassan, visited him and brought him books. On several occasions Natsir accompanied Hassan on these visits.[33] In 1934 Soekarno was exiled to the eastern Indonesian island of Flores. There, no longer under the pressure of day-to-day politics, he too continued his efforts to define his own thinking on Islam's current and future role in Indonesia's independence struggle. His evolving attitude was illustrated most clearly in a series of letters he wrote to Hassan between December 1934 and October 1936 (*Surat-Surat Islam dari Endeh*).

In these letters Soekarno analyzed the place of Islam in the modern world. He implicitly blamed Muslims themselves for their lack of social and political influence, bemoaning the fact that conservative Muslim groups closed their eyes to modern technological advances and harked back instead to an imagined earlier golden age of Islam. When looking at contemporary society, these Muslims, in his view, tended to focus merely on the restrictions imposed by their religion, ignoring its ability to adapt to changing times:

> How much better it would be if the Islamic community remembered rather what is tolerated and neutral! How good it would be if they remembered that in worldly matters, in matters of statesmanship, "one may criticize (*berqias*), one may speak heresy (*berbidah*), one may abandon earlier customs, one may adopt new customs, one may have a radio, one may fly in an airplane, one

---

[33] Rosidi, *M. Natsir*, p. 253. In his *Editor* interview, Natsir emphasized that while Soekarno was in Sukamiskin jail, it was the Persis members who visited him, not those from the PNI. See Hakiem, ed., *Pemimpin Pulang*, p. 242.

> may use electricity, one may be modern, one may be hyper-hyper modern"
> so long as this is not clearly forbidden or pronounced sinful by Allah and
> his Prophet.[34]

At the end of the decade, after the Dutch transferred him from Endeh
in eastern Indonesia to Bengkulu in southwest Sumatra, Soekarno was still
exploring the subject of Islam's place in modern governments and society. He
focused on the issue in two 1940 articles published in *Pandji Islam*: "Why
Turkey has Separated Religion from the State [Apa Sebab Turki Memisahkan
Agama dari Negara]" and "Society in the Age of the Camel and Society in the
Age of the Airplane [Masjarakat Onta dan Masjarakat Kapal-Udara]."[35] In these
essays he again urged that the strictures of the Prophet Mohammad be viewed
in the context of contemporary society and called on the Muslim community
to use their intellect in applying the Prophet's teachings correctly.

Soekarno frequently used Mustafa Kemal's Turkey as an example of a state
where religion was accorded its proper place and cited it in his arguments for
separating religion from government. He suggested that independent Indonesia
would be faced with two alternatives: "unity of religion and state but without
democracy, or democracy, but with the state separated from religion." He wrote:
"I [would] free Islam from the state, so that Islam can be strong and I [would]
free the state from religion so that the state can be strong."[36]

As Bernhard Dahm has noted, Natsir used Soekarno's articles as a point of
departure for contesting the older leader's arguments and indicating what Natsir
saw as the inherent dangers in Soekarno's way of thinking. They also spurred
him to consider what would be the best form of government for an independent
Indonesian state. In an article entitled, "Islam's attitude toward Freethinking,"
Natsir agreed with Soekarno that Mohammad viewed the intellect as an
instrument in reaching an understanding of God's word.[37] But he went on to
stress the limits of independent thought:

> He acknowledged that by independent thinking faith could be strengthened
> and much of the superstition that clung to religion could be eliminated
> without great difficulties. A free intellect would open the windows of the

---

[34] Soekarno, *Dibawah Bendera Revolusi* (Jakarta: Panitiya Penerbit Dibawah Bendera Revolusi,
1959), p, 334. Unfortunately I have not been able to see Hassan's responses, but there is no
indication from Soekarno's letters that the older scholar reacted too critically. The letters were
published by Hassan and later appeared in ibid., pp. 325–44.

[35] Ibid., pp. 403–45, 483–91.

[36] Sukarno, *Dibawah Bendera Revolusi*, p. 406.

[37] Mohammad Natsir, "Sikap 'Islam' terhadap 'Kemerdekaan-Berfikir'," in *Capita Selecta* [I]
(Bandung, The Hague: Van Hoeve), pp. 206–29.

study and let in the fresh air. But ... this gust of fresh air could become a storm, which would throw everything in the study into confusion and which could also shake the foundations of religion. 'Freedom without discipline produces terrible confusion; freedom without authority is anarchy.'[38]

In his later writing Natsir consistently pursued this theme of the dangers posed by unbridled "freedom" or unrestrained action in any sphere, whether in individual thinking or, politically, in the implementation of a democratic order.

Arguing forcefully against any possibility that religion could be separated from the governance of a Muslim country, Natsir wrote, also in *Pandji Islam*: "According to our outlook as a Muslim community, Islam is not merely an addition, an 'extra' that has to be incorporated in the state, but in our view it is the state that is the apparatus and instrument for Islam." As consistently in his writings throughout his life, Natsir was then emphasizing that the state was not a goal but an instrument (*staat, bagi kita, boekan toedjoean, melainkan alat*) for achieving the people's ideals.[39]

At the same time he did recognize that there were many aspects of a modern state that were outside the Islamic frame of reference. The role of religion, he specified, did not concern factors that alter with time, but was limited to those that are fixed and constant, including

> ... the rights and duties between the ruler and the ruled, the principle that certain ills of society be eliminated — such as the drinking of intoxicants, theft, gambling, prostitution, regulations for the harmony of home life, on marriage and divorce and on inheritance; rules to combat poverty, such as to distribute wealth through zakat and fitrah, to prohibit excessive interest on loans.

He asserted that such rules would not hamper progress, and in all other matters governance of a Muslim country could draw on examples from other countries: "We have the right to adopt good laws from England, or Japan, from Uruguay or Finland if they are not in conflict with our religion." But he disputed Soekarno's portrayal of the Turkey of Mustafa Kemal as a model to be followed by Muslim majority states.

In this series of articles, published under the alias of A. Moechlis in *Pandji Islam* in mid-1940, Natsir focused on refuting Soekarno's idealization of Mustafa Kemal's rule. He acknowledged the weaknesses of the Caliphate

---

[38] Bernhard Dahm, *Sukarno and the Struggle for Indonesian Independence* (Ithaca: Cornell University Press, 1969), p. 193. See Natsir, "Sikap 'Islam'," p. 210.

[39] Mohammad Natsir [A.Moechlis], "Persatuan Agama dengan Negara, II–III," *Pandji Islam* #27–36, July 8–September 9, 1940, p. 8215.

in decline in the 19th and 20th centuries but criticized Soekarno for his willingness to adopt European caricatures of an Islamic form of government based on the Caliphate's final decadent years. Rebutting Soekarno's arguments, Natsir contended that, though some of the Caliphs were tyrants, this did not reflect on their religion, for tyrants "can use any philosophy or religion to mask their tyranny." He asserted that once tyranny exists, religion and the state have already been separated and according to Islamic teaching the people then have the right to overthrow the tyrannical government.

While acknowledging the virtues of democracy, he also recognized its drawbacks, and contended that an Islamic system had superior characteristics:

> Democracy is good [*bagus.*] But the Islamic state system does <u>not</u> make all matters depend on the mercy of democratic institutions. The progress of democracy from century to century has demonstrated its different good characteristics. But it is also not free from several bad and also dangerous characteristics. We Muslims know well enough what is the result when that democracy has eroded to become a "party"-cracy or a "clique"-cracy complete with games of self-defense and sleights of hand behind the scenes, matters which Kemal Pasja for instance is himself very skilled and crafty at using in the political game. Because of this, because Islam does <u>not</u> want all its decisions and laws to rest on this so-called democracy, Islam does not want to be labeled democratic. We can surrender that [*itoe terserah*]. Islam is one idea, one understanding, one concept [*begrip*] in its own right that has its own characteristics, Islam is not 100% democracy, it is not 100% autocracy. Islam is … yes *Islam*. It can be viewed as a synthesis from these two antitheses….[40]

At the same time, he mocked Sukarno's portrayal of Kemal Mustafa's rule as democratic,

> "Democracy" in the country of Kemal Pasha? What is the meaning of democracy in the hands of the dictator Kemal Pasha? What is the meaning of a *vrij spel der krachten* ["free play of forces"] — freedom when all power is in the hands of a single man, the "State president" who is at the same time "Leader" of the only "Volksparty" that exists in his state, or strength in the hand of a "Fuehrer" Mustafa Kemal? What is the meaning of *freedom of the press* in the hands of this "Duce" Kemal Mustafa?

Natsir continued that, though Kemal had replaced Islamic law with laws based on the Swiss and Italian constitutions, "he has asked the people to be patient for 10 or 20 years before democracy can be implemented."[41]

---

[40] Ibid., p. 8239.
[41] Ibid.

Many of the arguments he advanced here against Kemal's government Natsir was to put forward against Soekarno himself in the 1950s when as Indonesia's president Soekarno tried to implement his ideas for a "Guided Democracy." But in contrast to his later stance, in 1940 Natsir was strongly advocating an "Islamic" not merely a "democratic" state. He was at the same time, however, in agreement with Soekarno's emphasis on the democratic nature of Islam, asserting, despite what he said above, that Islam is "democratic in the sense that it is anti-despotism, anti-absolutism, anti-arbitrary measures."

The conflict of ideas between Natsir and Soekarno was to continue until Soekarno's fall from power, though, despite their intellectual disagreements, they were able to work harmoniously together during the Republic's independence struggle against the Dutch. The two men did share some common attitudes: both had admiration for Mohammad Abduh and Jamal al-Din al-Afghani;[42] both embraced the progressive and egalitarian nature of Islam; and Soekarno always acknowledged the important role Islam had played in the early nationalist movement, writing as early as 1925:

> Many of our nationalists forget that the nationalist and Islamic movements in Indonesia ... had the same origin.... Both originated in a strong desire to resist the West, or, more precisely, Western capitalism and imperialism. So they are really not enemies, but allies.[43]

Both Natsir and Soekarno also opposed certain characteristics of Western democracy, such as government by a 50 + 1 majority in Parliament, stressing instead, though to different degrees, the idea of achieving a consensus among the competing parties. Natsir later also recognized how far the political situation dictated Soekarno's attitude toward Islam. Speaking in 1971 of the former president's attitude toward religion, Natsir stated:

> Soekarno had a considerable knowledge and understanding of Islam, but was not himself religious, nor attracted to Islam in a positive sense. He saw it as an objective factor operating in Indonesia with which he had to come

---

[42] Mohammad Abduh (1848–1905) was a follower of Jamal al-Din al-Afghani (1838[?]–97), who had argued that the Muslims' first task "was to free themselves from British dominance. Only afterward would it make sense for Muslims to determine the course of reform most appropriate for carrying out their mission in the modern world." John Kelsay, *Arguing the Just War in Islam* (Cambridge: Harvard University Press, 2007), p. 79. Abduh himself "tried to walk a careful line by which political independence and religious reform might be combined." He was founder of the Egyptian modernist school and a reformer of Islamic practices and ideas.

[43] Soekarno, *Dibawah Bendera Revolusi*, p. 42.

to terms, this being so both in the period of the nationalist movement and afterwards.[44]

Soekarno's major emphasis was always on the similarities between, and the need to establish harmony among, the three groups that he saw as making up Indonesian political society — nationalists, Muslims and Marxists. Only through these groups working together, he argued, could a firm basis be laid for an independent Indonesia. Natsir, however, vigorously opposed what he saw as Soekarno's moving too far in this direction and criticized his "deliberate simplifications [of Islam] *in order to find a common denominator*."[45] Essentially, for Soekarno religion was an individual matter, while for Natsir, Islam was "a religion of belief and action ... a social system, a system of life ... a complete civilization."[46] Its laws had the potential for ordering the state and the individuals within it, though within a democratic framework.

Western and Religious Influences

Natsir's struggles in trying to work out the relationship between Islam and democracy and between Islam and nationalism are in line with his ambivalence regarding the influence of Western powers and Western thought. As with many of the reformist Muslim thinkers who influenced him, and especially Haji Agus Salim who had worked so closely with leading members of the Dutch colonial administration, Natsir was torn between an admiration and embrace of the "positive sides of Western culture" and a strong opposition to Western imperialism and what he saw in the Netherlands East Indies as its efforts to Christianize the people it governed.

His views diverged from those of many of his educated contemporaries, in both the Islamic and religiously neutral political parties, at least in part because of the nature of his education, which, as in the case of Soekarno, he had received exclusively in the Netherlands East Indies. In this he differed from much of the nationalist leadership, including his fellow Minangkabau students Mohammad Hatta and Sutan Sjahrir who, after their schooling in Bandung and Batavia, had continued their education in the Netherlands and had there experienced the political free-for-all of a democratic society. Natsir had little perception of how religion operated in such a context, and disagreed with them

---

[44] Natsir interview, Jakarta, January 28, 1971.

[45] Dahm, *Sukarno*, p. 195.

[46] Transcript of interview of Merle Ricklefs with Mohammad Natsir, August 14, 1977, p. 4. I am grateful to Professor Ricklefs for giving me a copy of this transcript.

in their insistence on avoiding religiously based political parties. Nevertheless, as we have seen, the Western classical education he received in Bandung had a life-long influence on his way of thinking. It not only had the negative impact of intensifying his fear that the Dutch were using this education to Christianize their students, but also had the more positive influence of opening his mind to some of the most enlightened Western thinkers on human rights and democracy.[47]

At the same time, Natsir also differed from those of his contemporaries who had been educated in the Middle East and on their return to the Netherlands Indies strictly adhered either to the reformist stream of teachings in Cairo or the more traditionalist views espoused in Mecca.

Like Natsir, many religious thinkers in the Middle East in the early decades of the 20th century were searching for an acceptable relationship between nationalism and religion. This was particularly the case in Egypt where, during the struggle against British rule, Muslim nationalists, including such influential teachers as Rasjid Rida, were confronting the conflict between their desire for an independent Egypt and their loyalty to a disintegrating Caliphate, which lingered on as "a symbol of Islamic internationalism, daily losing ground to the competing ideologies of nationalism and communism."[48]

Although he was not to visit the Middle East until after Indonesian independence, Natsir in the pre-World War II years was influenced by the writings of these modernist Islamic thinkers, particularly Mohammad Abduh and to a lesser extent by his more radical disciple, Rasjid Rida.[49] (Natsir had

---

[47] Two of his teachers at the AMS in Bandung personified these differences. While Natsir believed that one of them (Christoffels) sought to undermine the students' religion, he warmly praised his Latin teacher (Van Bessem), who had protected the students' religious rights, for example opening his classroom to the Jong Islamieten Bond (JIB) to hold meetings that had been forbidden by the school's authorities. Natsir interview, Jakarta, January 30, 1971. See also Mrazek, *Sjahrir*, p. 47, n.99, where Natsir is reported as saying that it was the rector of the AMS who allowed the JIB to meet in the school "lest the watchdogs of the regime notice."

[48] Laffan, *Islamic Nationhood and Colonial Indonesia*, p. 214.

[49] Rasjid Rida (1865–1935), a Syrian, was an enthusiastic adherent of Abduh and founder of the influential periodical *Al-Munir* [The Lighthouse] in Cairo. He had a strong influence on many young men from Malaya and the Netherlands East Indies who studied at Al Azhar University in Cairo. See ibid., p. 81; William Roff, *The Origins of Malay Nationalism* (New Haven: Yale University Press, 1967), pp. 60–2; H.A.R. Gibb, *Modern Trends in Islam* (Chicago: University of Chicago Press, 1947), pp. 27–9, 33–5; H.A.R. Gibb and J.H. Kramers, *Shorter Encyclopaedia of Islam* (Ithaca: Cornell University Press, 1953), pp. 85–7, 405–7; Noer, *Modernist Muslim Movement*, pp. 32–3.

reportedly been introduced to Abduh's work by Syaikh Ahmad Soorkhati, a Sudanese teacher at Al-Irsyad.[50]) With respect to Abduh, Natsir later said: "the thing about him that attracted me most was his stand against colonialism…. Islam does not allow its followers to be colonized." Natsir added that Abduh also "showed Islam as a social system … which can be used as a starting point for solving problems."[51] Clearly Natsir was also close to Abduh in his realization of the importance of reforming Muslim education, especially higher education. Abduh argued for "a broad reform of education, both at the elite level of the training of members of the learned class, and at the level of educating lay experts in scientific and technical matters."[52] As H.A.R. Gibb has written, Abduh

> bridged, at least temporarily, the widening gap between the traditional learning and the new rationalism introduced from the West, and made it possible for the Muslim graduate of the Western universities to prosecute his studies without being conscious of a fear, or incurring the reproach, that he had abjured his faith.[53]

Natsir stressed that Abduh "tried to understand Western culture. He tried to show the positive sides of Islam and Western culture, not their antagonisms. He was not a nationalist in any real sense but an anti-racialist."[54]

Many students from the Netherlands East Indies, studying at al-Azhar, Cairo's famous university, were influenced by Rasjid Rida's espousal of "the seemingly contradictory goals of both a Muslim community undivided and a new world of independent Muslim countries."[55] Though Natsir acknowledged being influenced by Rida, he never seems to have been attracted to his advocacy for a while of establishing "a universal *khalifat*, which would control the holy cities of Mecca and Medina, oversee the pilgrimage, and, on occasion, intervene as a kind of *primus inter pares* authority in Shari'a debates."[56] Despite recognizing affinities with his co-religionists throughout the world, Natsir conceived

---

[50] Rosidi, *M. Natsir*, p. 167. According to Rosidi, Hassan had introduced Natsir to Syaikh Soorkhati. In later writings, Natsir cited Soorkhati (Syoekati), together with Hassan and Agus Salim, as the teachers who most influenced him.

[51] Natsir, interview, Jakarta, January 30, 1971.

[52] Kelsay, *Arguing the Just War in Islam*, p. 81.

[53] Gibb, *Modern Trends*, pp. 42–3.

[54] Interview, Jakarta, January 30, 1971.

[55] Kelsay, *Arguing the Just War*, p. 234.

[56] Ibid., pp. 89–90. Rida, however, did impose limits on the type of *khalifat* he was advocating, arguing that it should not "possess the kind of imperial political control wielded by the Abbasids or Ottoman or Mughal rulers. That kind of authority would be left to "the more regional communities that Europeans and North Americans call nations."

of the Indonesian nation almost exclusively in terms of its colonially defined boundaries rather than in the broader sweep of "separate Eastern Muslim homelands joined to their fellow Muslims above the winds by the experience of Western colonialism."[57] He saw Islam as a unifying factor for the peoples within the Netherlands East Indies but did not see it unifying them with other Islamic countries under colonial rule. At the end of the 1930s he dismissed Dutch fears of the spread of Pan-Islamic ideas, stating that, outside Egypt, all other Muslim communities were concerned with more immediate problems than those of the Caliphate.[58] Nor did he view the presence of other religions within the borders of the Netherlands East Indies as an obstacle to its unity, for to him an Islamic government was a tolerant government in which Christians and members of other religions were free to follow their own faiths.

But he also did not go along with other graduates of al-Azhar, "Cairo's most famous teaching-mosque,"[59] from his home region of West Sumatra, who founded the Permi party (Partai Muslimin Indonesia) there in 1930. Attracting a broad spectrum of political activists from that region and beyond, Permi espoused the twin pillars of Islam and Nationalism.[60] Natsir rejected this twin basis of struggle and called on Permi leaders to take Islam as the sole basis of their movement for independence.[61]

Throughout his polemic with Soekarno during the 1930s and early 1940s, as well as in his broader exploration of the relationship of Islam and nationalism, Natsir consistently expressed the belief that Islam was the natural bond among the peoples of the archipelago. He argued that it had always been in the vanguard of Indonesian nationalism and was the appropriate vehicle to unite Indonesians fighting for their independence:

> Long before the Budi Utomo had accepted non-Javanese members, long before the Pasundan movement had given up its provincialism, long before the local movements in West Java, in East Java, in Ambon, and in Central Sumatra looked beyond the boundaries of their own regions, long before there was any mention of an 'Indonesian nation,' the PSII [Partai Sarekat

---

[57] Laffan, *Islamic Nationhood*, p. 220.

[58] Natsir, "Oleh-oleh dari Algiers," *Pandji Islam*, July 1939, in *Capita Selecta* [I], pp. 153–67, esp. pp. 162–3.

[59] Laffan, *Islamic Nationhood*, p. 2.

[60] On the Permi, its influence, and its leaders (Iljas Jacub, Djalaluddin Thaib, and Muchtar Luthfi), see Audrey Kahin, *Rebellion to Integration*, especially pp. 53–7. It is noteworthy that Permi leaders, especially Muchtar Luthfi, maintained close ties with Soekarno and the Partindo.

[61] Mohammad Natsir [Is], "Koerang tegas jang meragoekan," *Pembela Islam*, no. 35 (October 1931): 2–7.

Islam Indonesia] and the Muhammadiyah had hundreds of thousands of members in their branches throughout Indonesia. These organizations, founded exclusively on the principles of Islam, embodied the concept of Indonesian unity....

It was the Muslim movement that, by breaking down the barriers of provincial thinking, first implanted the idea of Indonesian unity. It was the Muslim movement, holding aloft the banner of Islam, that first inspired a sense of solidarity with the peoples of other colonial countries.[62]

With this perception of the ties that bound the peoples of the archipelago, Natsir considered that Soekarno's efforts to evoke earlier Hindu kingdoms such as Majapahit as a basis on which to build Indonesian nationalism were misguided and an extension of Javanism, which would alienate all ethnic groups outside Java.

Pendidikan Islam

After graduating from AMS, Natsir began to teach in the local MULO, where he got no salary, and he also gave courses to railway workers.[63] But he was unhappy with the lack of religious instruction in the schools where he taught, and, with other Muslim scholars, came to believe that a purely Western education drew young people away from their religious beliefs. ("The Western education given by the Dutch colonials merely filled the brain. The spirit was left empty.") On the other hand, he recognized that, while Islamic *pesantren* and *madrasah* provided their pupils with a good religious grounding, the education offered there usually left them blind to world developments. He had become acquainted with the branch of the Taman Siswa of Ki Hadjar Dewantara in Bandung, but felt it was too Java-centric and emphasized nationalism and Javanese culture to too great an extent.[64] So he determined to start his own school which could provide a balance between a solid education and a study of religion: "Its students would study modern subjects such as are taught in Dutch schools but their awareness and pride as Muslims would be cultivated and extended while their knowledge of the religion they embraced would be deepened."[65] For such an endeavor he needed to develop his own teaching skills, and seek financial capital and help from his friends and supporters.

---

[62] *Pembela Islam*, no. 36 (October 1931), cited in "Persatuan Islam" (typescript, n.d.), p. 48.

[63] Natsir, *Politik*, p. 11.

[64] Rosidi, *M. Natsir*, pp. 159–60.

[65] Ibid., p. 160.

He entered teachers' training school from 1931–2 and gained a teaching diploma, while writing articles, continuing his teaching, and enlisting his friends to help him in founding a school. In 1932, he established a school that he called the Pendidikan Islam (Pendis, Islamic Education). Haji Muhammad Yunus, a rich trader and one of the founders of Persis,[66] lent him money to buy desks and benches, and then helped him rent a small stone building for the school, while another rich friend donated a hectare of land to it. His friend Ummi Nur-Nahar, then teaching at the government-supported Arjuna school, willingly left this reasonably well-paid employment to become a teacher at the Pendidikan Islam.

Ummi too was from West Sumatra and from a family that was much more active in the political history of the region than Natsir's. Her father, Marzuki Datuk Seri Maharadjo, was a *penghulu kepala* [clan head] in Kamang and had been one of the leaders of the 1908 rebellion. Captured by the Dutch, he had been brought to Jakarta and imprisoned in Glodok jail, where he died. Ummi, who was born on May 24, 1905 in Bukittinggi, was five years old at the time of her father's death. Raised by her mother, she graduated from the Bukittinggi HIS when she was about fifteen and won a scholarship to Santa Ursula School in Batavia. After graduating from the Batavia school Ummi returned to Padang and taught home economics. When her sister Nurniar married in about 1926 and moved to Bandung, Ummi accompanied her and got a job teaching in the Arjuna school there. Her brother-in-law introduced her to Natsir, one of whose friends was married to a friend of Nurniar. When she agreed to teach at Natsir's Pendis school, Ummi accepted wages below those she was currently earning. After about a couple of years, in 1934 she and Natsir married, a marriage that would last until Ummi's death nearly sixty years later. After they wed Ummi continued to help Natsir in the school, not only teaching the lower grades but on several occasions pawning her bracelet in order to keep the school financially afloat, redeeming it whenever monetary pressures eased.[67]

In contrast to the Muhammadiyah schools, which were "characterized by a combination of traditional religious education and [a] modern school system,"[68] Pendis's curriculum approximated that of Dutch schools with the addition of classes in Islam. It also incorporated new liberal trends in education, such as were then being developed in the German Arbeid Schulen emphasizing practical

---

[66] Noer, *Modernist Muslim Movement*, p. 84.

[67] Most of this account is based on an interview with Natsir and Ummi's children, Jakarta, October 28, 2008. They also noted that on the maternal side, Ummi's family came from Natal.

[68] Nakamura, "Crescent Arises," p. 144.

education. Thus in the garden attached to the school, the students were trained in such skills as crop cultivation and marketing. Instruction was also offered in music and the arts, with Natsir himself teaching the violin.[69] Friday prayers were held within the school building. Starting from a small class of five pupils in a rented room, the Pendidikan Islam school gradually expanded. Natsir later estimated that its 7-year primary school came to enroll an average of about 80 students, its 3-year secondary school averaged about 90 pupils, and its 2-year teachers training school had an average of about 30 pupils. The schools were co-educational with the students separated only during recreation periods.[70] By 1938 Pendis schools had been established in five other locations in West Java and they remained open till the Japanese closed all private schools in 1942 after their invasion of Java.

Political Context

As noted above, in the early 1930s the religiously neutral nationalist movement had splintered under the weight of Dutch repression of the political parties and the arrest of their leaders. Harsh government restrictions on the activities of political organizations removed open opposition to colonial rule from the options most nationalists felt they could embrace unless they wanted to join their leaders in jail. Those nationalist politicians who were willing to act within the parameters laid down by the Dutch were allowed to participate in a minor way in the legislative advisory bodies established by the colonial government. But the impact even the most cooperative of Indonesians could exert was minimal, and up until the eve of the Japanese invasion, the Dutch authorities refused all Indonesian requests, however mild, for a greater role in the colony's political affairs.[71]

Attitudes in the Muslim community paralleled those among the religiously neutral nationalists, as disagreements arose regarding the stance they should adopt toward independence and toward the restrictive policies of the colonial

---

[69] See Natsir, *Politik*, p. 11, where he writes: "You know, Islam does not forbid art, including dramatic performances. I myself taught the violin."

[70] Interview, Jakarta, May 31, 1971. He noted that after the occupation most of the students continued their studies in education, but some went into the army. A few later became rectors in secondary schools and one girl became a judge.

[71] For example, they rejected both the Soetardjo Petition in 1938 and the requests for an Indonesian parliament in 1939. On Natsir's reactions to these, see below as well as his "Disekitar Petisi-Sutardjo" (*Capita Selecta* [I], pp. 233–7) and "Parlemen Indonesia" (ibid., pp. 253–78).

government. In the 1910s much of the nationalist movement — both secular and religious — had been unified within the loose federation of the Sarekat Islam, or Islamic League, which did not demand that its members pledge sole allegiance to the League, but allowed them also to participate in other nationalist parties and organizations. However, when, immediately after World War I, the SI leadership began to emphasize its purely Islamic character and ceased to tolerate other more secular nationalist streams, the League soon split. This disintegration did not cease with the expulsion of the Communists in 1921 and the Muhammadiyah in 1927, but continued after the party changed its name to Partai Sarekat Islam Indonesia in 1930 and its outstanding leader, Oemar Said Tjokroaminoto, died in 1933. At that time, the rifts within the PSII became more pronounced, especially between Tjokroaminoto's brother, Abikusno Tjokrosuyoso, and Haji Agus Salim, who with Tjokroaminoto had headed the party and shared the allegiance of most of its members.

One critical issue dividing the party membership was that of non-cooperation with the colonial government, or *hijrah*,[72] which had been the party's policy since the early 1920s. Two major splits over this issue occurred in the years leading up to World War II. In 1935 Salim proposed abandoning the *hijrah* stance in order to join with other nationalist coalitions, a position rejected by the faction headed by Abikusno, which insisted instead on the policy's continued full implementation. When Abikusno chose the party's general secretary, Sekarmadji Maridjan Kartosuwirjo, to be his deputy he charged him with producing a pamphlet outlining the intellectual justification for continuing the PSII's *hijrah* policy. Kartosuwirjo published a two-part pamphlet "Sikap Hijrah Partai Sarekat Islam," in November 1936, which was distributed to party members.[73] Salim, however, continued to reject the arguments outlined there and was expelled from the PSII in early 1937, after which, together with his followers, he established a new party, the Badan Penyadar PSII [Body to Awaken Consciousness in the PSII].

Shortly afterwards, in 1939, Kartosuwirjo, too, became estranged from the PSII leadership, when Abikusno changed his earlier stance, deciding to put aside the non-cooperation policy and join in the broader nationalist political

---

[72] A reference to Mohammad's withdrawal from Mecca to Medina in AD 622.

[73] Holk H. Dengel, *Darul Islam dan Kartosuwirjo: Langkah Perwujudan Angan-Angan yang Gagal* (Jakarta: Pustaka Sinar Harapan, 1995), pp. 18–23. The first part of the pamphlet discussed the relations between man and religion and between religion and politics, and the second explained the meaning of *hijrah* and why it needed to be embraced by the PSII. See also Chiara Formichi, "Pan-Islam and Religious Nationalism: The Case of Kartosuwiryo and Negara Islam Indonesia," *Indonesia* 90 (October 2010): 125-46, esp. p. 135.

coalition Gapi (Gabungan Politiek Indonesia, Federation of Indonesian Political Parties) demanding an Indonesian parliament. Defying the PSII's about-face on the issue, Kartosuwirjo continued to adhere to the *hijrah* policy. He was then expelled from the party, and in 1939 established what he described as the Komite Pembela Kebenaran PSII (KPK-PSII), or what was termed the "real PSII," with its base in West Java.[74] Although it was "impossible to estimate the extent of the support Kartosuwirjo and his Second PSII enjoyed,"[75] the PSII headed by Abikusno was clearly weakened, a situation that was exacerbated by the growing competition among its former members.

Disturbed by this factionalism among the Islamic politicians during the closing years of colonial rule, Muslim religious leaders, both the traditionalists of the Nahdlatul Ulama[76] and the reformists of the Muhammadiyah, made efforts to bridge the conflicts and compromise among themselves, an effort that bore initial fruit with the establishment of the Majelis Islam A'la Indonesia (MIAI – Supreme Council of Muslims of Indonesia) in September 1937. Originally formed in opposition to a marriage ordinance that the Dutch government was attempting to introduce,[77] this new federation stressed the need for unity among Indonesian Muslims whatever their political or theological orientation.

A further effort to bridge the internal divisions within the reformist Muslim community was made in December of the following year with the foundation of the Partai Islam Indonesia (PII), headed by Wiwoho Purbohadidjojo, a former JIB head and member of the Volksraad. Members of the Muhammadiyah dominated the central board of the PII but its branches also incorporated both Persis and Permi adherents. In the years leading up to the Japanese invasion, both the PII and the MIAI federation, while operating mainly in the religious field, willingly cooperated with religiously neutral nationalist groups in the

---

[74] Dengel, *Darul Islam dan Kartosuwirjo*, pp. 21–2. Several PSII members apparently accused him of misuse of party funds.

[75] C. Van Dijk, *Rebellion under the Banner of Islam* (The Hague: Nijhoff, 1981), p. 36.

[76] The Nahdlatul Ulama (NU, Revival of the Religious Scholars) was an organization founded in Surabaya in 1926 by Wahab Chasbullah (1888[?]–1971) and K.H. Hasyim Asyari (1871–1947), to represent traditionalist interests and resist the rise of modernism in Indonesian Islam. It had a strong following in East and Central Java. See Greg Fealy, "Wahab Chasbullah, Traditionalism and the Political Development of Nahdlatul Ulama," in *Nahdlatul Ulama, Traditional Islam and Modernity in Indonesia*, ed. Greg Barton and Greg Fealy (Clayton, Vic.: Monash Asia Institute, 1996), pp. 1–41.

[77] The proposed marriage law would have permitted Muslims to enter into a civil marriage, would have forbidden more than one wife, and would ensure that divorce take place before a judge of the secular court. See Greg Fealy and Virginia Hooker, *Voices of Islam in Southeast Asia* (Singapore: ISEAS, 2006), p. 43.

political arena to press for a larger role for Indonesians in the government of their country. In May 1939 the PII became a member of the political coalition, Gapi, which was calling for Indonesia's right to self-determination, for a democratically elected Indonesian parliament and for solidarity with the Netherlands "in order to maintain a strong anti-Fascist front."[78]

As internal divisions weakened the PSII, Natsir distanced himself from the party and largely avoided involvement in the tensions and rifts that developed within the Islamic community. Nevertheless, in addition to his educational activities, he remained very active as head of the Bandung branch of the JIB (Union of Young Muslims), and when the Partai Islam Indonesia (PII) was formed at the end of 1938 he agreed to head its Bandung branch.

With his entry into the PII, Natsir's major focus of attention shifted from his educational duties in West Java to broader political issues, especially colonial policies in Indonesia and the reluctance of the Dutch government to cede any real autonomy to the Indonesian people. He recognized that, while the PII had assumed a neutral position in the dispute regarding whether or not to cooperate with the Dutch, it clearly leant toward the cooperative position, and he argued consistently for the Dutch to accede to Indonesian demands for a more equal status in the governance of Indonesia.

In an article written immediately after the formation of the Partai Islam Indonesia, he focused attention on the Soetardjo petition of 1936, which had requested "that a conference be convened to discuss plans for the evolutionary development of Indonesia over a ten-year period toward self-government within the limits of the existing Dutch Constitution."[79] Only at the end of 1938 did the Dutch government respond to the petition, bluntly and completely rejecting it. In writing on the issue, Natsir contended that the government's blunt refusal was more important than the petition itself, in that it alerted the people to the hollowness of Dutch protestations of working together (*pekerdjaan bersama*) with the Indonesian people to face the threat now emerging from the fascist powers in Europe and Asia.[80] Thus, he said, the Dutch attitude had the unintended consequence of offending both the cooperating and non-cooperating groups, uniting them in their struggle.

In subsequent articles he went on to argue that, by rejecting moderate demands such as those in the Soetardjo petition, the Dutch government was pushing even cooperative groups to assume radical positions. And by cracking

---

[78] Kahin, *Nationalism and Revolution*, p. 97.
[79] Ibid., p. 95.
[80] Natsir, "Disekitar Petisi-Sutardjo"(December 1938) in *Capita Selecta* [I], pp. 233–7.

down on legal demonstrations and interpreting laws as strictly as possible, the government was inviting Indonesians to go beyond legal bounds in seeking their rights.[81]

The Dutch rebuffed not only the Soetardjo petition, but also the demands by the "Indonesia berparlemen" movement. In response to the movement's request that the Volksraad be changed "into a broadly based representative body to which the government would be responsible," the Netherlands Indies government stated that all administrative and political changes must be postponed until after the war. To the even more moderate Wiwoho Resolution asking for less sweeping changes in the Volksraad,[82] the government only replied after several months that it would appoint an investigative committee, the Visman Commission, to look into the matter.

In discussing the issue, Natsir pointed out that the Dutch proposal to form the Visman commission highlighted the lack of progress that had been achieved over the previous twenty years, in that establishment of the commission merely duplicated actions taken in 1920 when the government had established the Carpentier Alting commission with a similar mandate. Indeed, he stated, the current Dutch proposal was even less broad, for the earlier 30-man commission had incorporated respected Dutch figures and its 30 per cent Indonesian membership had included such well-known personalities as Haji Agus Salim and Dr. Radjiman. In contrast, the 7-member Visman commission established in 1940 included only government officials and its Indonesian members had no ties to the *pergerakan* (nationalist movement). The lack of progress over the previous twenty years, he contended, was further demonstrated by the fact that the colonial government had largely ignored the recommendations of the earlier commission that:

> the international situation, the development of the Eastern country [*negeri Timur* i.e. Indonesia], the reality of the colonial politics of the Dutch state itself, the increasingly sharp intelligence (*ketjerdasan*) of the country's population, — all these push for Indonesia to be given autonomy.[83]

Despite these recommendations, twenty years later the colonial government had taken only the smallest steps to realize such a goal.

Natsir's preoccupation in his writings thus focused on highlighting the unwillingness of the Dutch over the previous twenty years to cede any greater freedoms to the Indonesian people irrespective of the situation prevailing in

---

[81] Natsir, "Selingan I" (February, March 1940), in ibid., pp. 279–92, esp. pp. 287–8.
[82] Kahin, *Nationalism*, p. 98.
[83] Natsir, "Hervormingscommissie ke II" (November 1940), in *Capita Selecta* [I], p. 327.

the country at any particular stage. In making his arguments he turned back to exploring the question of nationalism. Recognizing the perilous situation brought about by the rise of fascism in Europe and Asia, he contended that the Dutch should realize that the more strongly the Indonesian people adhered to love of their country (*kebangsaan*), the more likely it was that they would join with the colonial power in confronting any outside threat. He pointed out that different communities within the Indies, such as the Arabs and Chinese and even the Indo-Europeans, were uniting against the common enemy and that the best method the Dutch could employ in defending their Indies colony was to respect the sentiments that tied the people of that colony together: "The ideals of wanting to live together, to live and die together existing among all the people in Indonesia, that above all should be advanced as a basis for protecting these Dutch Indies in the Far East."[84]

He was thus returning to the arguments he had been making earlier in his polemic with Soekarno, again relying on Renan's definition of nationalism, but now expanding it to include not only the different religious and ethnic groups but also the immigrant Arab and Chinese communities, and even the resident Dutch community, who shared interests with the indigenous people. These joint interests were recognized by Indonesian groups such as Gerindo, which had opened its membership to Indo-Europeans as it

> began to understand '*kebangsaan*' not with the sense of skin color, or language but in the spiritual sense with the desire and ideal of living and dying together ('le desir de vivre ensemble,' Renan).[85]

Natsir recognized that expanding the meaning of *kebangsaan* so widely stemmed from the special situation in which Indonesia found itself and said he could not foretell whether or not such shared interests were enough to guarantee a unified country that could fulfill the interests and needs of all groups involved or maintain national unity in the future among groups with different ideals and ideologies. But he contrasted the recognition of these joint interests which united all peoples in the East Indies with the limited "association" (*assosiatie*) policies that the Dutch had been pursuing since the turn of the century, where such association only embraced a few of the top Indonesian leaders as "compatriots" — with the effect of alienating these leaders from their own people.[86]

---

[84] Natsir, "Aliran Assosiasi Exit?" (January 1939), in ibid., p. 241.
[85] Natsir, "'Associatie' atau 'Belangengemeenschap'?" ibid., pp 298–304, esp. p. 302.
[86] Ibid., p. 298.

While uncertain as to how far any feelings of unity could last once the outside threat was removed, Natsir argued that by far the best course for the Dutch in the present situation would be to encourage such patriotic sentiments. He argued for "elimination of the colonial system that has become an obstacle to any sense of unity and sharing the same fate and destiny among the various groups" in Indonesia, and he pleaded that the Dutch "replace [this system] with an order and relationship that is more in accord with humanity and democratic foundations that are also the basis of Dutch life in Europe."[87] Expressing Indonesian disappointment with the Dutch stubborn refusal to meet even their most modest requests, he contrasted the frustration of the Indonesian people with the situation in other Asian countries under colonial rule. He cited the Vietnamese under the French, and the Indians under the British and especially the loyalty the Americans were able to elicit from the Filipinos in the struggle against the Japanese because they had trusted and granted wide measures of autonomy to the people of the Philippines during the previous decades.[88]

Thus, in presenting his arguments for the Dutch to grant the Indonesians greater autonomy, by the early 1940s Natsir was embracing a moderate position that was in accord with that of the religiously neutral parties. He was emphasizing the ties that bound together all the peoples who lived in the archipelago and displayed few signs of promoting the Muslim community in particular. In many ways the position he adopted on the eve of the Japanese invasion stood in sharp contrast to his previous attitude toward non-religious Indonesian nationalist leaders and movements. But it was a stance that would characterize his actions and priorities over the subsequent decade, when he collaborated fully with Soekarno and the other nationalists with whom he had disagreed during the 1930s. This would often lead to tensions between him and his Muslim followers. Throughout these years he viewed achieving the independence of Indonesia as a far higher priority than pursuing the individual aims of any of its constituent groups, including those of the religious community.

---

[87] Natsir, "Don't Miss the Bus," in *Capita Selecta* [I], p. 356.
[88] Natsir, "Rempah-Rempah," in ibid., pp. 374–6.

$$3$$

Entering the Political Arena, 1942–50

The Japanese Occupation

In mid-February 1942 the first Japanese troops parachuted into South Sumatra and on March 1 they landed in Java. Within eight days Lt. Gen. Ter Poorten, the Dutch commander on Java, surrendered to the invading forces.

The Japanese invasion marked a decisive turning point in the history of Indonesia, revealing the weakness of the Dutch and providing leaders of the Indonesian nationalist movement with the means for eventually achieving the independence of their country from their colonial overlord.

From the beginning of their occupation, the Japanese authorities were conscious of the important role Islam played in the lives of most Indonesians and they considered religion to be "one of the most effective means to penetrate into the spiritual recesses of Indonesian life and to infuse the influence of their own ideas and ideals at the bottom of the society."[1] They also realized that a smooth-running administrative organization in Java required cooperation from Islamic leaders, and so, as Harry Benda has written, Indonesian Muslims for the first time were faced with colonial rulers who were "actively interested in winning their support."[2] Their widespread influence in Indonesian society thus gave Muslim leaders a certain amount of bargaining power with the occupying authorities.

---

[1] M.A. Aziz, *Japan's Colonialism and Indonesia* (The Hague: Martinus Nijhoff, 1955), p. 200.

[2] Harry J. Benda, *The Crescent and the Rising Sun: Indonesian Islam under the Japanese Occupation 1942–1945* (The Hague and Bandung: Van Heuve, 1958), p. 107.

In an effort to court Muslim allegiance, the Japanese allowed the MIAI (Majelis Islam A'la Indonesia), the federation of Islamic groups formed in 1937, to be re-established on July 13, 1942.[3] They were, however, always uneasy with the organization, whose leadership was largely made up of "radical" PSII personnel. As the federation had initially been founded with the aim of opposing a marriage law the Dutch were attempting to introduce, the Japanese feared that this basic anti-Dutch stance might change to a more general "anti-foreign" orientation.[4] Eventually, in October 1943, the Japanese authorities again dissolved the MIAI. A month earlier, they had granted recognition to the more moderate and less political organizations Muhammadiyah and Nahdlatul Ulama (NU), and it was the leadership of these two bodies that formed the core of the Japanese-sponsored Masjumi, which was founded in late November 1943 as a non-political coordinating religious body "with the almost sole aim of supporting the Japanese war effort."[5]

At the same time, religious leaders were accorded prominent roles in the administration. The Department of Religious Affairs was placed under Indonesian leadership in November 1943 and a bureau of religious affairs was set up in every Residency (*shu*), giving religious leaders an accepted place within the bureaucracy. As M.A. Aziz has written:

> Islam obtained a privileged position in the political system in which, next to the secular administration, a religious apparatus had been created. The Japanese thus brought about a fundamental change in the traditional method of governing, by the increase of power for Islam.[6]

This was not, however, true in all fields. The Japanese were particularly keen to gain the loyalty and enthusiastic support of young people in the lands they occupied; so they were determined not to let either religious or nationalist teachers guide the education of Indonesian youth. Thus, while Islamic leaders were granted a greater role in the quasi-political organizations sponsored by the Japanese, they were restricted in running their own schools. The Japanese authorities retained the Guru Ordinance introduced by the Dutch in 1925, which limited the freedom of private schools, and they reinstated *priyayi* administrators in their supervisory roles over local religious schools.[7]

---

[3] It had been briefly banned after the invasion. Aziz, *Japan's Colonialism*, pp. 204–5.

[4] Ibid., p. 205.

[5] Benda, *Crescent and the Rising Sun*, p. 151. See also Deliar Noer, *Partai Islam di Pentas Nasional* (Jakarta: Grafiti, 1987), p. 26. It should be noted that the Masjumi was only established in Java, not on the other islands.

[6] Aziz, *Japanese Colonialism*, p. 206.

[7] Benda, *Crescent and the Rising Sun*, pp.128–9.

In Bandung, as elsewhere in the Netherlands East Indies, many of the local people at first welcomed the Japanese soldiers as liberators. But, in contrast to many other parts of the archipelago, in Bandung this enthusiasm did not rapidly turn to disillusionment and opposition. The better Indonesian–Japanese relations there were in part a result of the fact that Resident Aneha, the man appointed as Military Governor for West Java (which had Bandung as its capital city), had in the 1930s been the Japanese consul in Surabaya where he had developed some knowledge of and sympathy for the local people. He named an Indonesian *priyayi* (member of the Javanese aristocracy), Raden Admadinata, as Mayor of Bandung,[8] and allowed several *bupati* (district heads) to play a strong role in the city's government, although they were always partnered with a Japanese official. It was the new mayor Admadinata who invited Mohammad Natsir to head the education department in the city.

Over the previous decade Natsir had not only become a recognized Islamic thinker, but had been deeply involved in the administration of Islamic education in Bandung as well as in running his own Pendidikan Islam school, so he was well qualified to take charge of the city's educational affairs. Under the Japanese all educational institutions, both private and public, became government schools, but, after a brief transition period in the immediate aftermath of the invasion during which all schools were closed, religious schools were allowed to reopen alongside the public schools. Gradually, the Islamic *madrasah* in Bandung reappeared, and they operated with little Japanese interference.

Administration of the schools was decentralized under the occupation, with each Residency (*shu*) having its own Education Service.[9] In Bandung Natsir enjoyed considerable freedom of action in running educational affairs, especially as the local authorities there, in contrast with those in other regions, generally left critical tasks such as compiling the school curriculum to him and his colleagues. The Japanese administration on Java initially tried to suppress the use of Arabic in the schools, but by the end of 1942 they realized they could not forbid the teaching of the Qur'an in Arabic. But though from then on they allowed Arabic to be taught, its use in religious instruction was made "conditional on the acceptance of their [the Japanese] own standard curriculum in non-religious subjects and — more important still — on the teaching of their own language in addition to Arabic."[10] The administration also stipulated

---

[8] Indonesian mayors were appointed to all except three (Jakarta, Semarang, Surabaya) Javanese cities in November 1942. George Kanahele, "The Japanese Occupation of Indonesia: Prelude to Independence," PhD. Dissertation, Cornell University, 1967, pp. 61, 280.

[9] Benda, *Crescent and the Rising Sun*, p. 244.

[10] Ibid., p. 127.

that Japanese *taiso* (physical exercise, closely allied to Japanese ideals) as well as Japanese songs be included in the curriculum. The use of Dutch was banned, and was replaced by Indonesian as the language of instruction, with the local dialect of Sundanese also taught in the elementary and middle schools. Natsir later stressed that he always attempted to ensure that the schools were infused with an Indonesian not a Japanese spirit, and he resisted further efforts at Japanization.

Natsir was able to establish and head an Islamic council (Majlis Islam), which became a coordinating body for teachers and religious leaders throughout the municipality of Bandung. Through this body, which was housed in a building near the City Hall, he was able to maintain contact with other religious leaders and keep them *au courant* with the government's activities. When the government sponsored training programs for *kyai* (Muslim clerics) from other parts of Java Natsir was one of the organizers. The Japanese intended these programs to provide instruction on "Japanese ideas and beliefs, educational methods and even sports," but Natsir and his colleagues apparently used them also to discuss Islamic beliefs and "play down — and often contradict — much of the Japanese public teaching and propaganda, particularly the doctrines of chosen race and the divinity of the emperor."[11] As a leading member of the prewar MIAI and PII, Natsir was appointed to the Masjumi's organizing committee when it was formed, and from there he was able to keep in touch with former colleagues from MIAI and other pre-war Muslim organizations.

The people of Bandung, then, seem to have enjoyed greater freedom than their compatriots in most other parts of the archipelago. But friction still did erupt between the Japanese authorities and Muslim leaders over a number of issues, especially over the Japanese belief in the divinity of their emperor and their insistence that Indonesians participate in the habitual ceremony of bowing in the direction of the imperial palace in Tokyo. Such obeisance offended Muslims, for the deep bow, or *saikeirei*, prescribed for the ceremony closely resembled the ritual bow of Muslims toward Mecca. Few Muslims, however, had the courage not to participate. The striking exception was the respected Minangkabau Islamic leader, Haji Abdul Karim Amrullah, who had been jailed by the Dutch in the final years of their rule, and was now being courted by the Japanese. In early 1943 at a meeting in Bandung of *kyai* from all over Java, Amrullah was given a place of honor and was seated among the Japanese participants. When the rest of the gathering rose to perform the *saikeirei*, he

---

[11] Howard M. Federspiel, *Persatuan Islam: Islamic Reform in Twentieth Century Indonesia* (Ithaca: CMIP, 1970), pp. 113–4.

alone remained seated.[12] The respect for Haji Amrullah among both Indonesians and Japanese was apparently so high that this act of defiance led to no reprisals against him.

Natsir never displayed similar courage, though, according to his recollections, he himself usually avoided participating in the ceremony by arriving late whenever it was scheduled. Perhaps as a result of Haji Amrullah's action, the Islamic community grew increasingly resentful at Japanese insistence on performance of the *saikeirei*, and finally in October of that year the government gave Muslims permission not to participate in the ceremony.[13]

From early 1944, the impact of Japanese military reverses began to influence their policies toward the people under their occupation. To enlist Indonesian support against what they anticipated would be an imminent counterattack from the Allied forces, the Japanese had established volunteer Indonesian militias in late 1943 — the Pembela Tanah Air (Peta, Defenders of the Fatherland) on Java and Gyu gun in Sumatra and Kalimantan, many of whose top leaders were Muslim. It has been estimated that perhaps 30 or 40 per cent of the battalion commanders "had a strong Islamic background."[14] On March 1, 1944, they also set up an organizational body, the Java Hokokai, drawn mostly from recognized religiously neutral Indonesians, predominantly *pangreh praja* (administrative officials), with Muslims enjoying only minor representation.[15] After Prime Minister Kuniaki Koiso made a statement on September 5, 1944 promising to grant Indonesia eventual independence within the Greater East Asian Co-prosperity Sphere, the Japanese acceded to a request of the Java Hokokai and instituted a special youth corps, the Pioneer Corps (Barisan Pelopor) directly under nationalist leadership.[16]

During 1944 Islamic leaders were strengthened *vis-à-vis* the *priyayi* as the Japanese encouraged Muslims to identify their goals with those of the Japanese and proclaim a Holy War in pursuit of them.[17] In December 1944, shortly after establishment of the Pioneer Corps, Japanese authorities balanced this secular militia with a special Islamic volunteer corps, known as the Hizbullah (or Army

---

[12] Hamka, *Ajahku*, 3rd printing (Jakarta: Penerbit Djajamurni, 1967), pp. 192–3. Benda, *Crescent and Rising Sun*, pp. 123–4.

[13] Benda, *Crescent and the Rising Sun*, p. 126.

[14] David Jenkins, "Soeharto and the Japanese Occupation," *Indonesia* 88 (October 2009): 1–103, esp. p. 47.

[15] The Hokokai was essentially an organization aimed at providing a structure in which most of the Japanese-sponsored associations on Java could be incorporated. Exceptions were the Masjumi and NU. Kanahele, "Japanese Occupation," pp. 142–3.

[16] Ibid., p. 166.

[17] Ibid., pp. 141, 164.

of Allah). The Japanese recruited and trained five hundred young Indonesian Muslims to lead this paramilitary force, which was "designed to harness Islamic support behind the Japanese" in anticipation of a future Allied invasion of Java.[18] Its first training camp was officially opened in West Java on February 18, 1945. The Hizbullah was tied directly to the Islamic political leaders in the Masjumi "to whom its members had to swear unswerving allegiance."[19]

Natsir's growing prominence in educational affairs in Bandung and his earlier activity in the Jong Islamieten Bond where he had come to know such nationalist Islamic leaders as Haji Agus Salim, Prawoto Mangkusasmito, Mohamad Roem and Jusuf Wibisono,[20] brought him to the notice of Mohammad Hatta. Only after his return from internal exile at the beginning of the Japanese occupation, did Hatta first encounter the young Muslim teacher, though he had met some of his friends nearly ten years earlier.[21] Recognized as one of the two paramount leaders of the Indonesian nationalist movement, second only to Soekarno, Hatta was one of the Indonesians most influential with the Japanese authorities. In early 1945, the Japanese allowed him to set up and head a tertiary institution for Islamic education in Jakarta, the Sekolah Tinggi Islam (STI, Islamic High School),[22] and in April of that year Hatta chose Natsir to be the secretary for the school, in charge of its administration.[23] In the closing months of the occupation Natsir traveled frequently between Bandung and Jakarta to teach at the school and conduct its business.[24]

---

[18] Jenkins, "Soeharto and the Japanese Occupation," p. 29.

[19] Benda, *Crescent and Rising Sun*, p. 179.

[20] Prawoto and Wibisono were active members of the Studenten Islam Studieclub (SIS) before the war, as well as of the JIB. They were also among the JIB group that Natsir used to meet with at Haji Salim's house and, with Roem, they became some of his closest colleagues in the Masjumi Party. See *Mohamad Roem 70 Tahun, Pejuang-Perunding* (Jakarta: Bulan Bintang, 1978), pp. 202–14, and Deliar Noer, *Aku Bagian Ummat Aku Bagian Bangsa: Otobiografi* (Bandung: Penerbit Mizan, 1996), pp. 222–4.

[21] See Mohammad Hatta, "Mohammad Natsir dan Mr. Mohamad Roem 70 Tahun," in *Mohamad Roem 70 Tahun, Pejuang-Perunding*, pp. 202–3, where he also recalls meeting Roem at Haji Salim's house in 1932. Hatta had been interned on Banda Neira with Sutan Sjahrir, from 1934 until the Dutch brought him back to Jakarta immediately before the Japanese invasion.

[22] This was one of three Sekolah Tinggi that the Japanese permitted to offer social studies as well as Islamic teaching. Deliar Noer, *Aku Bagian Ummat*, p. 223; Hatta, "Mohammad Natsir dan Mr. Mohamad Roem 70 Tahun," pp. 319–20.

[23] Deliar Noer, *Mohammad Hatta: Biografi Politik* (Jakarta: LP3ES, 1990), p. 194. Natsir's official title was Kepala Tata Usaha, or head of administration.

[24] Reportedly one of his students at the time was Pramoedya Ananta Toer. *Sabili* Edisi Khusus, p. 25.

During this period tensions were again growing between the religiously neutral nationalists and the Islamic leaders. In the Japanese-sponsored Investigatory Body for Preparatory Work for Indonesian Independence (Badan Penyelidik Usaha Persiapan Kemerdekaan Indonesia, BPUPKI), leaders from both groups began to discuss the basis of a future Indonesian state. In this body, on June 1, 1945, Soekarno first laid out the "Five Principles" or *Pancasila* that would become Indonesia's state ideology. These principles were nationalism, internationalism or humanitarianism, democracy, social justice and belief in God.[25] In elucidating the *Pancasila*, Soekarno rejected demands for an Islamic state, and directly challenged the Muslim community to follow a democratic course if they wished to realize that ideal, stating

> If we are really an Islamic people, let us work hard so that most of the seats in the people's representative body we will create are occupied by Islamic delegates ... then the laws made by this representative body will naturally be Islamic laws, too, ... We say that ninety per cent of us are Islamic in religion, but look around you in this gathering and see what percentage give their votes to Islam?... To me it is proof that Islam does not yet flourish among the masses.[26]

Islamic leaders felt that the *Pancasila* did not fully guarantee their position, but they eventually on June 22 reached a compromise expounded in the so-called "Jakarta Charter," which positioned Belief in God as the first principle in the *Pancasila* and included in the draft constitution a phrase that came to be known as the "seven words": *"dengan kewadjiban mendjalankan Sjari'at Islam bagi pemeluk-pemeluknja"* (with the obligation for adherents of Islam to practice Islamic law). The Committee placed these words in the draft constitution's preamble,[27] but at the initiative of Mohammad Hatta they were dropped in the provisional Constitution adopted on August 18, 1945 by the Indonesian Independence Preparatory Committee (Panitia Persiapan Kemerdekaan Indonesia,

---

[25] See Adnan Buyung Nasution, *The Aspiration for Constitutional Government in Indonesia* (Jakarta: Sinar Harapan, 1992), p. 10. Nasution sees Soekarno's speech as an effort to overcome the conflict between proponents of a secular state and those of an Islamic state. See also Muhammad Yamin, *Naskah-Persiapan Undang-Undang Dasar 1945* (Jakarta: Jajasan Prapantja, 1959) and George McT. Kahin, *Nationalism and Revolution in Indonesia* (Ithaca: Cornell University Press, 1951), pp. 122–7.

[26] Kanahele, "Japanese Occupation," p 198. This is a somewhat spurious argument as it is difficult to see how the committee's members can be described in any real sense as "representative" of the Indonesian people.

[27] B.J. Boland, *The Struggle of Islam in Modern Indonesia* (The Hague: Martinus Nijhoff, 1971), p. 27.

PPKI), which succeeded the earlier body.[28] This new 21-member body "was overwhelmingly dominated by non-Islamic politicians of the older generation," and had only two representatives of Islamic organizations (Ki Bagus Hadikusumo and Kiyai Wahid Hasjim, the leaders of the Muhammadiyah and NU), from the traditionalist and reformist streams.[29]

Dissension within the Islamic community over omission of the "seven words" from the Indonesian Constitution would convulse Indonesian politics over subsequent decades as religious and secular groups struggled over the place Islam would occupy in the new state.[30] Immediately after the Japanese surrender, the PPKI was itself transformed into the Central Indonesian National Committee (KNIP), which became Indonesia's Parliament during the early years of independence.

The Japanese defeat came too swiftly for the victorious Allied forces to achieve a transfer of power smooth enough to guarantee Dutch reassertion of control over their former colony. In July 1945 the Allied leaders at Potsdam had shifted responsibility for operations in most of the Netherlands East Indies from US General Douglas McArthur to the South East Asia Command (SEAC) of Admiral Louis Mountbatten, whose authority had previously extended from mainland Southeast Asia only to Sumatra. The sudden Japanese collapse in the wake of the atomic bombing of Hiroshima and Nagasaki on August 6 and 9, prevented Mountbatten's British and Indian forces from mustering the manpower, transport and military intelligence needed to embark on their task of repatriating the Japanese and liberating Allied prisoners of war on Java and Sumatra until at least late September. By that time Soekarno and Hatta

---

[28] Hatta intervened to have the seven words omitted, because, according to his own account, a Japanese naval officer (*opsis kaigun*) had assured him that Protestants and Catholics in the eastern archipelago strongly objected to the earlier formulation, viewing it as discriminating against minority religious groups. Fearing that islands outside Java and Sumatra would break from the Republic if the phrase were used, Hatta persuaded other members of the Committee to remove the words. Mohammad Hatta, *Sekitar Proklamasi* (Jakarta: Tintamas, 1970), pp. 66–70.

[29] A prewar NU and MIAI leader, Wahid was "the son and mouthpiece for his father, Hasyim Asy'ari, the most powerful traditionalist ulama in the country." Greg Fealy, personal communication, April 2011. (He was also the father of Abdurrahman Wahid, who became president of Indonesia in 1999.) Hadikusumo had headed Muhammadiyah since 1942 and had been a leading figure in Muslim education and politics since the 1920s. See also Benedict R. O'G. Anderson, *Java in a Time of Revolution* (Ithaca: Cornell University Press, 1972), p. 64; Noer, *Partai Islam di Pentas Nasional*, p. 38.

[30] For a full discussion of the place of the "seven words" in the Constitution and Hatta's role, see R.E. Elson, "Another Look at the Jakarta Charter Controversy of 1945," *Indonesia* 88 (October 2009): 105–30.

had proclaimed Indonesia's independence and hasty measures had begun in the capital and other parts of Java and Sumatra to create a functioning Republican state apparatus. Australian forces were already strongly established in Kalimantan and New Guinea (Irian Barat), however, and immediately after the Japanese surrender they moved to help the Dutch reassert their authority in much of the eastern archipelago.

Up until this time, Natsir had been known as one of the most promising of the young Islamic intellectuals and a leading figure in religious education in Bandung. He was also identified in many people's minds with the strictest of the modernist Islamic organizations, the Persatuan Islam, and the attitudes and thoughts of its best-known leader, Ahmad Hassan. In the years leading up to the invasion, he had shown an interest in and understanding of national and international politics through his leadership position in the Partai Islam Indonesia and through the articles he published in *Pandji Islam* on Dutch policies toward the Netherlands East Indies.[31] But from the end of the Japanese occupation, he was drawn directly into national politics, and not as a spokesman for Islamic grievances at Islam's subservient position in the new Indonesian Republic, nor as a champion for an Islamic state, but as a loyal and enthusiastic partner of the Republic's paramount leaders, Natsir's former antagonist Soekarno and Mohammad Hatta, a devout Muslim, but a man who had based his political career on the principle of religiously neutral political parties.

Unfortunately, the years of occupation and revolution were the one period in his life when Natsir, absorbed in his political activities, seems to have written little other than the official pronouncements that his job called for. So the picture of him during this period has to depend largely on his official writings, together with his recollections from several decades later, and the accounts of those, both Indonesians and outsiders, who came into contact with him as a member of the Republican government.

Revolution 1945–49

It was by chance that Natsir first mounted the national stage. As he himself recounts, on one of his visits to Jakarta in September 1945 he was staying at the house of Kahar Muzakkir, a prominent Muhammadiyah youth leader,[32] who

---

[31] See Chapter 2.

[32] Also known as A. Kahar Mudjakkir (1908–73), he had been trained in Cairo. After returning to Indonesia in the mid-1930s he was appointed to various posts in Jakarta under the Japanese. See Nakamura, "Crescent Rises," pp. 140, 173, 199.

took him along to a meeting of the central branch of the Indonesian National Committee (KNIP, Komite Nasional Indonesia Pusat).

> When we arrived in front of the Gedung Komidi [a theater where the meeting was being held] I wanted just to wait outside, but Pak Kahar Muzakkir urged me to accompany him inside. He said to the guard 'This is Saudara Mohammad Natsir.' Thus the guard wrote my name in the list of the participants. And from that time, I became a member of the KNIP.[33]

According to Natsir's account, two months later, when the number of Committee members had reached an unmanageable 232, he, Dr. Sarwono and Sudarsono were asked to form a working body (Badan Pekerja) to meet on a regular basis as a core group of the council.[34]

Allied forces under British command began landing in Jakarta on September 29, with the assigned tasks of accepting the surrender of the Japanese armed forces, releasing Allied war prisoners and civilian internees, and disarming and concentrating the Japanese soldiers in preparation for their repatriation to Japan.[35] Under protection of the Allies, Dutch troops too began to land in Java. From November 1945, the Allied command controlled the radio facilities in Jakarta, allowing the Dutch and Republic limited opportunities to broadcast over the airwaves. The only radio under Republican control at that time was the one in Bandung, so, according to Natsir, he used this connection to establish links overseas: "Every evening about 9 pm we would telephone Bandung and let them know what we wanted to broadcast, and Bandung spread this abroad, particularly to Radio India."[36] He wrote that they also kept in touch with students overseas, especially in the Middle East, recalling that he helped some of the Indonesian students in Baghdad to publish a monthly journal *Merdeka*, founded with the aim of introducing Indonesia to the outside world.[37]

Natsir considered that in these early months he was in fact performing much of the work of an information minister, and it was apparently no great surprise to him when on January 3, 1946, Prime Minister Sutan Sjahrir appointed him to replace Amir Sjarifuddin as the Republic's official minister

---

[33] Mohammad Natsir, *Politik Melalui Jalur Dakwah* (Jakarta: Media Da'wah, 2008), p. 17.

[34] Ibid., pp. 17–8. I have found no other accounts of the period that assign Natsir this role in formation of the Working Committee of the KNIP. He was apparently not one of its founding members, though Dr. Sudarsono, a close follower of Sjahrir, was. See Anderson, *Java in a Time of Revolution*, pp. 174–5. Natsir did become a member in September 1945, but resigned on being appointed minister of information in January 1946.

[35] Kahin, *Nationalism and Revolution*, p. 141.

[36] Natsir, *Politik*, p. 20.

[37] Ibid., pp. 20–1.

of information, a position he would hold for much of the Revolution.[38] It was, however, a surprise to many others, for he lacked his predecessor's reputation and experience and, although well known in the religious community, he was very new to the field of practical politics other than through his writings. He had, however, played a leading role in the establishment of the Muslim political party, Masjumi, at the Indonesian Muslim Congress (Kongres Umat Islam Indonesia) in November 1945.

In appointing him minister of information, Sjahrir must have been drawing in part on his knowledge of Natsir's character through his family ties with Natsir's wife, Ummi.[39] Natsir and Sjahrir had probably also come to know each other well when they were fellow students in Bandung (1927–9), though they were in different classes there. But Sjahrir was not alone in perceiving the political strengths of the young Muslim leader. President Soekarno, too, enthusiastically supported the appointment. In recounting his renewed relations with Soekarno after their prewar public disputes, Natsir recalls:

> When Sjahrir first proposed to Bung Karno that I become Minister of Information, Bung Karno responded "*Hij is de man.*" [He's the (right) man]. I didn't meet with him at the time. Then when we did meet in Yogya, we first pretended not to remember what had happened earlier. It was better to confront the current situation and let go of what was in the past, because we were now facing a great struggle. "How about us? We certainly clashed earlier," Bung Karno then said. "Yes," I replied rather jokingly. "Now that serves no purpose, later we can resume it." So from then on we were indeed close.[40]

Natsir took over his post at a time when the growing numbers of Dutch soldiers landing in Jakarta were making the situation untenable for the Republican government. Indonesian political leaders decided to leave the capital, and the day after his appointment Natsir withdrew with them to the Republic's new capital of Yogyakarta in Central Java, though he continued to commute between there and Jakarta as his work demanded. As information

---

[38] After being appointed toward the end of the first Sjahrir cabinet, he held the position in the second and third Sjahrir cabinets (March 1946–June 1947), and in the Hatta cabinet formed in January 1948 after the Renville agreements. Susan Finch and Daniel S. Lev, *Republic of Indonesia Cabinets 1945–1965* (Ithaca: Cornell Modern Indonesia Project, 1965), pp. 4–9,14–5. Amir was appointed to the post of minister of defense.

[39] Both Sjahrir and Ummi had family in Natal and Sjahrir's older brother, St. Nur Alamsyah was married to Ummi's older sister (Puteri Amna) who died fairly young. Interview with Natsir's children, October 28, 2008.

[40] Natsir, *Politik*, pp. 22–3.

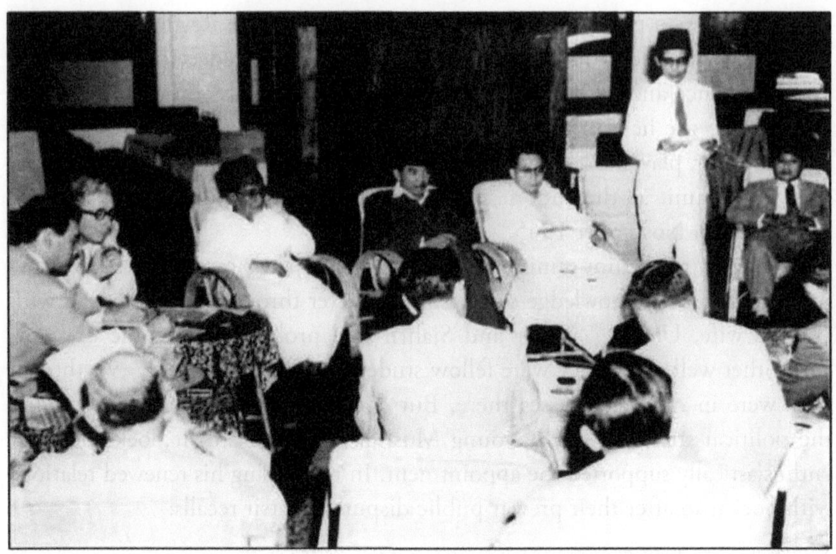

Natsir addresses press conference, 1946
(seated from L to R: H. Agus Salim, President Soekarno,
Vice President Mohammad Hatta).

minister, he worked on a daily basis with both Soekarno and Hatta, writing Soekarno's Independence Day speeches and being involved in preparing all the important statements issued by the president and vice president. The three worked collectively in keeping the people of the new Republic informed of the government's policies and activities.

Natsir saw his major function as communicating the government's policies to its followers: "I was the one who had to sell bread to the people." In performing this function, he was remarkably successful, in large part because of his honesty and openness. He was always willing to meet with journalists, maintaining good relations with them and frankly discussing the political and military situation. "The journalists would come to Natsir to ask about every incident in the revolutionary struggle, both concerning the government's opinion and the attitude of the Dutch and so on. Natsir frequently gave press interviews. The number of these interviews expanded the Ministry of Information's influence among the people."[41]

As information minister, Natsir was also the government's major intermediary in explaining its policies to its restless adherents in other parts of Java

---

[41] "Mohammad Natsir," in St. Rais Alamsjah, *10 Orang Indonesia terbesar Sekarang* (Bukittinggi and Jakarta: Mutiara, 1952), p. 91.

and Sumatra. He was a member of the delegation, headed by Defense Minister Amir Sjarifuddin that was sent in April 1946 to calm the "social revolution" that had broken out in East Sumatra as well as smaller outbreaks in other parts of the island. Though having little influence over the left-wing forces that were responsible for much of this unrest, Natsir's strongest cards in negotiating with impatient and dissident elements in Sumatra were the respect he enjoyed in the Muslim community as a whole, as well as his roots outside of Java. Though his status as a Muslim leader meant little in the 1946 revolts in East Sumatra, it carried greater weight the following year when in the aftermath of the signing of the Linggajati agreements[42] he tried to mediate a more limited revolt in his home region of West Sumatra.

The controversial talks at Linggajati, held under Allied auspices, stretched from December 1946 to March 1947, and engendered growing unrest in much of Sumatra and Java, as well as among Republicans in the other Dutch-occupied islands, over the concessions the Republic was making to Dutch demands. When the two sides finally reached an agreement, it involved the Republic surrendering its claims to authority over much of the "Outer Islands" in exchange for Dutch recognition of the Republic as the *de facto* authority in Java and Sumatra. But this recognition of the Republic's limited authority was coupled with an agreement that the Indonesian army would withdraw from major urban areas, leaving only a small contingent of police and a skeletal administration within these towns. The denial of Republican claims to nation-wide authority met with widespread opposition in many parts of the archipelago and Linggajati was in any case soon overturned by the first Dutch "police action" of July 1947, which violated its terms only four months after the agreement had been signed.

Republican willingness to cede territory to Dutch forces under this agreement was opposed in particular by some of the irregular militias that had sprung up in the early days of the Revolution, including the Islamic Hizbullah and Sabilillah, which were especially strong in West Java, Aceh and West Sumatra. On March 3 units drawn from these Muslim militias, planning to seize power from the military and civilian leadership of the Republic, rose up against the administration in Bukittinggi and other towns of West Sumatra. The rebels were rapidly suppressed, and their leaders, including members of the Masjumi and Hizbullah, arrested. When reports of the largely Muslim

---

[42] Under British auspices, representatives of the Netherlands and the Republic initialed the Linggajati agreement on November 12, 1946, and signed it on May 25, 1947 as a settlement to the Indonesian–Dutch dispute. It soon broke down.

rebellion reached Java on the final days of ratifying the Linggajati agreements, they caused consternation among top leaders of the Masjumi party. Three weeks later Natsir led an investigation team to Bukittinggi to find out how far the Masjumi's local branch had been involved in the revolt. The team finally reached the conclusion that, as a whole, the local Masjumi was not responsible for the attempted power seizure, though some of its members had actively participated. Nevertheless, it found considerable dissatisfaction among the Muslim politicians and militias with both the local and national Republican leadership. Reluctant to further alienate these groups, the local authorities took minimal actions against them and only two of their leaders were eventually brought to trial.[43]

In the field of foreign relations, while Sjahrir, as foreign minister, headed the official efforts abroad to gain international recognition for the nascent Republic, Natsir was its major intermediary at home with its foreign sympathizers. As such, his simplicity and general demeanor seem to have impressed overseas visitors. A young British supporter of the new Republic, who ran the Dutch blockade in order to come to Yogyakarta in early 1948, wrote that in the Ministry of Information he encountered

> a soft-voiced Sumatran of about forty, with very gentle manners.... I formed the impression that Natsir was a sincere, kindly man, who would be incapable of harshness or injustice. He at once gave the impression that he consequently and invariably confirmed: here was a man of a modest, deep and controlled sincerity. With his black eyes and high forehead, and with his pale face topped by unruly greying hair, he had something of the quality of Jimmy Maxton, though he had none of the latter's external fanaticism.... I liked him instinctively.[44]

It was Natsir's simplicity of dress that struck George Kahin when he first met him:

> When the next day I called at the Ministry of Information to see Mohammad Natsir I encountered a modest unpretentious man whose clothes certainly didn't make him look like a Government Minister. Indeed, he was attired in one of the most mended shirts I'd seen on any official in a government where simplicity of dress was the norm. Later I found that some of his staff had felt

---

[43] On this incident, see Audrey Kahin, *Rebellion to Integration: West Sumatra and the Indonesian Polity* (Amsterdam: Amsterdam University Press, 1999), pp. 123–6.

[44] John Coast, *Recruit to Revolution* (London: Christophers, 1952), p. 97. Born in Glasgow, James Maxton (1885–1946) was a leading member of the Independent Labour Party in Britain between the wars, with a reputation as one of the best parliamentary orators of his generation.

obliged to take up a collection so that their Minister could have one set of proper clothes to wear on important occasions.[45]

While Natsir retained close working relations with Soekarno throughout the Revolution, he was closer in background, attitude and temperament to the two other most prominent leaders of the early Republic, Vice President Mohammad Hatta and Socialist Party head and first prime minister, Sutan Sjahrir. As Bernard Dahm has written, Natsir's "breadth of culture suggests comparison with Sjahrir and Hatta, who also came from West Sumatra; but unlike them, he was concerned for the renewal of Muslim life in a changing world."[46] Sharing Minangkabau culture — all were born in West Sumatra: Hatta in 1902 and Sjahrir in 1909, the year after Natsir — the three had the basis for a working relationship as well as a personal friendship. Hatta's early schooling in West Sumatra was similar to Natsir's — a mix of formal Western education and additional courses in the religious schools run by the notable *ulama* of the region. In contrast, Sjahrir's family left West Sumatra when he was only a year old, and most of his early education was in the cosmopolitan city of Medan in North Sumatra.[47]

All three received Western secondary education (Hatta at the Prins Hendrikschool in Batavia, and Sjahrir and Natsir at the AMS in Bandung, where Sjahrir was a year ahead of Natsir), and it was only after they graduated that their paths diverged, with Hatta and Sjahrir going on to Holland to continue their studies and eventually form a nationalist political party, the New PNI (PNI Baru), while Natsir chose to abandon his legal studies, remaining in Bandung to devote himself to Islamic education.

Yet, this choice and emphasis did not cut Natsir off from his fellow Minangkabau. As a politician in the years after 1945, his political perspective grew closer to that of Hatta than to his earlier mentor, Ahmad Hassan. His personal and political ties were perhaps strongest with Sjahrir. In his approach to political organization he always favored the establishment of cadre and the education of party members as the firmest and most reliable bases for developing a political party, an approach similar to that pursued by Sjahrir in

---

[45] George McT. Kahin, "Mohammad Natsir," in *Muhammad Natsir 70 Tahun: Kenang-kenangan Kehidupan dan Perjuangan*, ed. Yusuf Abdullah Puar, *et al.* (Jakarta: Pustaka Antara, 1978), p. 330.

[46] Bernhard Dahm, *History of Indonesia in the Twentieth Century* (NewYork: Praeger, 1971), pp. 151–2.

[47] See Mavis Rose, *Indonesia Free: A Political Biography of Mohammad Hatta* (Ithaca: Cornell Modern Indonesia Project, 1987), pp. 6–10; Rudolf Mrazek, *Sjahrir: Politics and Exile in Indonesia* (Ithaca: Cornell Southeast Asia Program, 1994), pp. 23–4.

organizing his Socialist Party (PSI) and by both Sjahrir and Hatta in the early 1930s in forming the PNI Baru.

Natsir's strong religious affiliation was never in doubt, and he led a pious and humble life, consistent with his understanding of Islam, but he was regarded as a moderate member of the Muslim community. He had actively participated in founding the Masjumi party in November 1945, and headed the group known as the "religious socialists" within the party. George Kahin described Natsir and his faction this way:

> The Religious Socialists drew much of their inspiration from the teachings of Mohammad Abduh. However, the views of this young and dynamic group were in large measure their own and new. They represented the impact of the Indonesian revolution upon sincere young Mohammedans possessed of enlightened minds and a strong sense of their duty to serve society. Their principal leaders — Mohammad Natsir, Mr. Sjafruddin Prawiranegara, Mr. Mohammad Roem, Mr. Jusuf Wibisono, and Dr. Abu Hanifah — found considerable common ground with the moderate socialists who followed Sjahrir and with such progressive leaders of the small but effective Christian Party as Dr. Leimena and Mr. Tambunan.[48]

Later, however, Natsir explained that the term "religious socialists" was something of a misnomer "for the socio-economic formula which he and these colleagues espoused called for a mixed economy, encompassing socialist, co-operative, and private components, but with it being understood that attached to private property went the social responsibility to use it in a way that would promote the welfare of the community as well as that of the owner."[49]

This political philosophy, especially its emphasis on a mixed economy and the importance it assigned to the idea of cooperatives, was closest to that of Vice President Hatta. Indeed in outlook and philosophy Natsir and Hatta were very similar, though, at least until the early years of the Suharto regime, Hatta always rejected the idea of a political party based on religion,[50] while Natsir was a leading member of the Islam-based Masjumi. With both Hatta and Sjahrir, Natsir shared a strong belief in representative democracy as the best form of government for the newly-independent Indonesian state.

In providing the public face of the Republican government, Hatta and Natsir probably exerted something of a brake on the more mercurial Soekarno.

---

[48] Kahin, *Nationalism and Revolution*, p. 157.

[49] Kahin, "In Memoriam: Mohammad Natsir," *Indonesia* 56 (October 1993): 161–2.

[50] As noted earlier, Hatta was responsible for removing the "seven words" of the Jakarta Charter from the Preamble to the 1945 Constitution, and he was also the prime proponent for removing the provision that the Head of State should be a Muslim. See Nasution, *Aspiration for Constitutional Government*, p. 64.

It is interesting to note that each attributed to the other the pivotal role in guiding Soekarno's policies and utterances, Natsir writing:

> Hatta decided everything important. Bung Karno never wanted to issue a statement if Bung Hatta didn't agree. For instance, in facing difficult problems, such as the Madiun affair [the Communist uprising of September 1948] and other affairs, Bung Hatta was the one to decide the policy.[51]

For his part, Hatta recalled, "Bung Karno didn't want to sign any government declaration if it had not been prepared by Saudara Natsir,"[52] and he later described Natsir as "Sukarno's golden boy during the revolution."[53]

Though in political philosophy and religious adherence Hatta and Natsir were very much in harmony, they do not appear to have been personally close. Hatta's description of the relationship between Soekarno and Natsir indicates perhaps a degree of cynicism toward Natsir, and certainly during the later regional rebellion Natsir felt disappointed and disillusioned at Hatta's stance.[54] It is likely that the feeling was mutual. In personality and behavior there were clearly wide differences between them. Deliar Noer many years later pinpointed one contrast between the two, writing:

> He [Natsir] differed ... from another Indonesian leader, Mohammad Hatta.... People respected Hatta because he guarded his time so carefully. Natsir was admired because the door of his house was always open, whenever and to whomever. Lines of people wanting to meet with him were like queues outside a successful doctor's office. Among them were people from all levels of society, ordinary people [*awam*], religious teachers [*ulama*], intellectuals, businessmen, laborers, farmers, students, and young people.[55]

Natsir seemed to feel greater affinity with Socialist Party head Sutan Sjahrir not only in their socio-economic views but also on a personal basis. Though Sjahrir was much more worldly, the two were life-long friends and neighbors, and in the political sphere, the Natsir faction of the Masjumi always seemed most in tune with the Sjahrir-led faction of the Socialist Party.

In carrying out his official duties, especially in implementing the largely non-confrontational policies of the Republican government, Natsir had to

---

[51] Natsir, *Politik*, p. 24.

[52] Hamka, "Persahabatan 47 Tahun," in *Muhammad Natsir 70 Tahun*, p. 320; Mohamad Roem, *Bunga Rampai dari Sejarah* 3 (Jakarta: Bulan Bintang, 1983), p. 176.

[53] Taufik Abdullah, *Indonesia towards Democracy* (Singapore: ISEAS, 2009), p. 334.

[54] See, for example, Natsir's speech of February 10, 1959, "Bagaimana Sikap Bung Hatta?" in *Capita Selecta III*, pp. 169–74.

[55] Deliar Noer, "Kedudukan Natsir Masa Kini," *Panji Masyarakat* 691, August 1–10, 1991, p. 28.

perform something of a balancing act in order to maintain support within the Muslim community. But he was not alone in attempting to harmonize Muslim demands with government policy, for even his more rigid mentor, Ahmad Hassan, in the early months of the Revolution, published articles aimed at convincing impatient Muslims that they should support their leadership's decision to cooperate with the Soekarno government and not press too hard at this stage for their specific religious aims. Arguing that Muslims should be grateful to the nationalists for their major role in creating an independent nation, Hassan stressed the need for unity in the current situation, stating that Muslims should have patience with the shortcomings of a secular state. Until they had the opportunity to help formulate a permanent constitution "it was incumbent upon the Muslim groups to 'honor the government and its policies' and not undertake action detrimental to it."[56]

Since the proclamation of the Indonesian Republic in August 1945, Islamic groups had been trying to subordinate their specifically religious stances to the prime aim of gaining independence. But the tensions evident in balancing Muslim demands with national policy were reflected within the Masjumi — the major political party formed to represent Indonesian Muslims during the Revolution. Established in November 1945, the Masjumi was a loose federation of Muslim groups, subsuming both reformist and traditionalist Muslim organizations, including the Muhammadiyah and Nahdlatul Ulama (NU), as well as the prewar Muslim political parties, including the PSII. When Abdul Hassan's Persatuan Islam was re-established in 1948 it entered the Masjumi as an "extraordinary member" and its adherents were also urged to join the party on an individual basis.[57] But the initial unity of Muslim forces personified in the Masjumi party did not last.

Natsir was little involved personally in the machinations and disagreements that wracked the Muslim political ranks as the independence struggle proceeded, but as a leading member of the faction in the Masjumi that was identified most closely with the moderate policies adopted by the Republican government, and in his role as the government's minister of information, he became a target of the dissatisfaction of the many Muslims who disagreed with the government's stance.

In June 1947 the Socialist Party (PS) split between the faction headed by Sjahrir and that led by Amir Sjarifuddin who then succeeded Sjahrir as prime minister. Shortly afterwards members of the Islamic League (PSII) broke from

---

[56] Federspiel, *Persatuan Islam*, p. 117, quoting Ahmad Hassan, *Mereboet Kekuasaan* (Malang: Toko "Timoer," 1946), p.19.
[57] Federspiel, *Persatuan Islam*, p. 155.

the Masjumi to reform their old party[58] and several of its members accepted posts within the Amir Sjarifuddin cabinet.[59] A member of the PSII then replaced Natsir as information minister. Six months later, however, Natsir was recalled to his earlier position when Vice President Hatta was asked to form a presidential cabinet in January 1948, after Amir had been forced to resign in the aftermath of the Renville Agreements with the Dutch.

In their first "police action" mounted in July 1947 in defiance of the Linggajati Agreements, Dutch forces had overrun large tracts of land in both Java and Sumatra. The world community generally condemned these actions and in the latter part of the year the Security Council of the United Nations set up a Good Offices Committee with the task of settling the Dutch/Indonesian conflict through peaceful means. Under the Committee's auspices Dutch and Indonesian representatives met on the US ship *Renville* anchored off the coast of Java and in January 1948 reached a compromise, the so-called Renville Agreement that Prime Minister Amir Sjarifuddin felt compelled to sign. Under this agreement a ceasefire was proclaimed between the two sides, with the Republic acknowledging Dutch control over the areas their forces had overrun, on condition that a plebiscite was later held in these territories to determine the wishes of the people as to which side would eventually rule there.[60] Widespread opposition to the agreements among the Indonesian people led to the fall of Amir's cabinet, and Soekarno appointed Hatta to replace him at the head of a presidential cabinet. Hatta reappointed Natsir to the position of minister of information and he resumed his close working relationship with Hatta and Soekarno, cooperating with them in their strategy not only in Dutch Indonesian relations, but also against the Communist Party and in confronting the Madiun uprising of September 1948.

Not only the rift in the Masjumi, but also the split in the Socialist Party and the signing of the Renville Agreement all had widespread repercussions within the Muslim community. When the Islamic League (PSII) separated from the Masjumi party in July 1947, it was accused of opportunism, because

---

[58] On the prewar splits within the Islamic League, see Chapter 2; Holk Dengel, *Darul Islam dan Kartosuwirjo: langkah perwujudan angan-angan yang gagal* (Jakarta: Pustaka Sinar Harapan, 1995), pp. 16–26; and C. van Dijk, *Rebellion under the Banner of Islam: The Darul Islam in Indonesia* (The Hague: Martinus Nijhoff, 1981), pp. 3–6.

[59] Five members of the PSII were included in Amir's cabinet. See Kahin, *Nationalism and Revolution*, pp. 210–1.

[60] On these agreements, see Alistair M. Taylor, *Indonesian Independence and the United Nations* (Ithaca: Cornell University Press, 1960), pp. 93–7, 311–21; Kahin, *Nationalism and Revolution*, pp. 215–29.

several of its members then entered Amir's cabinet.[61] The fact that the Masjumi leadership had previously refused to enter the new cabinet meant that Amir would have been unable to form his new government without the defection of these PSII members.

Among those Masjumi leaders approached by Amir to enter his cabinet was S.M. Kartosuwirjo, who was offered the post of second vice minister of defense. Kartosuwirjo had been a leading member of the Islamic League in the prewar period, and had been expelled in 1939 for his adherence to the policy of non-cooperation with the Dutch.[62] He was also one of the founders of the new Masjumi party in 1945. At the last moment he refused Amir's cabinet offer, saying that he had not joined the PSII and was still tied to the Masjumi.[63] His relationship with the Masjumi party, however, was by then very tense, for he was deeply disappointed in its willingness to accommodate with the Republican government's policies.[64]

Kartosuwirjo's dissatisfaction reached a peak in January 1948 after the signing of the Renville Agreement. West Java was one of those regions from which Indonesian government leaders agreed to withdraw their military forces. In compliance with Renville, around 30,000 regular Siliwangi division troops retreated from West to Central Java, while about 4,000 soldiers, mostly from the irregular Islamic units of Sabilillah and Hizbullah, refused to be evacuated.[65] On February 10, 1948, as Siliwangi units withdrew, Muslim militia leaders and representatives of Islamic organizations in West Java held a conference where they expressed their opposition to the Renville Agreement and the retreat of Republican forces. They transformed the local Masjumi party into an Islamic Council (Majlis Islam) headed by Kartosuwirjo, which was to establish "a provisional Islamic government in West Java." They also formed a Tentara Islam Indonesia (TII, Indonesian Islamic army), made up of Hizbullah, Sabilillah and other Muslim units.[66] This army would become the military arm of the Islamic state that Kartosuwirjo would eventually proclaim in West Java the following year.

Although the Masjumi had opposed the Renville concessions, several of its leaders, including Natsir, were nevertheless willing to accept cabinet positions

---

[61] See Kahin, *Nationalism and Revolution*, pp. 209–11.

[62] See Chapter 2.

[63] Dengel, *Darul Islam dan Kartosuwirjo*, pp. 59–60. Dengel speculates that Kartosuwirjo was also reluctant because he didn't approve of Amir's policies and because the post offered him was only vice-minister of defense, while Amir retained the post of minister.

[64] On these tensions, see ibid., and van Dijk, *Rebellion under the Banner of Islam*, pp. 82–7.

[65] Kahin, *Nationalism and Revolution*, p. 234.

[66] Dengel, *Darul Islam dan Kartosuwirjo*, pp. 65–7.

within the Hatta government that was charged with implementing the agreements. Natsir continued his cooperation with the Soekarno-Hatta government throughout 1948, although he must have been conscious of the restiveness and open opposition in the Muslim community at many of the policies the Republic was pursuing. Throughout these months both he and Hatta maintained close relations with Kartosuwirjo, apparently believing he was still loyal to the Republic despite his open refusal to accept the terms of the Renville Agreements. According to Natsir, on several occasions Kartosuwirjo traveled from West Java to meet with Hatta who "gave him assistance so that [he] could cool the [feelings] of the West Javanese who felt abandoned by the Republic. Unofficially Bung Hatta helped when Kartosuwirjo came to Yogyakarta to ask for funds, food assistance or social necessities for the people in the jungle."[67]

The hard work and tension of his position took a toll on Natsir's health, and although he participated in the futile discussions between the Republic and the Dutch during November/December 1948, his overwork landed him in hospital. He was confined there at the time of the second Dutch "police action" of December 19, when Dutch forces overran Yogyakarta and arrested the Republican leadership. Leaving the hospital, Natsir attended the cabinet meeting held at 10 a.m. that morning in Soekarno's palace in Yogyakarta, shortly before the Dutch entered the city. Subsequently Natsir drew up one of the three statements (the others were written by Soekarno and Hatta) that the Republican leadership tried to broadcast to the Indonesian people before their arrest. The Dutch bombing and destruction of the Yogyakarta radio station prevented them from making their speeches, but the texts were reproduced and distributed throughout the occupied territories. In his speech Natsir "set forth the government's specific instruction to the population, showing the way to be followed in the struggle by those who were indecisive or confused as to what the most effective course was."[68] He called on the people to organize a battle strategy independent of the central administration that would obstruct and sabotage Dutch efforts to consolidate their control.[69]

The End of the Revolution

Together with the rest of the cabinet, Natsir was taken into custody by the Dutch and sent into internal exile on the island of Bangka off Sumatra's southeast coast, until a ceasefire was negotiated.

---

[67] Natsir, *Politik*, pp. 28–9. See also Dengel, *Darul Islam dan Kartosuwirjo*, pp. 88–9.
[68] Kahin, *Nationalism and Revolution*, p. 393.
[69] Ibid., pp. 394–5.

The Republic's Leadership on Bangka, 1949.

L to R:
H. Agus Salim, Mohammad Natsir, Mohamad Roem, Dr. A. Halim, H.F. Laoh, Mr. Asmaun, Rh. Kusnan, Mr. Ali Sastroamidjojo, Ir. Soekarno, Mr. Assaat, Mohammad Hatta, Mr. Saubari, Dr. Leimena, Dr. Darmasetiawan, Karta Wijaya, A.G. Pringgodigdo, and Sumarto

Dutch forces advanced rapidly after their initial assault of December 19 and soon occupied most of the major cities in Java and Sumatra. Nevertheless, they were unable to consolidate their control over the regions they overran. This failure was due in large part to the strong guerrilla resistance mounted by the Republican forces, under the military leadership of General Sudirman in Java and the civilian leadership of the Republic's Emergency Government (PDRI, Pemerintah Darurat Republik Indonesia), headed by Sjafruddin Prawiranegara, which was set up in Sumatra on December 22, 1948 immediately after the Dutch occupied Yogyakarta.[70]

The Dutch gradually realized that their early military success had not led to political victory, and, pressed by the United Nations, they reluctantly took the first steps toward a compromise with the Republican leaders. In doing so, however, the Netherlands authorities ignored the Republic's Emergency Government in Sumatra, which was heading the resistance to the Dutch occupation. Nor did they attempt to negotiate with its military commander in chief, General Sudirman, in Java. Instead, they made contact with Soekarno and the other Republican officials whom they had imprisoned on Bangka. Without any consultation with the Emergency Government, Soekarno then appointed Mr. Mohamad Roem, the Masjumi leader and former interior minister of the Republic, to head a delegation to negotiate with the Dutch, whose delegation was led by Dr. H. Van Royen.

When they heard of the Roem-Van Royen talks, Sjafruddin and Sudirman strongly protested both the discussions and the agreements the two sides eventually reached, arguing that the imprisoned leadership had no idea of the actual situation on the ground and were making unnecessary concessions to the Dutch.[71] Their vociferous opposition worried Soekarno and the other leaders on Bangka, and in an effort at conciliation, first Hatta then Natsir were sent to speak with Sjafruddin to persuade him to accept the situation. Hatta went to Aceh to meet with him, believing that he had his headquarters there, but had to return empty-handed when he found that Sjafruddin and the leaders of the Emergency Government were in fact based not in Aceh but in West Sumatra.

---

[70] Vice President Hatta had sent Sjafruddin to Sumatra in November 1948 to establish a government presence there should the Dutch succeed in overrunning Java.

[71] Interview with Sjafruddin Prawiranegara (Jakarta, September 30, 1976). Sjafruddin stated that he and Sudirman were in accord in opposing the talks, as the leaders on Bangka were "political prisoners" and "accepted the talks with the Dutch as if we were in a weak position. But we were convinced we were in a very strong position ... we were convinced that we could demand that the Dutch leave much larger areas. Our de facto power, the de facto authority of the Emergency Government was stronger and encompassed a much larger area than the Dutch presented."

So a new delegation was dispatched, this one headed by Mohammad Natsir and with Leimena and Halim as members.

Natsir and his delegation flew to Bukittinggi where they received radio instructions to proceed to the market town of Payakumbuh, from where under cover of a very uneasy local ceasefire they made their way north. As Natsir described it:

> Someone said that Sjafruddin was outside Payakumbuh. We asked the commander for a car … and were accompanied by two tanks … at one point the local commander said you can go where you want; we are not responsible for what happens to you. The lower echelons [of the Republican forces] were not informed [of our arrival] so some platoon came at us with guns; we waved our hands and handkerchiefs. I had a Minangkabau cap that was brown [usually they were black] and the soldiers recognized the cap and that was what saved us. One officer asked if I was Pak Natsir. After an hour a messenger came to inform the platoon that we were in the region.
>
> Then we met Sjafruddin; he was very angry. He was not willing to listen to us: "What are you doing?" he said, "You are selling out the whole thing."[72]

The delegation met with Sjafruddin in Padang Jepang, near Payakumbuh, and spent the night persuading him to agree to the *fait accompli*. Finally the following morning, Sjafruddin "asked me what should be done. I said it was up to him. 'If you don't accept this we will stay and fight with you. Either you go with us or we stay with you.'"[73] After consulting with his local supporters Sjafruddin agreed to return to Yogyakarta with Natsir and his delegation, realizing, as did Sudirman on Java, that they had no other choice if the Republic was to remain unified. On July 13 Sjafruddin flew to Yogyakarta and returned his mandate to President Soekarno who proclaimed a ceasefire to go into effect on August 17, 1949.

As the Revolution drew to an end and the Republic was pressured to make even further compromises before the Dutch were willing to transfer sovereignty to the new state, Natsir finally became estranged from the stance of the moderate Republican leadership, especially of Mohammad Hatta, who was largely framing the government's policies. Two major problems strained the relationship. The first was the number of concessions that the government

---

[72] Interview with Mohammad Natsir, Jakarta, October 16, 1976.

[73] Ibid. This also accords with Sjafruddin's account. According to him, Natsir "was also against that agreement, but he had to speak his master's voice. When he knew the situation he was against that agreement [but] we decided to go along with Soekarno." Interview, Jakarta, September 30, 1976.

Sjafruddin Prawiranegara returning to Yogyakarta, July 1949. Natsir standing at the plane's door.

was willing to make to the Dutch, especially over the matter of West Irian. The second concerned the policies to be adopted *vis-à-vis* Kartosuwirjo and the Darul Islam (lit. Abode of Islam) movement that was growing in strength in West Java.[74]

Natsir had been appointed as an adviser to the Indonesian delegation to the Round Table discussions with the Dutch that were held from August to December in The Hague to discuss the handover of power to the Indonesians. He did not, however, accompany the delegation to the Netherlands, and when he heard that, under the terms of the agreement being reached there, West Irian would be exempted from the transfer of sovereignty, he angrily cabled Hatta to express his disagreement.[75] He threatened to resign from the cabinet should this provision go through and when the agreement went ahead he refused to reassume his post as minister of information, stating that he would find it impossible to explain to the Indonesian people why West Irian had not been returned.[76]

So he ended the Revolution, again outside the government but still very involved in Indonesia's political life. It seemed that he would now have to turn his attention away from building consensus in support of the newly independent Indonesian state and toward the specific problems of the religious community he had long represented. In 1949 he was elected as chairman of the Masjumi party, now the largest political party in the Republic, and when he left the government he turned his major attention to developing the party and leading it in the new Parliament.

---

[74] The issue of the Darul Islam will be dealt with in the next chapter.
[75] According to Natsir, Haji Agus Salim also opposed it.
[76] St. Rais Alamsjah, *10 Orang Indonesia*, p. 92; Natsir, *Politik*, p. 25.

4

Leading the Government, 1950–51

From Federated to Unitary State

On January 16, 1950, the Dutch transferred sovereignty, not to the Indonesian Republic that had been its adversary for the previous five years, but to the Federated States of Indonesia (RIS, Republik Indonesia Serikat) made up of both the Republic and the BFO (Bijeenkomst voor Federaal Overleg, Federal Consultative Assembly), a federation of states, mostly outside Java and Sumatra, which had been sponsored by the Dutch during the Revolution in an effort to curb the power of the Indonesian Republic. In the new RIS, the Republic, although its population of perhaps 31 million made it by far the largest entity, was merely one of sixteen component states, the smallest of which had a population of only about 100,000.[1] Indonesia was now faced with an even more difficult task than freeing itself from colonial governance — bringing together such a disparate set of societies and cultures to create a viable country.

Because of his opposition to some of the concessions made in the Round Table agreements that had led to the transfer of sovereignty, Natsir had refused to join the new RIS government headed by Mohammad Hatta. Several other Masjumi members did, however, hold cabinet posts.[2] Meanwhile, Natsir

---

[1] See George McT. Kahin, *Nationalism and Revolution in Indonesia* (Ithaca: Cornell University Press, 1951), pp. 446–7.

[2] Sjafruddin Prawiranegara was minister of finance, Abu Hanifah, minister of education and culture, K.H. Wahid Hasjim headed the religious affairs ministry, and Mohamad Roem was initially a minister of state.

remained as head of the Masjumi party, sat in Parliament, and at times acted as Hatta's emissary in efforts to calm unrest in West Java.

Almost as soon as the federal order was established, public pressure arose for it to be replaced by a unitary state. Many of the Republicans who had been fighting the Dutch since 1945 saw the Federated States largely as a colonial construct that betrayed many of the ideals for which they had fought. This pressure sparked a "unitarian movement" that grew up during the first six months of 1950, spearheading Republican demands for the federal structure to be dissolved.

The dissatisfaction expressed by this movement intensified after Indonesian and Dutch members of the Royal Netherlands Indies Army (KNIL) mounted a series of uprisings and attempted coups and assassinations against Hatta's government. The first and most minatory of these attempts was a military attack launched in Bandung on January 23, 1950, with immediate follow-up actions in Jakarta, where the plotters planned to kidnap members of the cabinet and assassinate three of them, including the defense minister, Sultan Hamengku Buwono. In both Jakarta and Bandung a disaffected Dutch officer, Captain R.P.P. "Turk" Westerling, notorious for the massacres he had conducted in South Sulawesi during the Revolution, headed the anti-government actions.[3] It was soon discovered that Sultan Hamid II, head of the federal state of West Kalimantan and a minister in the RIS cabinet, also supported and even perhaps had instigated the coup attempts.[4] Although the rebel forces were driven out of both Bandung and Jakarta before they could pose any real danger, the Westerling plot exacerbated Indonesian mistrust of the Dutch,[5] and increased antagonism toward the federal states. Anti-Dutch sentiment within these states themselves led to requests from most of them to be incorporated into the Republic, as a first step toward complete unification of the country.

But at the same time the Republican-supported "unitarian movement" raised fears, especially in eastern Indonesia, about becoming subject to a central government on Java, along with doubts as to whether the oldest and strongest of

---

[3] For his own account of the campaign in South Sulawesi, see Raymond "Turk" Westerling, *Challenge to Terror* (London: William Kimber, 1952), pp. 88–123; see also Ulf Sundhausen, *The Road to Power: Indonesian Military Politics 1945–1967* (Kuala Lumpur: Oxford University Press, 1982), p. 55; George Kahin, "Indonesian Politics and Nationalism," in *Asian Nationalism and the West*, ed. William L. Holland (New York: Macmillan, 1953), pp. 121–2.

[4] See Herbert Feith, *The Decline of Constitutional Democracy in Indonesia* (Ithaca: Cornell University Press, 1962), pp. 62–3; Sundhaussen, *Road to Power*, p. 57; Taufik Abdullah, *Indonesia towards Democracy* (Singapore: ISEAS, 2009), pp. 195–6.

[5] Westerling himself was smuggled out of Indonesia in a Dutch military plane. Feith, *Decline*, p. 62.

the federated states, the State of East Indonesia (NIT, Negara Indonesia Timur), would be able to maintain its autonomy in the face of pressure for unification within the Republic. In April 1950 Netherlands Indies Army (KNIL) units awaiting demobilization in Makassar rebelled against the Republic and in support of the East Indonesian State (NIT). Later that month, in protest to the declaration of Anak Agung Gde Sukowati, president of the NIT, that he would in principle be willing to join a unitary state, dissident elements in eastern Indonesia proclaimed an independent Republic of the South Moluccas (RMS, Republik Maluku Selatan) based in Ambon. For several months, this government managed to maintain control of the Ambonese islands in the face of Republican military assaults against them, until central government forces finally succeeded in occupying the town of Ambon in December 1950.[6]

Fearing that amidst conflicting pressures the new Indonesian state could fall apart, Hatta, as prime minister of the Federated States (RIS), had held a meeting in early May 1950 with the heads of the East Indonesian State (NIT) and of the other strongest member of the RIS, the State of East Sumatra (PST). At that meeting all three leaders agreed to the establishment of a unitary state. But though the NIT and PST were willing to move toward unification, they requested that this should be achieved by the federal states first allying with one another before joining together with the Republic in a new unitary state. The Republicans, on the other hand, were pressing for the remaining federal states to be amalgamated within the existing Republic. (In other words, while the RIS wanted its component states to join the new Republic of Indonesia as a separate entity, the Republican representatives wished them to liquidate themselves first, and then be absorbed within the Republic.) To bridge these opposing positions, Natsir proposed a "*mosi integral*" which called for all of the states, including the Republic, to liquidate prior to formation of the new unitary state. Both sides viewed this proposal as a compromise they were willing to accept, as it would mean that all the states would enter the new Republic on an equal footing.[7]

---

[6] The Republican army launched an attack against the islands in September 1950, but only three months later, after much killing and destruction, was it able to occupy the town of Ambon. On these events, see Richard Chauvel, "Ambon: not a revolution but a counterrevolution," in *Regional Dynamics of the Indonesian Revolution*, ed. Audrey Kahin (Honolulu: University of Hawaii Press, 1985), pp. 254–61.

[7] The clearest elucidation of these events appears in St. Rais Alamsjah *10 Orang Indonesia Terbesar Sekarang* (Bukittinggi & Jakarta: Mutiara, 1952), pp. 93–4. In his moves toward reaching agreement on a new state, Natsir was reportedly allied with Kasimo from the Catholic Party and Tambunan from the Christian Party (Partai Kristen). Adian Husain, "Sang Pemersatu yang Terlupakan Sejarah," in *Pemimpin Pulang: Rekaman Peristiwa Wafatnya M. Natsir* ed. Lukman Hakiem (Jakarta: Yayasan Piranti Ilmu, 1993), p. 118.

     Islam, Nationalism and Democracy

President Soekarno with Natsir after his appointment as prime minister.

Representatives of the federal and Republican parliaments worked out a draft Provisional Constitution for the new state, which was ratified by the two parliaments in mid-August. By August 17, 1950, the fifth anniversary of the Proclamation of Indonesian Independence, the new Republic of Indonesia had come into existence, embracing the whole archipelago with the exception of West Irian. Five days later, on August 22, President Soekarno invited Mohammad Natsir to form its first government.[8]

Natsir as Prime Minister

Natsir entered office with the full support of the president. According to one account, when asked by a reporter who should become prime minister, Soekarno had replied: "Ya, who else but Natsir of the Masjumi. They have a concept for saving the Republic constitutionally."[9] But this did not mean that

---

[8] Mohammad Hatta, the prime minister of the RIS, was left with the more prestigious but less powerful position of vice president of the Republic.

[9] See Mohammad Natsir, *Politik melalui Jalur Dakwah* (Jakarta: Media Da'wah, 2008), p. 34, where Soekarno's words appear: "Ya, siapa lagi kalau bukan Natsir dari Masyumi. Mereka punya konsepsi untuk menyelamatkan Republik melalui konstitusi."

the way to formation of a new government was clear, for on his appointment, Natsir had to enter into long negotiations with other party leaders, especially those from the National Party (PNI), over the composition of his cabinet. It was generally assumed that, until elections could be arranged for creation of a representative government, it would be best to form a coalition between the two largest parties, the Masjumi and the PNI. The two parties were judged to be about equal in strength, but, as prime minister, Natsir tried to ensure that the Masjumi had most influence, with six cabinet seats against the PNI's four.[10] Unwilling to accept a division of power that favored the Masjumi, PNI leaders fought hard for control of some of the most important ministries, including education, interior and defense.

Negotiations proved so difficult that Natsir was tempted to return his mandate. Soekarno, however, refused his offer and urged him to continue his efforts to form a government. Deciding to confront the PNI directly, Natsir threatened to "go it alone" and form a cabinet without the National Party if its leaders were unwilling to compromise. He apparently hoped that this threat would provoke the PNI into making some concessions, but instead it threw his own Masjumi party into disarray. Both the group headed by Dr. Sukiman Wirjosandjojo and the Nahdlatul Ulama faction openly expressed their fears that, if Natsir carried out his threat, the PNI would be forced into the communist camp. The PNI leaders apparently thought that this opposition within his own party would deter Natsir from proceeding with his plan. They therefore stuck to their earlier demands, in effect daring him to carry out his threat. Natsir took up the challenge and informed President Soekarno that he had formed a cabinet without PNI participation, "an extraordinarily bold act," according to St. Rais Alamsjah.[11]

This act, however, also made his cabinet weaker and the PNI stronger, for, as Natsir's critics within the Masjumi had foreseen, the Nationalists thereafter headed a formidable opposition coalition of leftist parties, including the Indonesian Communist Party (PKI), which could frustrate many of the government's initiatives.

To create a cabinet without Indonesia's other major political party, Natsir had to reach well beyond Masjumi leaders such as Mohamad Roem, Sjafruddin

---

[10] Deliar Noer, *Partai Islam di Pentas Nasional* (Jakarta: Grafiti, 1987), p. 203. Natsir proposed that the Masjumi should have the prime minister-ship, interior, finance, defense, education and religious affairs, while the PNI was offered foreign affairs and the information, public works and labor posts. Feith, *Decline*, p. 148.

[11] St. Rais Alamsjah, *10 Orang Indonesia*, p. 96. Most of this account is based on that of Feith in *Decline*, pp. 149–50.

President Soekarno and Vice President Hatta with Natsir's cabinet,
September 6, 1950.

Prawiranegara and K.H. Wahid Hasjim.[12] He also had to draw his ministers from some of the smaller parties including the Sjahrir socialists, and from respected figures who had no official party affiliation, such as Sultan Hamengku Buwono of Yogyakarta, Ir. Djuanda Kartawidjaja, Dr. A. Halim and Mr. Assaat. Many observers, however, viewed the cabinet he formed as basically a coalition between Natsir's Masjumi and Sjahrir's Socialist Party (PSI). Herbert Feith, for instance, argued that all the officially "non-party" members had PSI sympathies "in one or another degree,"[13] while future foreign minister Adam Malik stated that "Natsir, when composing his cabinet, consulted more with Subadio Sastrosatomo from the party of Soetan Sjahrir than with Jusuf Wibisono from

---

[12] Hasjim, who became minister of religion, was from the NU faction, Roem, who became foreign minister, had been a leading figure in the negotiations for the transfer of sovereignty and Sjafruddin, who became finance minister, was a long-time colleague of Natsir and had headed the Emergency Government of Indonesia in early 1949 after the Dutch occupation of Yogyakarta. (See Chapter 3.)

[13] Feith, *Decline*, p. 151. This echoes criticisms made at the time by Natsir's colleague, Sukiman, and in the newspaper *Merdeka*. See Noer, *Partai Islam*, p. 208. The only cabinet member who was actually a member of the PSI was Prof. Sumitro Djojohadikusumo who held the post of minister of trade and industry.

his own party."[14] This fact led to alienation of sections of Natsir's own Masjumi party, to such an extent that two of his closest colleagues, Jusuf Wibisono and Burhanuddin Harahap, both absented themselves from the confidence vote that was taken in Parliament on October 25.[15] Thus, although by September 6, 1950, Natsir had finally succeeded in swearing in his cabinet, in the process he had clashed not only with the Nationalist Party but also with important elements in his own party. In addition his cabinet faced a host of problems, few of them offering easy solutions.

Natsir came to the prime minister-ship with a number of both advantages and disadvantages. Most strongly in his favor were his reputation for integrity and the fact that he headed what was generally regarded as the largest of the political parties. The latter fact was yet to be proven, for other than at the local level none of the political parties had faced an electoral test. Nor were they to do so for another five years.

In addition, the strength of the Masjumi was undermined by the fact that by the time Natsir became prime minister the party had largely fractured into an uneasy alliance of disparate factions and was close to breaking apart. Tensions within the Masjumi had been exacerbated by the difficult negotiations involved in forming the cabinet. As we saw in the previous chapter, it had always been a loosely knit organization which was openly riven by factional disagreements and which "exacted little discipline from its members."[16] While all its adherents shared Islam as a political ideology, the party embraced no single set of policies to which its members could subscribe. As Howard Federspiel has written:

> … Muslim organizations which often represented mutually contrary views were also federated members and held disciplinary control over many members of Masjumi, thus ensuring a permanent mechanism … for the perpetuation of difference and factionalism. The Muhammadijah, with its concern for social progress and its modernist viewpoint in religious matters, was almost the exact opposite of the Nahdlatul Ulama, which wanted to preserve the traditional religious system that had been dominant in Indonesia before the entry of modernist Muslim thought. These two groups formed the nucleus for two wings or factions within the party, with the Muhammadijah

---

[14] See Rudolf Mrazek, *Sjahrir: Politics and Exile in Indonesia* (Ithaca: Cornell Southeast Asia Program, 1994), p. 407.

[15] Feith, *Decline*, p. 152. According to Yusril Ihza Mahendra, these two Masjumi leaders had disagreed so strongly with the makeup and program of the cabinet that they had walked out. See *Pemikiran dan Perjuangan Mohammad Natsir* ed. Anwar Harjono dkk. (Jakarta: Pustaka Firdaus, 2001), p. 122.

[16] Feith, *Decline*, p. 134.

representing what came to be known as the moderate wing and the Nahdlatul Ulama representing the conservative wing.[17]

In addition, there was a largely generational divide within the "modernist" group between Natsir's faction and the one headed by Dr. Sukiman Wirjosandjojo, with Natsir deriving much of his support from outside Java and from young men who had come of age during the Revolution, while Sukiman's adherents were drawn largely from older more traditional Javanese Muslims. Other differences divided the two factions: Natsir was closer to Sjahrir's Socialists (PSI) in philosophy, while Sukiman was closer to the nationalist PNI and also had ties to the Nahdlatul Ulama.

Within the party, Muhammadiyah and other modernist organizations provided the basis of support for Natsir, as chairman of its executive council, and also for Sukiman, who was chairman of its legislative council. According to Feith, these two leaders were also supported by propertied groups. But the traditionalist faction, the Nahdlatul Ulama (NU), headed by Wahab Chasbullah and K.H. Wahid Hasjim and largely based in Central and East Java, was increasingly alienated by the modernists' domination of policy and the feeling among the NU leaders that the traditionalists were being excluded from access to strategic positions and patronage opportunities.[18] At the opposite fringe of the party were the "radical fundamentalists," who formed a "more militant, illiberal and anti-secularist current,"[19] mostly drawn from members of the Persatuan Islam (Persis), with which Natsir had been allied before the war. These fundamentalists recognized as mentors both Abdul Hassan, who had headed the Persis in the 1930s, and Isa Anshari, who had succeeded him as chairman of that organization.[20] The Persatuan Islam "while it was fundamentalist in religious matters and thus frequently allied with the reforming or moderate wing on many points, ... was so uncompromising on other matters that it often was regarded as an arch-conservative faction," and also often described itself as "revolutionary-radical."[21]

---

[17] Howard Federspiel, *Persatuan Islam: Islamic Reform in Twentieth Century Indonesia* (Ithaca: Cornell Modern Indonesia Project, 1970), p. 157.

[18] Greg Fealy, "Wahab Chasbullah: Traditionalism and the Political Development of Nahdlatuhl Ulama," in *Nahdlatul Ulama, Traditional Islam and Modernity in Indonesia*, ed. Greg Barton and Greg Fealy (Clayton, Vic.: Monash Asia Institute, 1996), pp. 21–2.

[19] Feith, *Decline*, p. 136.

[20] On Isa Anshari, see B.J. Boland, *The Struggle of Islam in Modern Indonesia* (The Hague: Martinus Nijhoff, 1971), pp. 78–9; Federspiel, *Persatuan Islam*, pp. 124–5.

[21] Federspiel, *Persatuan Islam*, p. 157.

Natsir's somewhat debatable advantages when he assumed office were balanced, or perhaps outweighed, by equal or stronger disadvantages. First, post-independence Indonesia was still rent by disagreements over the degree of centralization the new unitary state should impose. For despite the dissolution of the Federated States, many of the regions outside Java desired to retain a considerable degree of autonomy. Both Natsir and his Masjumi party were sympathetic to this sentiment, seeing a democratic Indonesia as dependent on a degree of decentralization and devolution of power from the Javanese center.

Combined with the pressure for greater regional autonomy was the question of the regional representative councils (DPRD, Dewan Perwakilan Rakyat Daerah), in most of which the Masjumi party had majority representation. These councils had been formed earlier in the year under the federal RIS government through an indirect system of election that was based on political parties and major occupational groups already existing in the local areas. An interior minister from the National Party (PNI) had drawn up Regulation No 39 establishing these regional legislative councils. Implementation of the law, however, resulted in a Masjumi majority in nearly all of the councils, because in most of the regions the number of organizations affiliated with the Masjumi was far greater than for any other party.[22] The PNI now pressed for Regulation 39 to be revoked and the local assemblies dissolved, while the Masjumi-dominated government was naturally reluctant to see them disappear. Masjumi leaders argued that: "if the DPRD [the local councils] were to be dissolved, there should first be laws governing their replacement, so a vacuum [of power] could be avoided."[23]

Nor was this the only disagreement on the form of the new state. Dissatisfaction with any moves toward greater centralization soon merged with the growing attraction of radical Muslim movements, most notably the Darul Islam in West Java and allied groups in Aceh and South Sulawesi. Headed by the former Islamic Association Party (PSII) leader, S.M. Kartosuwirjo,[24] the Darul Islam spearheaded demands both for greater regional autonomy and for an Islamic state.[25]

These were the issues that were of greatest concern to Natsir personally and in his role as head of the Masjumi, though the most immediate

---

[22] Ibid., pp. 165–7. See also Kahin, "Indonesian Politics and Nationalism," pp. 142–3.

[23] Natsir, *Politik*, p. 40.

[24] On Kartosuwirjo, see Chapter 2, pp. 31–2 and Chapter 3, pp. 56–7.

[25] The best treatment of the history of the Darul Islam during this period is Holk H. Dengel's *Darul Islam dan Kartosuwirjo: Langkah Perwujudan Angan-Angan yang Gagal* (Jakarta: Pustaka Sinar Harapan, 1995).

problems he faced as prime minister related to other economic, political, and international challenges. Among such challenges was the labor unrest that was already infecting the seaports and plantation estates when he came to office. These strikes and disorders were encouraged by the political opponents of his Masjumi government, especially by followers of the PNI and the Indonesian Communist Party (PKI). Labor dissatisfaction was exacerbated by the continuing control that Dutch interests were allowed to exert over Indonesia's domestic economy and also by the compromises the Indonesian representatives had made to the Dutch in the final negotiations in The Hague with regard to West Irian.

Equally challenging were the problems the government faced in creating a national military. The process involved the fate of both the remaining forces of the Netherlands Indies Army (KNIL) and the many independent bands of all political persuasions that had fought the guerrilla war for independence. The irregular forces included the Islamic militias of the Hizbullah and Sabilillah and the Communist and leftist militias of the Pesindo and Merapi Merbabu Complex (in Central Java), together with bands with little political affiliation, such as the Laskar Harimau Liar (the wild tiger militia) in northern Sumatra. During the final two years of the Revolution Vice President Hatta had worked with the senior army leadership, most notably A.H. Nasution who at the time headed West Java's Siliwangi division, in attempts to impose a "rationalization" process on the disparate bands that were defending the Republic in Java and Sumatra. Through this process many of the irregular soldiers were to be demobilized and their units incorporated within the Indonesian National Army or TNI (Tentara Nasional Indonesia). These efforts met with little success at the time and they had to be totally abandoned after the 2nd Dutch "police action" of December 19, 1948, when many of the irregular bands, especially in Sumatra, fought the ensuing guerrilla war much more effectively than did the regular army units.

After the transfer of sovereignty, Hatta and Nasution, who was now Army Chief of Staff, reinstated the rationalization program, as they felt that the irregular bands posed a threat to security in several regions, and needed to be either disarmed and demobilized, or incorporated within the post independence armed forces, together with the remaining Netherlands Indies Army (KNIL) units that had fought on the Dutch side during the independence struggle. At this time Natsir had good relations, not only with Hatta, but also with Nasution and other members of the army leadership. In a speech to Parliament at the end of October he outlined a policy to implement their rationalization program, stating that his government aimed to incorporate 30,000 members of the KNIL into the TNI and discharge about 30,750, while about 8,250 KNIL soldiers were expected to return to Holland.[26] Altogether the government's plans called for the army to be reduced to 200,000 men, which would mean the discharge of about 80,000 troops within three months.[27] This prospect dismayed large numbers of soldiers who had been fighting the Dutch throughout the revolutionary years and had no training for any other occupation.

These were the major problems absorbing the government's attention. In addition, in the wings, but attempting to move to center stage, was President Soekarno, increasingly frustrated at the curbs that a parliamentary system of government imposed upon his own authority. His frustration brought him and Natsir into a direct confrontation over the division of power in the new state.

During his few months in office, Natsir struggled, with varying degrees of success, to tackle these many challenges.

Labor Unrest

When the Natsir cabinet took office, it was faced with a rash of strikes and eruptions of violence between employers and workers in many industries and especially on the plantations of north Sumatra. The government dealt relatively successfully with this particular challenge, for all cabinet members recognized the necessity of improving the workers' situation. Under the trade and industry minister, Dr. Sumitro Djojohadikusumo, an agreement was reached with the labor unions, including the most radical, on substantially raising the minimum wage, fixing it at Rp.7.50 a day in cash and kind at the prevailing value of the rupiah (it had previously been Rp.1.50 per day).[28]

At the same time, under the fiscally responsible guidance of both Dr. Sumitro and Minister of Finance Sjafruddin Prawiranegara, Indonesia's economy was shifted onto a firmer financial footing. Helped by the Korean War boom, the banking system was reorganized to stimulate domestic production and trade and to finance long-term development. Measures were also passed to spread the banking system to loan cooperatives throughout the country. In the field

---

[26] Kabinet Pres. Arsip # 1295 *Djawaban Pemerintah* concerning Program of Natsir Cabinet, 12 October 1950, p. 27 (Arsip Nasional, Jakarta).

[27] Ibid. See also Van Dijk, *Rebellion*, pp. 110–1.

[28] Yusuf Abdullah Puar, ed., *Muhammad Natsir 70 Tahun: Kenang-kenangan Kehidupan dan Perjuangan* (Jakarta: Pustaka Antara, 1978), p. 111. At the time, however, the value of the rupiah had drastically fallen.

of development, the government emphasized not only large-scale industries, such as printing, cement, fertilizer factories, etc. but also small industries in the agricultural sector,[29] and laid down guidelines for reviving small industries and businesses.

But industrial unrest revived in early 1951, spurred by dissatisfaction among the Communists at Natsir's "gradualism" over the West Irian issue (see below). It was at least in part pressure within the Communist Party over this issue that resulted in D.N. Aidit replacing Alimin as head of the party in January 1951 and an ensuing intensification of strikes on estates and in ports.[30] The Natsir cabinet moved firmly in response to this crisis. It issued a temporary ban on all strikes and lockouts in what were described as "vital" economic enterprises, which included public communications and transport facilities and a wide range of other industries.[31] It was able to enforce this ban, thanks to the support Natsir's government enjoyed among senior army officers who were able to back it up with threats of military action. The cabinet was widely criticized for imposing the ban, which was viewed as a violation of basic human rights. Nevertheless, as Herbert Feith has written, "it was effective in achieving its immediate purpose."[32]

Darul Islam

An issue of great concern to Natsir, because it involved his friends, his religion and his Masjumi political party, was the continued alienation of Kartosuwirjo and his Darul Islam followers from the new Republic.

Kartosuwirjo and his Islamic Army of Indonesia (TII, Tentara Islam Indonesia) had controlled much of the territory of West Java since the Siliwangi forces had withdrawn in early 1948 in conformity with the Renville Agreements. When the government units attempted to return to the region in January 1949 after the Second Dutch "police action," they were repulsed by the TII,[33] leading the Siliwangi division to report: "the Darul Islam movement formed the greatest impediment to the independence struggle and was never

---

[29] Ibid., p. 122. See also Feith, *Decline*, pp. 173–4.

[30] See Donald Hindley, *The Communist Party of Indonesia, 1951–1963* (Berkeley: University of California Press, 1964), pp. 48–51.

[31] These included "harbor enterprises, the oil industry, hospitals, dispensaries, state printing offices, electricity and gas, the principal banks, and all establishments of the minister of Defense." Feith, *Decline*, pp. 174–5.

[32] Ibid., p. 175.

[33] Dengel, *Darul Islam dan Kartosuwirjo*, pp. 88–90.

willing to compromise." The report concluded that the TNI had to fight both the Dutch and the Darul Islam movement at the same time.[34] Kartosuwirjo remained in adamant opposition to the policies of the Hatta government and the concessions the Republic was making in the Roem-Van Royen talks and the opening of the Round Table negotiations.

In the summer of 1949, before the transfer of sovereignty from the Dutch, Prime Minister Hatta charged Natsir with the task of acting as the government's negotiator both with the Dutch-sponsored Pasundan state in West Java and with the Darul Islam. Natsir had come to know Kartosuwirjo during the time they were both students and had met at the house of Abdul Hassan, whom both regarded as a mentor. Natsir's mandate was to ask the Darul Islam leader to halt the DI's military actions against the Republic's armed forces. While staying at the Hotel Homan in Bandung in August 1949, however, Natsir heard that Kartosuwirjo was on the verge of proclaiming an Islamic state. In an effort to forestall this action, Natsir asked Hassan to carry a note to the Darul Islam leader urging him to refrain from issuing the proclamation. Natsir later recalled the course of events in his interview with *Tempo*:

> This letter reached the hands of Kartosuwirjo three days later, just when DI/TII was proclaimed. Yes it was late. This is called fate [*takdir Tuhan*]. Why was it late? Kartosuwirjo was indeed well guarded. No one was allowed to meet him. The guards only recognized Tuan Hassan after he introduced himself, "I am Hassan, Hassan from Bandung," after waiting three days. [Even] if it had not been late it would not have been easy to convince Kartosuwirjo. For him it was hard to eat his words [*menjilat ludah kembali*]. That's difficult. I met with his organization and many of its leaders in Bandung. They said that if Kartosuwirjo accepted, they would submit. But Kartosuwirjo didn't give the order to submit.[35]

Thus, on August 7, 1949, as the Revolution drew to a close, Kartosuwirjo continued to defy the Soekarno-Hatta government, proclaiming an Islamic State of Indonesia (Negara Islam Indonesia) and setting up a rudimentary governmental structure in West Java. The DI's military units, the "Islamic Army of Indonesia (Tentera Islam Indonesia)," became the NII's official army and this army in 1950 continued to control about a third of the countryside of West Java, mostly in the mountainous interior.

Subsequently, Hatta again used Natsir in his efforts to find a political solution to the problem of the Darul Islam, appointing him chairman of a

---

[34] Ibid., p. 90.
[35] Natsir, *Politik*, pp. 27–8.

committee with this mandate. But the committee failed to achieve any results and "simply faded out of existence."[36]

So when Natsir became prime minister a year later, the problem of the Darul Islam was high on his agenda. He hoped that with a recognized Muslim leader at the head of the government the rebels would be more likely to abandon their opposition to the Republic. This hope had been strengthened over the previous months, with the outbreak of the Korean War, when on the international scene the lines between the communist and non-communist worlds became starker and Kartosuwirjo began to see the communist nations replacing the Dutch as the greater threat.[37] In October 1950 after Indonesia entered the United Nations. Kartosuwirjo secretly sent a letter to Soekarno, with a copy to Natsir, approving their entry to the international body and welcoming the accession of Natsir's cabinet. He urged the government to pursue an openly anti-communist policy and also asked it to proclaim Indonesia as an Islamic state.[38] In a speech broadcast on November 14 Natsir gave his response, calling on armed guerrillas still in the mountains to realize that guerrilla warfare was no longer needed and urging that they should devote their thoughts and energy to a new struggle to develop and perfect their young country.[39] He proclaimed an amnesty, stating that, if the guerrillas in West Java surrendered and gave up their weapons before the middle of December, they could be admitted to the armed forces or police, should they so desire, and, if not, the government would help them find alternative employment.

The response to this offer was not overwhelmingly positive, as, according to some sources, only 1,180 soldiers reported by mid-December with a meager forty-six weapons.[40] Natsir's call was, however, welcomed in East Java.[41] And in

---

[36] Van Dijk, *Rebellion*, pp. 112–3. A biography of Hassan puts a more charitable light on Natsir's attempts. The author writes: "Natsir's recommendations reflected the view of the Indonesian Islamic community: they did not support Kartosuwirjo and didn't agree with his method of forming an Islamic State, but they also would not denounce him or ask the government to take harsh steps to destroy the movement. Part of the Islamic community worried that if the Darul Islam were denounced this would mean opposing the bases of an Islamic State and they believed that through the road of negotiations the government would be able to invite Kartosuwirjo to return to the Republic." Syafiq A. Mughni, *Hassan Bandung: Pemikir Islam Radikal* (Surabaya: PT Bina Ilmu, 1994), pp. 103–4.

[37] Dengel, *Darul Islam dan Kartosuwirjo*, p. 128.

[38] Boland, *Struggle of Islam*, p. 60. Boland includes the text of the letter in ibid., appendix II, pp. 244–9. See also Dengel, *Darul Islam dan Kartosuwirjo*, pp. 128–9.

[39] See Puar, ed., *Natsir 70 Tahun*, pp. 109–10. The full text of the speech is published in *Capita Selecta II* (Jakarta: Abadi, 2008), pp. 10–4.

[40] Van Dijk, *Rebellion*, pp. 110–1.

[41] Ibid., p. 117. See also Puar, *Natsir 70 Tahun*, p. 110.

Central Java serious negotiations were held with the local Darul Islam leader, Amir Fatah, that resulted in his surrender.[42] But Fatah's treatment at the hands of the TNI when, after his surrender, the soldiers threw him in jail, was not reassuring for other DI members and made them less willing to enter into talks with the government.[43]

In both June and December 1950, Natsir sent envoys to meet with Kartosuwirjo. On the second of these occasions, Kartosuwirjo refused to meet with the envoy, Kyai H. Muslich, sending a message that, although he would have liked to meet, he considered the messenger's status too low for them to conduct meaningful talks.[44] Kartosuwirjo reportedly sent two letters to Natsir, informing him that he was only willing to talk directly with Natsir or Soekarno after they recognized the Negara Islam Indonesia (NII).[45] In a private letter to Natsir he apparently said that, as prime minister, Natsir had authority to make the Republic of Indonesia (RI), the Islamic Republic of Indonesia (RII). If he did this he would have Kartosuwirjo's full support.[46]

On February 17 of the following year, Kartosuwirjo sent another letter to Soekarno, with a copy to Natsir, outlining a possible basis for agreement between the DI's aims and the position of the central government.[47] While still insisting on his right to proclaim an Islamic State of Indonesia, Kartosuwirjo wrote that he was willing to discuss practical questions concerning the boundaries of this state and he declared that it would be a friend to the Republic especially against any communist threats.

Despite this limited olive branch from Kartosuwirjo, Natsir's call for the guerrillas to come down from the hills had neither resulted in any large number of them surrendering their arms nor in their incorporation within the community. Consequently the government ended its offer of amnesty. Although conscious that the army did not share his willingness to be reconciled with the insurgents, Natsir later stated his belief that had he had more time in office, perhaps six months or longer, he might have succeeded in reconciling the two sides. But his policy's success depended not only on the rebels but on "the good

---

[42] Dengel, *Darul Islam dan Kartosuwirjo*, pp. 157–8.

[43] Hendra Gunawan, *M. Natsir & Darul Islam: Studi Kasus Aceh dan Sulawesi Selatan Tahun 1953–1958* (Jakarta: Media Da'wah, 2000), p. 23.

[44] Dengel, *Darul Islam dan Kartosuwirjo*, pp. 158 and 233, where there is a facsimile of Natsir's letter of December 23, 1950 authorizing H. Muslich to meet with Kartosuwirjo on his behalf.

[45] Gunawan, *M. Natsir*, p. 5.

[46] Dengel, *Darul Islam dan Kartosuwirjo*, p. 158.

[47] Boland, *Struggle of Islam*, pp. 60–1. Boland includes the text of the letter in the Appendices to his book, pp. 250–5.

will of the TNI to accept them and their weapons as comrades in the struggle," a condition that was not fulfilled as clashes broke out between the surrendering DI members and the TNI soldiers during several of the surrender attempts.[48]

With the breakdown of Natsir's efforts to settle the Darul Islam problem in West Java through peaceful means, the Republican Army resumed military attacks against guerrillas throughout the archipelago under the name Operation Freedom. Following Natsir's resignation these operations intensified under his successor, the Masjumi-PNI coalition headed by Sukiman, which had acceded to army demands for harsher military actions against the rebels. Kartosuwirjo adopted an equally intransigent stance. He issued a declaration that, with the fall of the Natsir cabinet, any possibility of an agreement between the Darul Islam and the Republic of Indonesia (that he was now calling the Communist Republic of Indonesia) had disappeared.[49]

Regional and Religious Issues

It was not only in West Java that the Natsir cabinet was faced with challenges from Islamic groups and their militias, allied on occasion with Kartosuwirjo's Darul Islam. In South Sulawesi government policies were more successful than in West Java, at least temporarily. There, Kahar Muzakkar, a former lieutenant colonel in the Indonesian (federal) army who had quarreled with the East Indonesian commander, Colonel Kawilarang, now headed a guerrilla force of over 20,000 men.[50] The Natsir cabinet issued a decree in November 1950 stipulating that the guerrillas in South Sulawesi be admitted into the Republican army as a unit that would ultimately form part of the Hasanuddin brigade.[51] Under a plan agreed to in March 1951, four battalions of these guerrillas would be integrated into the TNI the following August, with Kahar enjoying a measure of command authority over them.

Much more challenging was the situation in Aceh, where the Islamic dissidents were led by Teungku Muhammad Daud Beureu'eh, a respected *ulama* who had headed the All Aceh Ulama Association, PUSA, since its founding in 1939.[52] The PUSA acted as spokesman for Acehnese dissatisfaction at the

---

[48] Natsir, *Politik*, pp. 36–7.

[49] Puar, *Natsir 70 Tahun*, pp. 110–1.

[50] See Feith, *Decline*, pp. 212–3.

[51] See Barbara Harvey, "Tradition, Islam and Rebellion: South Sulawesi, 1950–1965," PhD dissertation, Cornell University, 1974, pp. 228–31; Van Dijk, *Rebellion*, pp. 176–7.

[52] See Boland, *Struggle of Islam*, pp. 69ff; Eric Morris, "Aceh: Social Revolution and the Islamic Vision," in *Regional Dynamics*, pp. 83–110.

agreement that had been reached between the Republic and the Federated States. Under this agreement Aceh was to be absorbed within the province of North Sumatra. (The new unitary Republic of Indonesia was to consist of ten provinces, with Sumatra divided into only three provinces [north, central and south].) Such an arrangement flew in the face of promises that Sjafruddin Prawiranegara had made to the Acehnese on the eve of the transfer of sovereignty.

After Sjafruddin had returned his mandate as president of the Emergency Government of the Republic (PDRI) to Soekarno in July 1949, the president had appointed him deputy prime minister and sent him to Aceh, giving him the authority to decree government regulations for Sumatra, subject to central government review. In December 1949 at the urging of Acehnese leaders, Sjafruddin had issued a government decree recognizing Aceh as a separate province, with PUSA head Daud Beureu'eh as its governor.[53] This confirmed the status Aceh had enjoyed throughout the independence struggle when the Dutch had never dared launch an attack against it and it had provided the Republic with indispensable financial support. Proud of this record, Acehnese leaders refused to accept any change in status.

During the closing months of 1950 a series of ministers, including Sjafruddin, Interior Minister Assaat and Vice President Hatta, traveled to the region in an effort to mediate the dispute, but they all failed to persuade Daud Beureu'eh and his followers to agree to Aceh's incorporation within North Sumatra. Finally, on December 22, Natsir received a telegram from Daud Beureu'eh threatening that if Aceh were not proclaimed an autonomous province by January 1, 1951 all officials from the governor down would resign. Natsir asked them to refrain from implementing this threat until he had the opportunity to explain the matter to them personally, and he planned an immediate visit to Aceh. But his departure was delayed by a deep personal tragedy when in early January his elder son, Abu Hanifah, was drowned in a swimming pool accident.

Natsir finally left for Kota Raja (now Banda Aceh) on January 23. During the visit, while rebuffing Natsir in his official capacity, Daud Beureu'eh showed his personal affection for the prime minister. He had sent condolences on the death of Natsir's son, and although he snubbed the government delegation by not meeting them at the airport, he sent his wife as his personal representative to welcome them. Natsir ignored the official slight, but did insist on staying at the Sultan's palace (*keraton*), where government delegations were usually housed,

---

[53] Morris, "Aceh," pp. 103–4.

although it had not been prepared for them. When Daud Beureu'eh finally came to the *keraton*, Natsir received him calmly and expressed his willingness to let the Acehnese leader decide who would be invited to attend the official talks with the government delegation.

Negotiations, however, soon broke down. For Daud Beureu'eh held to the position that Aceh was an autonomous province, while Natsir insisted that the government was bound by the agreement reached between the Republic and the Federated States in which Aceh formed a part of North Sumatra. Natsir stressed that although the government itself had no objection to Acehnese autonomy, it could not move to implement this until new laws were passed to supersede the agreement regarding Indonesia's constituent provinces.

Over breakfast the following morning, Natsir quietly informed the gathering that he would depart later that day and "When I arrive in Jakarta, I will report the result of our meeting to the President and the cabinet, then I will return my mandate to the President." Daud Beureu'eh expressed surprise and asked why he intended to resign. Natsir replied that, as he had been unable to reach an agreement with the Acehnese, their ultimatum was still in force. "In this situation," said Natsir,

> "I must choose between two alternatives. Firstly, that the Central Government take military steps against Aceh, because the ultimatum and its implementation actually form a challenge that cannot be ignored by any Government. Alternatively, I could resign my position before this happens. After pondering the choice I think it is better to choose the second alternative, because I could not bring myself to make war on Aceh. I am well aware that Aceh has been the prime capital for the Republic since the Proclamation."

Taken aback by Natsir's stance, Daud Beureu'eh and his followers withdrew for further consultations. Ultimately they sent a message to Natsir to explain the impossible situation in which they found themselves. Stating that all the people of Aceh wished for autonomy and had faith in their leaders, the message continued: "It is now clear that we cannot succeed in the way they hoped. So where can we hide our faces?" In response, Natsir expressed his understanding of their dilemma and offered to make a speech over the radio to explain the situation to the Acehnese people, outlining the problem and what he saw as the best path to a solution.[54]

---

[54] The above account is based on Puar, *Natsir 70 Tahun*, pp. 112–4. This is clearly Natsir's version of the events.

In his speech later that day, which was broadcast as widely as possible throughout the province, Natsir recalled Aceh's loyalty during the Revolution and reminded its people of the threats pro-Dutch forces had posed to the Republic since the transfer of sovereignty. He pleaded with them to view their inclusion within the province of North Sumatra "not as a door that closes off forever all other future possibilities, but as a step ... toward organizing our country into autonomous regions that possess duties and responsibilities in harmony with their individual strength and readiness...."[55]

Through this approach, Natsir was able to persuade Daud Beureu'eh and his followers to abandon their open opposition to the center's plans, but it was a hollow agreement. Daud Beureu'eh refused to take up the government post offered him and retired to his home village. Natsir returned to Jakarta, leaving a commitment that the central government would propose a law to Parliament under which Aceh would be able to exercise its right to autonomy. This was a promise he was unable to fulfill before his cabinet fell a few weeks later.

Through these actions with respect to Aceh, Natsir showed that, although he was sympathetic to regional aspirations, he was unwilling to let these threaten the unity of the state.

Again in his home region of West Sumatra, he demonstrated this determination to impose central over local authority. In October of 1950 his government rejected the provincial council's nominees for governor of Central Sumatra, on the ground that they lacked administrative experience. Instead, it appointed a Javanese, Roeslan Moeljohardjo, as acting governor. When the provincial council in its turn rejected Roeslan, the Natsir cabinet passed a law that suspended representative government in the region. It reinstated Moeljohardjo as acting governor, and the interior department appointed a six-man committee to assist him.[56] Although Natsir promised that the provincial council would be re-established in six months, his cabinet had fallen before these months expired, and, as with Aceh, the promise was not fulfilled. When later queried regarding this action, Natsir stated that Moeljohardjo "was a good Muslim and member of the Masjumi party, and should therefore have been acceptable to the people of West Sumatra."[57] But this arbitrary behavior became another source of local resentment against the central government in Jakarta.

---

[55] The full text of the speech appears in *Suara Penerangan*, January 30, 1951. See also Ajip Rosidi, *Sjafruddin Prawiranegara: Lebih Takut kepada Allah SWT* (Jakarta: Inti Idayu Press, 1986), p. 152.

[56] The law, (No. 1 of 1951), applied exclusively to the province of Central Sumatra. See Kahin, *Rebellion to Integration*, p. 172.

[57] Interview with Mohammad Natsir, Jakarta, October 16, 1976.

The International Milieu

It was the Republic's relationship to the former metropole that brought Prime Minister Natsir and President Soekarno into open confrontation; yet in the general field of foreign relations they were broadly in accord. Despite Natsir's strong anti-communism, his cabinet espoused "a free and active foreign policy" for the Republic, through which it was tied neither to the Western nor the Eastern bloc. Indonesia had become a member of the United Nations in September 1950 and participated actively in debates on the Korean War, abstaining on a motion that accused China of being the aggressor. While refusing military assistance from the United States, the Indonesian government did accept American technical and economic aid. On all these matters Soekarno and Natsir were in accord.

The clash between the two came more narrowly over the Republic's ties to the Netherlands. The two major challenges in this relationship sprang from the agreements reached at the Round Table Conference. First, with respect to the status of West Irian, the conference had agreed that Dutch authority was to be preserved only for a 12-month period before the territory's final status was determined. This period would expire on December 27, 1950, little over three months after Natsir assumed office, and there was no sign that the Dutch would adhere to the agreement. Tied to the West Irian problem was the special relationship between Indonesia and the Netherlands, embodied in the Netherlands Indonesian Union agreed upon at The Hague talks. As it became increasingly clear that the Netherlands would not in fact hand over West Irian by the specified date the Union became a major focus of Indonesian dissatisfaction.

This issue brought to a head the tensions that had been developing between Soekarno and Natsir over their relative powers. When Natsir became prime minister, his parliamentary cabinet replaced Hatta's presidential cabinet. In assuming office, Natsir had insisted to Soekarno that, as Indonesia had adopted a parliamentary system, responsibility for decision-making no longer lay with the president, but with the cabinet in agreement with the Parliament.

In early December Natsir heard that Soekarno intended to make a speech on the occasion of Mohammad's birthday, in which he would declare that if "before the cock crows on 1 January 1951 West Irian has not been returned to the Republic, then the Indonesian Dutch Union would be dissolved unilaterally."[58] Natsir asked to see the text of Soekarno's statement before he broadcast it and the president reluctantly agreed. Natsir was in accord with

---

[58] Puar, *Natsir 70 Tahun*, p. 108.

the president on the necessity of dissolving the Union but he believed that Indonesia's standing in the world dictated that abrogation of the agreement to form the Union had to be carried out in an orderly manner through a scheduled ministerial meeting between the Dutch and Indonesians, and not through a unilateral declaration by the president. Reminding the president of his earlier undertaking with respect to decision-making, Natsir proposed that there be joint discussions between the cabinet and the president on the issue. "Flushed with anger," Soekarno reluctantly agreed, and at the cabinet meeting, held in the palace, both he and Natsir presented their views, the president in an eloquent, 30-minute speech. However, in the ballot that was taken following their presentations, only 3 of the participants voted to dissolve the Union unilaterally in accordance with Soekarno's demands, while 12 voted for the action to be taken at a joint ministerial session with the Netherlands scheduled several months hence, in accordance with Natsir's proposal.

The president canceled his planned broadcast, and accepted what he viewed as a major blow to his authority. But he did not forgive Natsir. He renewed the complaints he had been voicing for months that his position as president was no more than a rubber stamp. From then on the personal relationship of respect and cooperation that Soekarno and Natsir had maintained throughout the Revolution, ended.

Resignation

From the beginning of 1951, then, not only did Natsir's government face formidable opposition in Parliament from the National and Communist parties, but, in addition, these two parties were increasingly allied with and supported by President Soekarno. Matters came to a head over the regional councils formed during the Revolution. As mentioned earlier, most of these councils were dominated by the Masjumi party, for in the uneasy times of the anti-Dutch struggle, the leaders who had gained the greatest respect in most regions came from the religious groups that had consistently opposed the colonial power. Also during the Revolution, the Masjumi party had been most active in forming social organizations and it was from these organizations that a majority of the council members were drawn. Because the other political parties in Parliament, most notably the National and Communist parties, believed that the Masjumi's local strength gave it an unfair advantage in any future national elections, they now demanded that these local councils should be dissolved. The cabinet acceded to the request, but Interior Minister Mr. Assaat resolved that their dissolution should be delayed until measures could be taken for their replacement.

The issue of the regional councils epitomized an important difference between the Masjumi and the other major parties (at that time, the PNI and PKI), namely the party's commitment to decentralization and some devolution of power from the Javanese center to the other Indonesian regions. Masjumi had by far the largest following in the non-Javanese islands. It is ironic that Natsir, who was not only strongly committed to a democratic form of government but also saw decentralization and regional autonomy as its necessary basis, should have been the prime minister to have moved most emphatically to enforce central power over the dissatisfied regions, especially Aceh and his home region of West Sumatra.[59]

When his government came to power, Natsir had viewed his prime mission as arranging and carrying out nationwide elections so that the Parliament sitting in Jakarta would reflect the actual will of the Indonesian people. The myriad of problems that had faced him since September 1950 meant that nothing had yet been achieved toward preparing for these elections. Nevertheless, his cabinet held that elections had to be the basis of representative government and he adhered to this stance also in the case of the local councils. The other political parties, understandably, felt that Natsir held to this position less because of his cabinet's commitment to decentralization and wish to avoid local power vacuums than because it believed these councils with their Masjumi majorities would strengthen the party's power base. Thus the opposition parties intensified their demands for immediate dissolution of the councils, boycotting sessions of Parliament in which the issue was scheduled for discussion. Unable to achieve a quorum, the cabinet reviewed the situation and decided that, in the face of this adamant opposition and in light of Soekarno's confrontational attitude toward Natsir's government, there was no alternative but for Natsir to return his mandate. The following day Natsir went to the Palace to offer his resignation to the president, who reportedly replied in Dutch that "I guessed from the beginning that this [would happen]."[60]

Natsir as Head of Government

Natsir's cabinet had lasted only six months, and he had been unable to achieve practically any of his major goals. No preparations had been made to arrange for elections to be held for a representative government, nor had Natsir been successful in reconciling either the Muslim dissidents or his political opponents

---

[59] On his moves to suspend represenative government ent in West Sumatra, see above, p. 81 and Kahin, *Rebellion to Integration*, pp. 171–4.

[60] "Saya sudah duga sejak semula." Natsir, *Politik*, p. 42.

in the ruling coalition and in the opposition. At the same time, he and Soekarno were no longer able to work together.

In later analyzing the achievements and failures of his government, Natsir laid much of the blame for its failures on the political system that then existed. He contended that, while Indonesia in a formal sense "already had democratic state institutions such as a head of state, a parliament, a cabinet that was responsible to Parliament, and a division of power between the executive, legislative and judiciary," these bodies in fact were only forms and, without an electoral law and a Parliament chosen by the people, they lacked any meaningful content. In his view, without a system under which a motion of no confidence in the government inevitably led to its fall and to a general election in which the people could express their will, there was no accountability. For in the situation existing in Indonesia in the early 1950s, a successful motion of no confidence in the cabinet merely led to power passing automatically from the governing party to the opposition. This meant merely a shuffling of positions at the top.

In Natsir's view a parliamentary system could only work if the political parties were accountable to the electorate. It was for this reason, he later argued, that Indonesia experienced four changes of government in five years, before the cabinet of Burhanuddin Harahap was finally able to draft an electoral law and organize and carry out nation-wide elections in 1955. Although Natsir had confronted Soekarno over the primacy of the legislative body in a parliamentary system, he nevertheless was of the opinion that in an unstable transition period, such as that following the transfer of sovereignty to Indonesia, a presidential cabinet, similar to the one that had existed under Vice President Hatta, would have been more suitable to the new state than the parliamentary cabinet that was in fact instituted.[61] He was to argue for returning Indonesia to this form of government for most of the rest of his time in Parliament. At the same time he would continue to refute accusations, put forward by Indonesians and foreign observers alike, that Indonesia was not "yet ripe for a democratic system."

The government's lack of accountability was not, however, the sole reason for the precipitate fall of Natsir's cabinet. Other factors played an important role. First among these were the political disagreements that developed and intensified between Natsir and Soekarno after the showdown over West Irian, undermining their earlier feelings of mutual affection and respect. Herbert Feith attributed the original basis of their growing antagonism in part to the fact that Natsir's cabinet pursued policies that accorded closely with the positions of Hatta and Sjahrir, the pragmatic "administrators" whom he contrasted with

---

[61] He made all these points in an interview with Yusuf Abdullah Puar, the editor of *Natsir 70 Tahun*, pp. 123–5.

the "solidarity makers" epitomized in the leadership style of Soekarno. The president's growing antagonism was exacerbated also by Natsir's persistent efforts "to confine Soekarno within the bounds of the figurehead President's role, a role to which Soekarno had never resigned himself."[62] As Feith further noted, after Soekarno was forced to yield over the West Irian issue, "he began to use his influence actively in support of PNI endeavors to bring the cabinet down."[63]

But some of the blame must also attach to the cabinet members, including Natsir himself. The leadership characteristics that he displayed during his tenure should be considered more closely, for these few months were the only period in which he had the opportunity to put into practice, under however difficult conditions, his philosophy of government and of the relationship between religion and the state.

As noted earlier, from the beginning Natsir was hampered by the fact that even within his own Masjumi party he headed a very uneasy coalition. Attempting to reach common ground among its disparate factions and between them and the NU that was still officially a part of the Masjumi, was in itself a daunting task. There were always tensions between Natsir and the more traditionalist and conservative leaders, not only of the NU but also of the Sukiman faction of the Masjumi. During his time as minister of information in the Revolution and then as prime minister, Natsir stood firmly in the moderate mainstream of Muslim politics. He worked easily with the nationalist leaders who were not allied with any religious parties, and after the transfer of sovereignty he maintained his close personal relationship to Socialist party leader Sjahrir.

In the political sphere he became an ever-more vocal advocate for democracy, and for Hatta to play a more central role in the vice presidency as a counterweight to the authoritarian proclivities of President Soekarno. His friendly relations particularly with the leaders of the PSI increasingly alienated him from the more puritanical Muslim faction headed by his mentor Ahmad Hassan and Isa Anshari. The fact that he no longer observed the narrow strictures of the more extreme wing of the Persatuan Islam, opened him to outspoken criticism from Hassan, who went so far as to publish a brochure

---

[62] Feith, *Decline*, pp. 170–1. In her biography of Mohammad Hatta, Mavis Rose agrees, writing that Natsir became "a thorn in Sukarno's flesh and almost as great a *bete noire* to him as was Sjahrir." She noted that "Natsir's insistence that the President remain a figurehead irritated Sukarno," as did his "developing rapport with the Sjahrir faction." Mavis Rose, *Indonesia Free* (Ithaca: Cornell Modern Indonesia Project, 1987), pp. 175, 184.

[63] Feith, *Decline*, pp. 170–1.

criticizing Natsir for allowing his daughters to wear Western clothes and socialize with their male friends, and being willing on occasions to serve his guests with drinks.[64]

Deliar Noer, who was one of Natsir's closest followers during the 1950s, was insightful in assessing the strengths and weaknesses in Natsir's later conduct of the affairs of the Dewan Da'wah under the Suharto regime. Some of these criticisms are perhaps applicable to his actions as prime minister, though in this earlier period he had more able subordinates on whom to rely.[65] Deliar's three major criticisms were: first, Natsir's lack of discipline in his willingness, and indeed eagerness, to welcome all who wished to speak with him, a characteristic he displayed throughout his life. While this openness tied him closely to people from all levels of society and made him a beloved figure to his followers, it was deleterious to the conduct of an effective organization, for it meant he paid "no attention to the demands of efficiency and management."[66] Second was Natsir's dislike of bureaucracy and his consequent unwillingness to delegate, taking on his own shoulders too much of the work of the organization he headed. Similarly, in Deliar's eyes, he tended to rely to too great an extent on those people closest to him in whom he had greatest trust, being reluctant to build an organizational system and develop a younger cadre of workers.[67]

In forming and leading his own government, Natsir did display some of these characteristics, certainly a tendency to rely on the people closest to him, whether of the Masjumi party or often of Sjahrir's socialist party and on others with no stated party affiliation. While his personal relationships with individuals of all political persuasions were frequently warm, in his dealings with political factions, especially those with whom he disagreed, he often appeared to show a degree of inflexibility — first in being unwilling to compromise with the PNI over formation of the cabinet, and later in his dealings especially with the more traditional elements within his own Masjumi party — not only with the NU

---

[64] Deliar Noer, *Aku Bagian Ummat Aku Bagian Bangsa* (Jakarta: Penerbit Mizan, 1996), p. 417.

[65] For example, it seems likely that the strong economic steps taken by Natsir's government were less attributable to him than to the less conciliatory Sumitro and Sjafruddin, who were largely dictating the direction of the economy.

[66] See Deliar Noer, "Kedudukan Natsir Masa Kini," *Panji Masyarakat*, August 1–10, 1991, pp. 25–9, esp. p. 26. Bernard Platzdasch, too, saw the "loose management style of the party" and the fact "that it did not impose high levels of discipline among its constituents," as weakening the Masjumi's effectiveness. Bernard Platzdasch, *Islamism in Indonesia* (Singapore: ISEAS, 2009), p. 36.

[67] Noer, "Kedudukan Natsir Masa Kini," pp. 28–9; also interview with Deliar Noer, Jakarta, January 10, 2004.

faction[68] but also with that of Sukiman. The tensions among the political parties and within the Muslim coalition became increasingly evident during Natsir's few months in office.

The respect Kartosuwirjo and his followers in the Darul Islam felt towards Natsir should have enabled him to broker some agreement with the Muslim dissidents, but it seemed to be more of a hindrance, for he was unable to persuade the military to his way of thinking and was suspect in their eyes because of his closeness with DI leaders. Although he had a good relationship with Nasution and other Muslim officers, the surrender agreements he tried to broker with the Darul Islam collapsed. This was in part because he was never able to persuade Kartosuwirjo to soften his stance.

In other negotiations he conducted, his favored method seems to have been to avoid confrontation and adopt what could be described as "unilateral disarmament," expressing his willingness to sacrifice his government's position and abandon his mission because of his fundamental agreement with his opponent's stance. This method he adopted with Sjafruddin in 1949, when he offered to stay with the Emergency Government (PDRI) in the jungle if Sjafruddin were unwilling to give up the struggle. Again with Daud Beureu'eh in 1951 he expressed his willingness to resign as prime minister if the Acehnese leader would not agree to the government's policy. In so doing he offered his own stature and integrity as a guarantee for an ultimately favorable outcome, rather than reaching an agreement that would have entailed compromise on both sides. In the case of Daud Beureu'eh at least, this method led to promises that could not be fulfilled.

This tactic was in accord with a general tendency toward rigidity and unwillingness to soften a fundamental stance, an apparent willingness to break rather than bend in any negotiations. As prime minister, he seemed to lack the flexibility of thought that might have enabled him to figure out the necessary compromises that might have brought about an acceptable solution to the problems he faced. This had not been the case in the critical weeks when the RIS was dissolved and the new unitary Republic was established in 1950. At that time he was able to fashion a formula acceptable to both sides. But during his prime minister-ship he seemed hidebound in insisting on the literal interpretation of any documents or agreements, especially The Hague Agreements and the ones transforming the RIS into the unitary Republic. In both cases he adhered so strictly to the letter of these agreements in his disputes with Soekarno and Daud Beureu'eh that he closed off the possibility of reaching an effective compromise between opposing positions.

---

[68] See Fealy, "Wahab Chasbullah," pp. 21–2.

During his few months in office, then, Natsir did not display many of the characteristics of an effective political head of government. But he did remain faithful to the pursuit of what he saw as the best interests of the newly independent state. The principles of government that he most consistently followed were maintenance of the unitary status of the Republic, its responsibility to all the people it served and the primacy of adhering to the letter of any agreement that had been reached. Neither his strong religious faith nor his belief in the merits of a decentralized political order seem to have diverted him from the major thrust of his government's policies, which were aimed at maintaining a unified and independent Indonesian state that held a respected place in the world community.

5

From Loyal Opposition to Rebellion, 1951–57

Parliamentary Maneuvering

Natsir's cabinet resigned on March 21, 1951, but at that time it was by no means clear that the move would end his leadership position in the government. He still headed the Masjumi, probably the strongest of the political parties, and there was no clear candidate to succeed him in the prime minister-ship. When President Soekarno invited Sartono of the National Party (PNI) to form a new PNI-Masjumi coalition, many in the modernist Islamic community were still hoping that Natsir would return as its prime minister. But, instead, Sukiman Wirjosandjojo, the leader of the traditionalist faction within the Masjumi party, who had a good relationship with Soekarno and was close to the PNI, was chosen to head the new government.[1] And when Sukiman announced his cabinet on April 26, not a single member of the Natsir faction of the party was included. It must have been difficult for Natsir to accept a subordinate position to his older colleague, whose base was in Java and whose views on politics and

---

[1] Sukiman was born in 1896 in Solo. He was a medical doctor who had graduated from the University of Amsterdam in 1925, and was Hatta's predecessor as chairman of the Perhimpunan Indonesia in the Netherlands. See Taufik Abdullah, *Indonesia Towards Democracy* (Singapore: ISEAS, 2009), p. 117. He first entered the PSII in 1927, then founded and headed the Partai Islam Indonesia (PII) in the immediate prewar period. He held various cabinet positions during the Revolution, including minister of the interior in the 1948 Hatta cabinet. See St. Rais Alamsjah, *10 Orang Indonesia terbesar sekarang* (Bukittinggi: Mutiara, 1952), pp. 68–81 and Mohamad Roem, *Bunga Rampai dari Sejarah* II (Jakarta: Bulan Bintang, 1977), pp. 194–202.

Indonesia's place in the world differed so markedly from his own, but Natsir and his modernist colleagues agreed to support the cabinet and give it a chance to implement its policies.[2]

On domestic policy, the most striking difference between Sukiman's government and that of Natsir lay in Sukiman's willingness to seek tough military solutions to the problems posed by the rebellious movements in various parts of the archipelago. Although Natsir was known to have closer relations with army leaders than Sukiman, he was opposed to reliance on military force, and always stressed the need to seek a negotiated solution to internal unrest, especially when dealing with the Darul Islam and other Muslim rebel movements.[3] He had provoked army displeasure during his tenure as prime minister when he had sent Masjumi leader, Kyai Muslich, as envoy both to the Darul Islam in Central Java and to Kartosuwirjo himself.[4] Further friction arose between him and the army when military officers arrested some Masjumi members suspected of being close to the Darul Islam.[5]

Natsir's government had also negotiated with Kahar Muzzakar, the Islamic militia leader in South Sulawesi who had cut ties with the army in July 1950. In early 1951, these negotiations had resulted in Kahar's units being incorporated into the National Reserve Corps. When he succeeded Natsir as prime minister, Sukiman followed through on these negotiations, but Kahar rebuffed him and instead, on August 17, 1951, left Makassar with his troops for the mountains. They made their allegiance clear in January of the following year when Kahar accepted an appointment as Sulawesi commander of Kartosuwirjo's Islamic Army of Indonesia, the official fighting force of the Darul Islam.[6] His action must have further soured Sukiman on the idea of negotiated settlements with rebel movements.

In its intolerance of internal opposition, the Sukiman cabinet went so far, in August 1951, as to arrest Ahmad Hassan and Isa Anshari, the two principal leaders of Natsir's former party, the Persatuan Islam. This was part of a general sweep, mostly against Communists whom the government accused of instigating

---

[2] See Natsir's speech to Parliament, May 31, 1951 in M. Natsir, *Capita Selecta II* (Jakarta: PT Abadi and Yayasan Capita Selecta, 2008 [1957]), pp. 26–33.

[3] See, for example, his "Soal 'Gerilya,'" [January 12, 1952], and "Lagi Soal 'Gerilya'" [February 2, 1952] in *Capita Selecta II* (Jakarta: Abadi, 2008), pp. 272–9.

[4] Holk Dengel, *Darul Islam dan Kartosuwirjo* (Jakarta: Pustaka Sinar Harapan, 1995), pp. 158–9.

[5] Herbert Feith, *Decline of Constitutional Democracy in Indonesia* (Ithaca: Cornell University Press, 1962), p. 189.

[6] Ibid., pp. 212–4.

labor unrest in some of Indonesia's most important ports,[7] but also against a few Muslims whom government leaders suspected of conspiring with the Darul Islam.[8] Although, in contrast to the PKI detainees, the two Muslim leaders were released within three days and no charges were brought against them, their arrest signaled a stark break with the conciliatory policies that the Natsir government had previously pursued.

Other than their contrasting approaches to internal unrest, Sukiman and Natsir also differed markedly in the field of foreign affairs. Sukiman was more militantly anti-Communist than Natsir and had a close relationship with the American ambassador, Merle Cochran. He urged that the Indonesian government align itself more firmly with the United States and the West. Natsir, when he was prime minister, had tried to follow a strictly non-aligned foreign policy, whereby Indonesia was tied to neither the Western nor the Eastern bloc. To this end he had rebuffed offers of American military aid and, although his government accepted Western technical and economic assistance, he had refused to allow any strings to be attached that would have made this aid conditional on Indonesia's alignment with the United States.

Under Sukiman, Indonesia drifted away from this "free and active foreign policy" into more direct alignment with the West, a shift that provoked considerable opposition not only in the cabinet, but also within the Masjumi party and the government as a whole. When it signed the Japanese Peace Treaty in September 1951, the government met opposition from an important minority of the cabinet (6 out of 16) and a substantial majority of Parliament.[9] The Masjumi party itself was badly split over the issue, and at its council held on September 4-6, the party officially came out in favor of signing the peace treaty only after "a major tussle of strength" between Sukiman's group which supported the treaty and that headed by Natsir which strongly opposed it. In the event, the Indonesian Parliament was never willing to ratify the agreement.[10]

The Sukiman cabinet's pro-West stance ultimately brought it down. In order to gain financial and military assistance under the so-called Mutual Security Act (MSA), Sukiman made concessions to the United States that were

---

[7] About 15,000 people were arrested in Jakarta and other major port cities. George McT. Kahin, "Indonesian Politics and Nationalism," in *Asian Nationalism and the West*, ed. William L. Holland (New York: Institute of Pacific Relations, 1953), pp. 65–196, esp. pp. 188–9.

[8] Howard M. Federspiel, *Persatuan Islam: Islamic Reform in Twentieth Century Indonesia* (Ithaca: Cornell Modern Indonesia Project, 1970), pp. 169–70.

[9] See Kahin, "Indonesian Politics and Nationalism," pp. 191–2.

[10] See Feith, *Decline*, pp. 195–6.

unacceptable to both the Indonesian public and the political parties. In January 1952 Foreign Minister Subardjo promised to "make a full contribution ... to the defensive strength of the free world" in return for American economic aid.[11] Such a promise flew even more directly in the face of the "free and active foreign policy" supported by a broad spectrum of Indonesian political opinion. A widespread outcry in the public and the press greeted announcement of the agreement. Led by Natsir, the Masjumi executive refused to accept it, and although the Masjumi did not withdraw its ministers from the cabinet, its open opposition sparked an exodus of ministers from other parties, forcing the Sukiman cabinet to resign on February 23, 1952.

The Masjumi retained considerable influence in the subsequent coalition cabinet headed by Wilopo of the National Party (PNI), in which Prawoto Mangkusasmito of the Masjumi was deputy prime minister and three other Masjumi members held cabinet posts.[12] But this cabinet's fall, in June 1953, was at least in part due to the growing hostility between the PNI and the Masjumi, and in the subsequent first Ali Sastroamidjojo cabinet (July 1953–July 1955) the PNI leader excluded the Masjumi from participation.

Natsir as Head of Masjumi

Rivalry between Natsir and Sukiman was evident not only in the conduct of government policy but also in the leadership of the Masjumi party. In the years leading up to World War II Natsir had been junior to Sukiman, heading the Bandung branch of the Partai Islam Indonesia (PII) while Sukiman headed its central office.[13] When the Masjumi was initially established at the end of 1945, effective leadership of the party was divided between the Presidium (Dewan Partai, lit. Party Council), which was made up of provincial representatives and special representatives, and a Party Leadership Council (Dewan Pimpinan Partai), which acted as the executive body. In addition, there was a Majelis Syuro (Consultative Council), dominated by traditional Islamic leaders mostly from the NU.[14] At the Masjumi congress of 1949 the younger modernists under Natsir came to dominate the party, with Natsir elected chairman while Sukiman headed the Presidium. At the same time the party's rules were changed, limiting the influence of the Majelis Syuro. Natsir

---

[11] Ibid., pp. 199–201.
[12] See Deliar Noer, *Partai Islam di Pentas Nasional 1945–1965* (Jakarta: Grafiti, 1987), p. 225.
[13] Ibid., p. 61.
[14] Federspiel, *Persatuan Islam*, p. 160.

and Sukiman held roughly equal power until the Masjumi's 1952 Congress after which Natsir became official leader of the party with Sukiman as his deputy.

Despite the rivalry between the Natsir and Sukiman factions, until mid-1952 the major friction in the Masjumi party was between the NU traditionalists at one end of the political spectrum and the Natsir reformists or modernists at the other. It had seemed that this internal party dissension might be eased in April 1951 when Sukiman took over as prime minister, for he had closer relations with NU leaders. Like Natsir, he had received a Western education, though, unlike Natsir, he had continued this schooling in the Netherlands. Nevertheless, he was able to maintain friendly relations with the NU, for he was not strongly identified with the reformist wing of the Masjumi nor was he noted for his scholarly understanding of Islam. Natsir, on the other hand, had been recognized as a leading modernist scholar in the prewar years. More importantly, in the eyes of NU leaders, members of the Natsir faction of the party were disdainful toward their more traditional colleagues and were systematically attempting to restrict the NU's influence within the Masjumi.[15]

The NU derived its strength from its position on the party council, the *ulama*-dominated Majelis Syuro, established in 1945, whose role, according to the traditionalists, was to review party leaders' decisions and judge them against Muslim legal standards. However, when the party was reorganized first in 1949 and later in 1952, the Majelis Syuro was stripped of all but advisory functions, and power was concentrated in the Central Leadership Council, dominated by the reformists.[16] The NU cited this change in the Majelis Syuro's status as the major reason for their leaving the Masjumi.

Many observers, however, have seen the principal cause for the NU's withdrawal from the Masjumi coalition as lying mainly in the disputes over the position of minister of religion in the Wilopo cabinet. The NU's Wahid Hasjim

---

[15] I am grateful to Greg Fealy for alerting me to the importance of this factor. Deliar Noer, however, noted that Idham Chalid did not feel that Natsir himself adopted such an attitude. According to Noer: "Much later, NU leader KH Idham Chalid, when he was speaking to NU trainees and criticizing the attitude of several Western-educated Masjumi leaders toward *pesantren* scholars [*ulama*] during the Masjumi Party Congress in Bogor in 1952, said that, although Natsir was Western educated, he was not like these other leaders. He acknowledged Natsir's wisdom in conducting that meeting. The leader of whom we now write [i.e. Natsir] indeed honored *ulama*, including those from the *pesantren*. But he was severe, even though silently, toward those who were not sincere and who say one thing but mean another [*yang lain di mulut lain di hati*]." Deliar Noer, "Kedudukan Natsir Masa Kini," *Panji Masyarakat*, August 1–10, 1991, pp. 25–9, esp. p. 29.

[16] Federspiel, *Persatuan Islam*, p. 160. See also Noer, *Partai Islam*, pp. 61–3.

had held this post since the time of the Hatta cabinet in 1950, but he came under strong parliamentary attack because of his alleged mismanagement of shipping negotiations for the haj pilgrims in 1951.[17] Sjafruddin Prawiranegara, supported by Natsir, led the attack on Hasjim, and both these reformist leaders were clearly determined to prevent Hasjim from retaining the religion ministry in future cabinets. But they also were unwilling to appoint another NU leader to the post, which meant that no NU member held a cabinet portfolio. Ultimately the Masjumi leaders succeeded in replacing Hasjim with Muhammadiyah leader, Fakih Usman.[18]

Their actions sparked anger in the NU. Wahab Chasbullah led the attack, demanding that the NU should be allotted both the religious affairs and defense portfolios, and subsequently meeting with other political leaders, including Soekarno, to plead the NU's cause.[19] At its congress held in Palembang on April 26, 1952 the NU decided in principle to disaffiliate from the Masjumi, but, reluctant to be seen as splitting Islamic unity, proceeded slowly in a series of stages over the subsequent months to loosen its ties. It officially withdrew from the party at the beginning of August, and on August 30, together with the Islamic League (PSII) and the small, Minangkabau-based traditionalist party Perti (Persatuan Tarbiyah Islamiyah, Islamic Education Association), it established the Indonesian Muslim League (Liga Muslimin Indonesia), a federation that the Masjumi refused to join and which had Wahid Hasjim as its first chairman.[20] The NU then formally cut all ties with the Masjumi, leaving the Sukiman and Natsir factions as the major components of the truncated party.

At the party's congress in 1952 the foreign policy disagreement between Natsir and Sukiman again erupted, with Sukiman contending that Indonesia should now align itself with the Western bloc. Natsir felt that such a policy would cause an adverse popular reaction which would play into the hands of Communists, for the average Indonesian would have difficulty in "accepting such a relationship with the white West with equanimity." A majority of the party sided with Natsir, and he retained the Masjumi leadership.[21]

The degree to which the departure of the NU had weakened the Masjumi and divided the Muslim community became clear with the formation of the first cabinet of Ali Sastroamidjojo in July 1953. The Muslim League (Liga

---

[17] *Antara*, October 26, 27, 1951.
[18] Feith, *Decline*, pp. 235–6; see also Fealy, "Wahab Chasbullah," pp. 21–3.
[19] Fealy, "Wahab Chasbullah," pp. 23–4.
[20] Noer, *Partai Islam*, p. 230.
[21] George Kahin interview with Natsir, Jakarta, November 19, 1954.

Muslimin Indonesia) accepted five seats in this cabinet, three of them held by the NU and two by the PSII. According to Noer, the PSII's participation caused a split in that party, with one of its principal leaders, Amelz, leaving it to join the Masjumi.[22] The Masjumi voted against parliamentary acceptance of the Ali cabinet, but was joined in its opposition only by the Catholic Party, while the NU, PSII and Perti, all voted to support it. As noted above, the advent of the Ali cabinet marked the first time the Masjumi had been excluded from the government.

Growing Opposition to Soekarno

After the fall of the Sukiman government and the formation of the Wilopo and subsequently the nationalist-dominated Ali Sastroamidjojo cabinets, Natsir moved from the position of moderate critic to that of outspoken opponent of the political trends in Indonesia, and in particular of Soekarno's growing power and his early steps toward introducing his concept of "Guided Democracy" to the country. Over the years, Natsir's criticisms of both Soekarno and the Parliament became more trenchant.

Criticisms of the president were also coming from many elements in the Islamic community, particularly after Soekarno's speech in January 1953 during a visit to Amuntai in South Kalimantan, where he voiced fears of Muslim extremism, pointing to the fact that more radical elements in the community were voicing demands for an Islamic state. The president repeated the misgivings, previously expressed by Hatta at the Preparatory meetings for Indonesian independence in 1945, that "if we establish a state based on Islam, many areas whose population is not Islamic, such as the Moluccas, Bali, Flores, Timor, the Kei Islands, and Sulawesi, will secede."[23] As John Legge has written, Soekarno's Amuntai speech was "not so much an example of Sukarno's tendency to take sides as an appeal to Islam to curb itself and fit into the Indonesian consensus he was anxious to achieve."[24] It certainly fitted with the opinions he had expressed in the pre-war period when he was examining Islam's place within the future Indonesian state.[25] But the Persatuan Islam leader, Isa

---

[22] Noer, *Partai Islam*, p. 235.

[23] Sukarno, "The National State and the Ideals of Islam (1953)," in *Indonesian Political Thinking, 1945–1965*, ed. Herbert Feith and Lance Castles (Ithaca: Cornell University Press, 1970), p. 164.

[24] J.D. Legge, *Sukarno: A Political Biography*, 3rd ed. (Singapore: Archipelago Press, 2003 [1972]), p. 281.

[25] See Chapter 2.

Anshari, responded harshly, declaring that "there is a cold war between Islam on the one hand and on the other are those who call themselves Islamic and are not."[26]

At the time, Natsir appears not to have openly expressed his reactions either to Soekarno's speech, or to Isa's intemperate words, and together with other moderate members of the party seemed eager to avoid a showdown with the president.[27] He recognized the threat posed to Indonesia's democratic development by extremists among the Muslim politicians as well as those coming from the left. This danger was not only evident in the expansion of the Darul Islam movement but also in the open advocacy by Isa Anshari and other members of the Persatuan Islam of an Islamic state.[28] Anshari's statements highlighted the cleavage within the Masjumi at this time between Natsir's reformists and what Allen Samson described as the "fundamentalists." Of the Natsir-associated faction, Samson wrote:

> Reformists ... were disposed to cooperate with secular forces so long as they felt they had a stake in the political order.... [Their] political goals were the establishment of a state based on Islamic tenets, decentralization with consequent devolution of power from a Javanese-dominated unitary government to one of wide local and regional autonomy, and the recognition of Islam as an influential and legitimate political force with a degree of political power commensurate with its numbers. Masyumi's reformist mainstream theoretically favored an Islamic state, but its urbanized, pragmatic character ensured it an influential role in secular politics and made it a moderating influence within Islam.[29]

In the months leading up to the 1955 elections, there was a drumbeat of criticism from the opposition parties against the government of Prime Minister

---

[26] Federspiel, *Persatuan Islam*, p. 172. On the attitudes within the Masjumi party toward both Soekarno's speech and Isa's reaction, see also Holk, *Darul Islam dan Kartosuwirjo*, pp. 162–5.

[27] Federspiel, *Persatuan Islam*, p. 173.

[28] In an interview on May 19, 1967, Natsir expressed the view that some fundamentalist Muslims had done damage to the Masjumi by "extreme statements concerning an Islamic state," not in accord with the views of the party leadership and that this should not be allowed to happen in any future Muslim party. He described Isa Anshari, the most vocal defender of the Darul Islam within the Masjumi party, as "our Joe McCarthy." See Chapter 8.

[29] Allan A. Samson, "Conceptions of Politics, Power, and Ideology in Contemporary Indonesian Islam," in *Political Power and Communications in Indonesia*, ed. Karl D. Jackson and Lucian W. Pye (Berkeley CA: University of California Press, 1978), p. 215; see also ibid., pp. 199–200.

Ali Sastroadmijojo, criticisms that gained traction because of the domestic economic difficulties and price rises that plagued the country during the early months of that year, and the growing tensions between the cabinet and the army.[30] Despite the success of the Bandung Conference of Asian African Nations[31] that he had done so much to organize, Ali was compelled to submit the resignation of his cabinet on July 18, 1955.

Two months later the Masjumi-led Burhanuddin Harahap cabinet, which succeeded the first Ali cabinet, was finally able to hold the long-awaited national elections, postponed for over five years since the transfer of sovereignty. But although the conduct of these elections was remarkably successful, and they were recognized as being democratic and largely free of corruption, they did not succeed in resolving the country's political dilemmas, for no one party emerged with a clear mandate. The National Party (PNI) garnered the largest number of votes (22.3%), with its strength lying largely in the heavily populated regions of Central and East Java. It was closely followed by the two Islamic parties, Masjumi (20.9%) and NU (18.4%), with the Communist Party (PKI) emerging as a strong fourth (16.4%), also with its major strength in Central and East Java. The vote was therefore roughly split evenly between religious and secular parties. The Masjumi was the only party that attracted a majority vote from the regions outside Java.

The Burhanuddin cabinet clung to power for five months after the elections but Burhanuddin was ultimately compelled to return his mandate to the president on March 3, 1956. After much jockeying among the three major parties (PNI, Masjumi and NU) over whether or not Communists should be included in the cabinet in view of their having received 16 per cent of the nationwide vote, the president again chose the PNI's Ali Sastroamidjojo as formateur of a new government. Ali put together his second cabinet, which was dominated by the National Party with the Masjumi and NU as equal, subordinated, partners.[32] In his second cabinet, Ali did not include any Communists, but rather gave an important role to the religious parties. Recognizing their achievement in gaining nearly 40 per cent of the vote between them he assigned five seats each to the Masjumi and the NU, as well as one seat to both the PSII and Perti. The Muslim parties then had a majority (12 out of 23 seats) in the cabinet, and had they been able to work together should have

---

[30] For extensive discussions of all these factors, see Feith, *Decline*, pp. 379–84, 394–409.

[31] On the conference, see George McT. Kahin, *The Asian-African Conference, Bandung, Indonesia* (Ithaca: Cornell University Press, 1956).

[32] Feith, *Decline*, pp. 466–8. Although the PNI had won the largest number of votes in the election, both the PNI and Masjumi had gained 57 parliamentary seats.

been able to decide the direction of government policy.[33] In the event, however, strong disagreements continued to divide them.

The failure of the general elections to provide a solution to the country's political and economic problems heightened Soekarno's frustration with the parliamentary system. From late 1956 he began to make moves to strengthen the president's power *vis-à-vis* that of Parliament, culminating in his February 1957 unveiling of his "*konsepsi*" of a Guided Democracy that Soekarno believed was more suited to Indonesian realities than was the Western form of democracy the country had previously been following.

Natsir versus Soekarno

It was as a protest to Soekarno's "concept" that Natsir began a frontal attack against the path the president was following, launching instead a strong defense of a democratic system of government. He expressed his views in February 1957 in his "First Reaction to the President's Concept."[34] Responding to the president's criticisms of democracy as a Western concept and unsuitable for Asian peoples, Natsir stated that one could not make a dichotomy between "Western democracy" and "Eastern democracy," affirming instead: "There is only 'democracy and non-democracy' [*jang ada hanja antara 'demokrasi dan bukan demokrasi'*]." It seemed, he said, that the "*konsepsi*" was aimed at creating a "democracy without an opposition." After noting that parallel influences passed from east to west and from west to east, he continued:

> Democracy in my view is a philosophy that is not limited to an administrative system, but democracy is a "way of life" that embraces spiritual and material fields. In this connection the late President Franklin D. Roosevelt formulated an understanding of democracy that I think can be accepted by every true democracy whether of the east or the west. A true democracy gives guarantees for:
>
> 1. Freedom of expression
> 2. Freedom of religion
> 3. Freedom from want
> 4. Freedom from fear.
>
> Democracy can also be divided into political democracy that guarantees freedom of thought, speech, assembly and religion, and economic democracy that guarantees social justice for all members of society.[35]

---

[33] Ibid., p. 250.

[34] Natsir,"Reaksi pertama terhadap 'Konsepsi Presiden'," February 19, 1957, *Capita Selecta III* (typescript [1961]), pp. 25–6.

[35] Ibid., pp. 31–2. He gives the four characteristics of democracy in both English and Indonesian.

No Indonesian leader ever gave a clearer and simpler portrayal of the basic principles of a democratic system of government.

In the months between this major defense of democracy and the speech he gave to the Constituent Assembly in November 1957 there appears to have been a major shift in Natsir's thinking regarding the Five Principles (*Pancasila*) that had been adopted in 1945 as Indonesia's state philosophy.[36] Up to late 1957 he seems to have been willing to view the *Pancasila* as an acceptable philosophy for the state, with the major proviso that belief in God remain the first of these five principles and that the "seven words" of the Jakarta Charter be again included in the Preamble. He had in fact defended the *Pancasila* on two major occasions: first, in an address he gave before the Pakistan Institute of World Affairs in 1954, and later that same year in an article in *Hikmah*, entitled "Is the Pancasila in Conflict with the Teachings of the Quran?" where he confronted the issue directly.[37] In his Pakistan speech he noted that, though the Indonesian Constitution makes no mention of Islam as the state's religion,

> it has put the monotheistic belief in the one and only God, at the head of the Pantjasila — The Five Principles adopted as the spiritual, moral and ethical foundation of the state and the nation.
>
> Thus for both our countries and peoples Islam has its very essential place in our lives.

In the article where he more broadly considered the relationship of *Pancasila* and the Qur'an, he stressed that there were no inherent contradictions or incompatibility between *Pancasila* and Islam:

> In the eyes of a Muslim, the formulation of the *Pancasila* does not appear *apriori* as "something foreign," that stands in opposition to the teachings of Islam. He sees in it a reflection of what is on his side. But this does not mean that the *Pancasila* is identical with, or contains all the teachings of Islam. *Pancasila* indeed contains the goals of Islam, but *Pancasila* does not mean Islam. We have a strong conviction [*berkeyakinan yang tak akan kunjung kering*] that in an Islamic country and atmosphere, *Pancasila* will thrive.[38]

---

[36] See Chapter 3, pp. 43–4.

[37] The first was published in the United States as *Some Observations concerning the Role of Islam in National and International Affairs* (Ithaca: Cornell Southeast Asia Program Data Paper Number 16, 1954), and the second, "Apakah Pancasila Bertentangan dengan Ajaran Al Qur'an?" that first appeared in *Hikmah* VII (May 29, 1954), was reproduced in *Capita Selecta II*, pp. 203–12.

[38] "Dimata seorang muslim, perumusan Pancasila bukan kelihatan *apriori* sebagai satu 'barang asing', yang berlawanan dengan ajaran Al Qur'an. Ia melihat dalamnya satu pencerminan dari sebagai yang ada pada sisinya. Tapi ini tidak berarti bahwa Pancasila itu sudah identik atau meliputi semua ajaran-ajaran Islam. Pancasila memang mengandung tujuan-tujuan Islam,

In the same article, however, Natsir did express some misgivings about the Pancasila formulation, recognizing its imprecision and fearing that it could be twisted because "each Indonesian feels the right to give his own contents to this formulation." He went on to say:

> We hope that the *Pancasila*, in its journey since its proclamation toward giving itself content, will not be filled with teachings that are opposed to the Qur'an, the Divine Revelation (*Wahyu Ilahi*) that for centuries has been the lifeblood for the majority of our people.[39]

By November 1957 Natsir seems to have become convinced that the dangers within the *Pancasila* outweighed its good qualities, and in arguing for Indonesia to be an "Islamic Democracy" he contended that the *Pancasila* was amorphous and essentially secular and thus unsuited for a Muslim nation such as Indonesia. This change almost certainly was occasioned by two major factors: first, as already mentioned, Soekarno's increasing efforts to introduce a more authoritarian order in Indonesia;[40] and second, the growing strength of the Communist Party (PKI) in the 1950s, which became evident in the 1955 elections and even more so in the 1957 local elections.[41] While on a personal basis Natsir was able to maintain cordial relations with leaders of the PKI, drinking coffee with Aidit and adhering to his general practice of agreeing to disagree, he opposed and increasingly feared the influence over Soekarno of communist philosophy, especially its anti-religion stance.

Both Natsir's outspoken criticisms of Soekarno on one hand, and his censure of the fundamentalist stream within the Islamic community, as represented by Isa Anshari, on the other, formed part of a strong defense of representative democracy that he continued to argue was the most suitable form of government for Indonesia. Until the debates in the Constituent Assembly in 1957 he would often stress the virtues of democratic as against authoritarian government and mute any particular advocacy of "Islamic democracy" as such. He did, however, always argue that values based on religion should be the ultimate source of the moral code of policy makers.[42] In a speech at the

---

tetapi Pancasila itu bukanlah berarti Islam. Kita berkeyakinan yang tak akan kunjung kering, bahwa diatas tanah dan dalam iklim Islamlah, Pancasila akan hidup subur" Natsir, "Apakah Pancasila Bertentangan dengan Ajaran Al Qur'an," *Capita Selecta II*, pp. 210–1.

[39] Ibid., p. 211.

[40] Natsir seems to have come to believe that the breadth and flexibility of the *Pancasila*'s principles allowed them to be fashioned into whatever form the president desired.

[41] Lev, *Transition to Guided Democracy*, pp. 96–101.

[42] Natsir, "Kemampuan Mengendalikan diri sjarat mutlak bagi Kemerdekaan," November 7, 1956, in *Capita Selecta III*, p. 12.

end of 1956 he contended that authoritarianism was not the answer to the weakness that had become evident in the democratic process in Indonesia, and in its political leaders. In a country so diverse and extensive, he stated, it was important for people of diverse ethnicities and cultures to recognize that they could bring their grievances to government attention through their representatives, "so that they can really feel that their government is from them, for them and responsible to them.... It is this feeling of belief and love that actually forms the true power that gathers the archipelago of Indonesia into a single state."[43]

But, as in his prewar writings, he warned against wild or unfettered democracy (*demokrasi jang liar*), which he thought would result in chaos. Before Soekarno formally presented his own "concept" Natsir had proposed a "guided democracy, not in the sense that this entire democratic system has to be controlled by one or several men who are all powerful and uncontrolled. But guided democracy in the sense that the adherents/supporters and implementers of this democratic system are guided and led by high moral values and philosophies."[44]

Within two months of this statement, the Masjumi withdrew its ministers from the Ali cabinet and moved into official opposition. Natsir explained that the party was doing so because of the inability of the government to overcome crises and the fact that it continued to ignore Masjumi advice. He stressed the party's desire to return to the *dwitunggal* of Soekarno-Hatta and stated that while the Masjumi had resigned from the cabinet, it hoped for continued cooperation with the other political parties.[45]

Constituent Assembly

On December 15, 1955, two months after the general elections, further elections had been held for a Constituent Assembly that would formulate a Constitution to replace the 1950 Provisional Constitution that had been hastily approved when the Federal States were abolished in favor of a Unitary State of Indonesia. The major difference between the two constitutions was that, under

---

[43] Ibid., p. 8.

[44] "Jang kita hendak tegakkan ialah demokrasi jang terpimpin, bukan dengan arti bahwa seluruh sistim demokrasi itu harus dikendalikan oleh seorang atau beberapa orang jang serba-kuasa jang tidak kenal kendali. Akan tetapi: demokrasi jang terpimpin dengan arti, bahwa pemeluk/pendukung dan pelaksana sistim demokrasi itu terpimpin dan terbimbing oleh nilai2 moral dan nilai2 hidup jang tinggi." Ibid., p. 13.

[45] Ibid., p. 20.

the 1950 Provisional Constitution of the Unitary State that replaced the 1949 Constitution of the federal order, Parliament, not the president, could topple the government and the president did not have the power to dissolve Parliament.[46] Many, including Natsir, hoped that in formulating a new Constitution in the late 1950s the Constituent Assembly's discussions, in which all political parties and beliefs were represented, could reach an agreement for the governance of Indonesia that would enable the country to evade the growing pressures for an authoritarian state under Soekarno's concept of Guided Democracy.

The sessions were held against a backdrop of accelerating moves toward creation of such a state. Martial law had been declared in March 1957, and Soekarno began moves toward "burying the political parties" and replacing them with an "emergency extra-parliamentary cabinet of experts," whose major allegiance was to the president. On April 9, Soekarno proclaimed a new government headed by a "Working Cabinet [Kabinet Karya]" with Djuanda Kartawidjaja, a respected figure with no party affiliation, as its prime minister. Previously the president had summoned the leaders of the major political parties to the palace to ask whether or not they would be willing to participate in such a cabinet. Natsir, along with other Masjumi leaders and those of the PSI, refused, "a depressing moment for Natsir because Sukarno treated him so kindly in the meeting," according to Taufik Abdullah.[47]

From November 1956, until it was dissolved by presidential decree on July 5, 1959, the Constituent Assembly's 544 members, elected in November 1955, debated the ideals of a constitutional state, but only during the first year was there any real chance of these debates bearing fruit.[48] Soekarno and his supporters exerted growing pressure on the Assembly to approve a return to the 1945 Constitution, under which presidential power would be greatly expanded, making it easier to introduce Soekarno's concept of Guided Democracy.

Natsir was active as a Masjumi party representative in the early sessions of the Assembly, presenting his party's position on the state order it envisaged for Indonesia. In his speeches he seems to have moved from his earlier position

---

[46] Adnan Buyung Nasution, *The Aspiration for Constitutional Government in Indonesia* (Jakarta: Pustaka Sinar Harapan, 1992), p. 28.

[47] Taufik Abdullah, *Indonesia towards Democracy* (Singapore: ISEAS, 2009), p. 280. This statement is presumably from an interview with Natsir. During the meeting, Abdullah continues: "It was as if the warm relationship the two leaders cultivated during the revolution had returned."

[48] The Constituent Assembly held seven plenary sessions, one in 1956, three in 1957, two in 1958 and one in 1959. The debates in 1957 were the most substantive for discussion of the philosophy and basis of the state. Nasution, *Aspiration for Constitutional Government*, p. 41.

Natsir speaking to the Constituent Assembly.

where he accepted the *Pancasila* and put all his energies into arguing for a democratic as against an authoritarian form of government. In these debates, in conjunction with other religious party members of the assembly, he now argued strongly in favor of an Islamic as against a secular state, which he identified with a state based on the *Pancasila*.[49] The foci of his major speech to the Constituent Assembly in November 1957 were the arguments that Islam not *Pancasila* should be the basis of the state, and that Islam and democracy complemented rather than contradicted each other. He initially expressed strong agreement with the imperative need for tolerance among members of the Constituent Assembly, but argued that this tolerance had to be based on sincere and frank expression of the opposing positions.

He opened his discussion of the Constitution by outlining his understanding of the meaning of the state as an institution that possessed, not only territory, people, administration, and sovereignty, but also a Constitution that provided the basis for other unwritten laws and powers. This Constitution "has to position the state in the closest possible proximity with the society that inhabits our country … and it has to be deeply rooted in the thought, feelings, faith and life philosophy of the people within our country." He stated that all

---

[49] Ibid., p. 71.

groups and streams (*aliran*), without exception, wanted the state to be founded on democracy. But he argued that, as the faith of the vast majority of Indonesia's people was Islam, "the state of our Republic of Indonesia should be based on Islam: a democratic state based on Islam."[50]

He contended that the first principle of democracy was for "the state to reflect the philosophy of life of the majority of its people" and secondly give living space for the groups that have differing beliefs from the majority (*ruang hidup bagi golongan-golongan jang berpendapat lain daripada majority*).

In confronting his opponents' position that Islam should not form the basis of the state because it was the faith of only one group in Indonesia, he argued that the *Pancasila*, too, was adhered to by only one group and did not reflect the beliefs (*paham hidup*) of the Islamic community (*Umat Islam*). He went on to examine the argument put forward by proponents of *Pancasila*, that it was the "meeting point" (*titik pertemuan*) for all groups in the society, contending instead that, in fact, various social groups rejected one or more of the principles or "*sila*"; for example the Communists rejected the principle of belief in God.

He continued:

> It is not merely on the basis of the Umat Islam forming the largest group among the Indonesian people that we propose Islam as the Basis of our state, but also because of our Conviction that the teachings of Islam form a structure for government and social life that has a character perfectly suited for the life of the state and society and can guarantee a life of mutual respect among the various groups in the state.[51]

Ultimately, he said, Assembly members were faced with basing the state either on secularism or on religion.

In arguing for religion as against secularism, which he now identified with the *Pancasila*, he turned to President Soekarno's speech on June 17, 1945, which had first outlined the concept of the *Pancasila*. Natsir used that speech to contend that the future president's description of religion there, whereby belief in God was irrelevant to later stages of human development, offended the vast majority of Muslims. After quoting extensively from the speech, he said that Soekarno was arguing that: "someone who is still at the stage of agrarian life needs God, but when he reaches the stage of industrialism he has no further need of God." Natsir likened this argument to the Marxist position that

---

[50] *Tentang Dasar Negara Republik Indonesia dalam Konstituante*, 3 vols. (Jakarta: Percetakan Negara, n.d.), vol. 1, pp. 112–3.
[51] Ibid., p. 116.

economic and social structure determines the religion, culture and philosophy of a society. In contesting this view, Natsir cited Alexis de Tocqueville and others who had, he stated, argued the merits of religion rather than secularism forming the foundation for a state. He continued to contend that secularism provided a fertile ground for relying on force in the pursuit of power, the standard of fascist regimes such as that of Nazi Germany.

He concluded that secularism does not provide a strong basis for social life, but rather weakens the connections between an individual and the society in which he lives.[52] He then referred back to President Soekarno's assertion that the *Pancasila* has "five bases or ideas, that are spread throughout the existing groups in Indonesia," and again pointed out that the Communists do not accept the principle of religion included therein. He continued that, while no one would contradict the fact that there are good ideas within the *Pancasila*, its supporters do not even agree among themselves as to what the *Pancasila* actually is. This is because, in his view, it is merely an abstraction or concept, trying to stand as neutral above all ideologies, a stance that prevented it having any roots among the people. Turning from Islam to *Pancasila* was "like leaping from firm ground to empty space."[53]

On this basis, he then argued that all the principles of the *Pancasila* already exist in Islam, but as values that have a real and clear substance. He went on to outline the benefits and also limitations of Islam within the state, turning back to arguments he had made in the 1930s that Islam is not concerned with state matters that are transitory, but only with those matters of principle that do not change over time. He stressed that, while in matters of man's relations with God "all is forbidden except what is allowed," in everyday matters and those of man's relationship with man "everything is allowed except what is forbidden."

He contended that, as Islam has no priesthood or hierarchy, a state based on Islam is not a theocracy but a "theistic democracy." All values that Indonesians take pride in, such as mutual help or "*gotong royong*" and the value of democracy or discussion (*nilai demokrasi atau musyawarah*) are protected under Islam.

On the surface, there appears to be a striking contrast between this speech and the positions Natsir had adhered to over the preceding years (and indeed adopted again later), when he had portrayed an Islamic state as an ideal that would take at least decades to realize and when he was willing to compromise with the secular parties in accepting the fundamental elements of the *Pancasila*.

---

[52] Ibid., p. 124.
[53] Ibid., pp. 127–9.

But the crux of his criticisms of the *Pancasila* lay <u>not</u> in its basic principles but in their amorphous nature and his conviction that Soekarno was manipulating them in order to maximize his own power. (This would also be the case later under the Suharto regime, when Natsir opposed that president's insistence on all parties and organizations having the *Pancasila* as their sole foundation.) As we have seen, he had always been wary of the ambiguity of some of the *Pancasila* principles and had realized that their value depended to a great degree on their interpretation.

Indeed it is unlikely that Natsir was now actually arguing for an Islamic state, but rather for a state in which there was a convergence between Islamic laws and democratic practices. Certainly he was very conscious of the difficulties that would attend any efforts to make Indonesia into an Islamic state. In 1971, he recalled that during the Constituent Assembly debates his Christian friends and colleagues had expressed fears of such a state, begging Masjumi leaders: "Only do not ask for an Islamic state. If this happened we would be your guests, and we are not your guests in this country." While holding that an Islamic state "is still an ideal to achieve," Natsir then stressed that "Muslims themselves are not yet living even in a transitional period" so "the ideal is very far from the present reality," and its realization, which had to take place through democratic means, could take at least one or two generations.[54]

Natsir drew a distinction between an "Islamic state" and a "Muslim nation" such as Indonesia, with a majority Muslim population, where a democratic form of government would ensure majority Muslim representation in Parliament and militate against any law being passed that contravened Islamic precepts.[55] It seems likely, therefore, that in his speech before the Assembly he was staking out a position for the Masjumi party that would provide a basis for negotiation with the other groups represented there. (It is noteworthy, however, that in the speech, he made no allowance for the different degrees of piety among the Indonesians making up the nominally Muslim majority.)

In later discussing the Constituent Assembly and the reasons for its failure, Natsir expressed a much more tolerant attitude than appeared in his major speeches before that body. In interviews in 1971, he stated that: "in the last months of the Constituent Assembly before Soekarno dissolved it, the Masjumi had come to agree to drop the insistence on an Islamic state and was moving

---

[54] Natsir interview, Jakarta, January 30, 1971. According to Mohammad Siddik (Superintendent [Ketua Pengawas] DDII), "Natsir felt the need to revive Islam in Indonesia and a rational approach toward it. He was for an Islamic state <u>and</u> Islamic constitution but the sense more than the form." Interview, Jakarta, October 29, 2008.

[55] Natsir interview, Jakarta, January 30, 1971.

toward an area of compromise with non-Islamic parties.... It began to explore possibilities that the *Pancasila* serve as the basis for the Constitution so long as it included the Jakarta Charter."[56] (One issue on which the party was never willing to compromise, however, was that the president had to be a Muslim, though it did not stress this, because "in a democratic country majority rule would prevail,"[57] and a Muslim would be elected.) "Before discussion could get underway toward some sort of compromise," he added, "Soekarno, backed strongly by the army, interrupted and dismissed the Constituent Assembly."[58]

Natsir stressed that in closed sessions following the first and second terms of the Assembly,

> people became closer and closer. We were able to talk in a relaxed way and gained quite a lot. If you propagate Islam throughout the country, to how many places would you have to go to meet a group such as this [the members of the Assembly]? We took the opportunity to show what Islam is. Prawoto [second chairman of the Constituent Assembly and chief of the Masjumi faction] and others showed people that they were not so far from each other.... The atmosphere of the discussions was so good that Soekarno did not like it. In closed debate the Communists were also reasonable — they could respond to logical argument. But the third factor was Soekarno interfering....

Admitting that a few members of the Masjumi, such as Isa Anshari, were as extreme on the right as the Communists were on the left, Natsir stated that: "We had sufficient confidence that given enough time we could convince people from both extremes. Isa Anshari after the Constituent Assembly debates modified his ideas — there was a change though it could not be a complete one."[59]

This later view, however, seems not to admit fully the bitterness that was increasingly affecting Indonesian political life in the fall of 1957. By November of that year, multiplying crises were pushing Indonesian society into rigid confrontational camps. Natsir must have felt that he had done all in his power to realize a truly democratic state within which Islam played a major role consistent with its dominance within Indonesian society. Increasingly he had seen President Soekarno, with the support of the secular parties (particularly the National and Communist Parties) take steps to monopolize political power

---

[56] Natsir interview, Jakarta, January 23, 1971.

[57] Natsir interviews, Jakarta, March 1 and May 26, 1971.

[58] Joint interview with Natsir and Osman Raliby, spokesman for the Masjumi in the Constituent Assembly after Natsir's departure, May 26, 1971 (correcting Natsir interview, Jakarta, February 24, 1971).

[59] Natsir interview, Jakarta, January 30, 1971.

within his own hands and be well on the way to creating a truly authoritarian state. In this situation, Natsir turned back to his earlier embrace of what he termed an Islamic democracy. The Masjumi party he headed followed him along this path to greater confrontation with the Soekarno government. Dan Lev described the situation as he perceived it in stark terms:

> Masjumi later blamed the PNI and Soekarno for scuttling all attempts to resolve the ideological conflict, but by the time the Konstituante [Constituent Assembly] debates began in mid-November [1957] Masjumi leaders themselves had begun to lose interest in a compromise. They were increasingly frustrated in their opposition to the government's regional, economic, and foreign policies. The Tjikini assassination attempt and the take-over of Dutch enterprises at the end of November and early December[60] threw the whole political situation out of kilter. For Masjumi a single dimension compromise on ideology was meaningless while no concessions were forthcoming from the Government or from other parties on more imperative political questions.[61]

We should then turn to consider in more detail the train of events that forced Natsir to abandon his political course and join the Sumatran dissidents who had been challenging the Soekarno government throughout 1957.

Decision to Flee Jakarta

On December 1, 1956, frustrated by the powerlessness of his office Mohammad Hatta had resigned as vice president.[62] That same month three Sumatran colonels — Ahmad Husein, Maludin Simbolon and Barlian — seized power in Central, North and South Sumatra, with Colonel Ventje Sumual following their lead in South Sulawesi the following March.[63]

After Soekarno initially put forward his *konsepsi* of Guided Democracy, also in March 1957, Natsir proposed that, to confront the crisis posed by the regional unrest, the joint leadership (*dwi tunggal*) of Soekarno/Hatta should be restored and a unity government installed, headed by former vice president Hatta and Hamengko Buwono, the Sultan of Yogyakarta. This proposal was reminiscent of Natsir's position at the time of the fall of the first Ali cabinet in July 1955, when the Masjumi party had argued for formation of a "Presidential cabinet" headed by Mohammad Hatta even if it were only a "caretaker cabinet,"

---

[60] See below, pp. 110–1.

[61] Daniel S. Lev, *The Transition to Guided Democracy: Indonesian Politics, 1957–1959* (Ithaca: Cornell Modern Indonesia Project, 1966), pp. 129–30.

[62] He had indicated his intention to do so nearly six months earlier.

[63] These events will be dealt with in Chapter 6.

with the limited functions of solving the military problem and conducting nationwide elections.[64]

No such cabinet had been formed in 1955. After the elections, with their inconclusive results, when the Burhanuddin cabinet finally was compelled to resign, the issue arose again. But again the idea did not materialize. In reaction to Soekarno's *konsepsi* and in an attempt to alert Indonesians to what he saw as the president's determination to destroy democracy and introduce a dictatorship, Natsir raised it once more and proposed a Hatta-led "presidential cabinet." In his view, the president's moves toward a more authoritarian state were the major danger threatening the country, and the dissidence that was spreading in the regions outside Java stemmed from the failure of the central government, and especially the president, to use democratic means to meet the challenges facing the newly independent Indonesia. Hatta's return to a position of leadership would help quell some of this mistrust and opposition. From Natsir's perspective, the solution proposed by the president in proclaiming his *konsepsi* was merely an attempt to expand his own power and create a "democracy without an opposition,"[65] which was not a cure to the problems the country faced, but a new disease.[66]

Throughout the early 1950s, the issue of the status of West Irian had remained stalled as the Dutch refused to loosen their hold on the territory. On November 29, 1957 the crisis atmosphere in Indonesia reached a new level when the UN General Assembly in New York again refused to put the issue of West Irian on its agenda. In response, Soekarno immediately ordered labor unions and the Indonesian army to take over Dutch-owned properties and called on the remaining Dutch residents of Indonesia to leave the country.

The following evening, November 30, a group of youths hurled grenades at President Soekarno's party when he was attending a night fair at his children's school in the Tjikini neighborhood of Jakarta. One of the president's aides pushed him to the ground as the grenades exploded and he narrowly survived, but eleven others in the crowd were killed and dozens wounded. Suspicion immediately fell on the former army intelligence chief and deputy chief of staff, Colonel Zulkifli Lubis,[67] because the youths carrying out the attack, most of them from the strongly Islamic regions of Bima and Dompo (on the

---

[64] Noer, *Partai Islam*, p. 243.

[65] "Reaksi pertama terhadap konsepsi presiden," February 19, 1957, in *Capita Selecta III*, p. 24.

[66] "Itu bukan obat tetapi penyakit baru," February 28, 1957, in ibid., p. 28.

[67] Col. Lubis had been a contender for the position of chief of staff in 1955 when Nasution was appointed to the post, and he had mounted a coup attempt in late 1956 against both

island of Sumbawa), were members of the Gerakan Anti-Komunis (GAK, Anti-Communist Movement), headed by Saleh Ibrahim, a close associate of Lubis.[68] As several of the young men also belonged to the youth wing of the Masjumi party, the leaders of the party then came under attack and several Jakarta newspapers accused Natsir, Sjafruddin Prawiranegara, then governor of the Bank of Indonesia, and former Prime Minister Burhanuddin Harahap of involvement in the assassination attempt. The government also arrested Natsir's nephew at his house, alleging that he was implicated in earlier bombings of the Communist Party headquarters.[69]

In the aftermath of the Tjikini incident, the Natsir wing of the Masjumi party further antagonized Soekarno by strongly opposing the proposed take-over of Dutch properties. At a meeting in the palace in late November, Natsir's close associate Sjafruddin warned that such a take-over would be disruptive of the economy and hard on the people, pointing out that 40 per cent of all foreign exchange was earned by Dutch companies. As Sjafruddin later described how his statements were received, "You could hear a pin drop. No one raised a voice in support, and of course Soekarno was very angry."[70] Accusations mounted that Sjafruddin was pro-Dutch and threats were issued against him and his family.[71]

From early December the harassment against Natsir also increased, mostly in the form of phone calls to his home, gangs shouting outside his house, and a series of articles attacking him in the left wing press, especially the Soekarno-controlled newspaper, *Pemuda*.[72] Natsir appealed for help to the attorney general,

---

Nasution and Soekarno. A devout Muslim, Lubis was an adviser to an anti-communist paramilitary group, with a membership made up mostly of radical young Muslims. See Kahin and Kahin, *Subversion*, pp. 112 –3. Also on Lubis, see Jenkins, "Soeharto and the Japanese Occupation," *Indonesia* 88, p. 68.

[68] C.K.H.R. Surjo Sediono, *Peristiwa Tjikini* (Jakarta: Soeroengan, 1958); see also Audrey Kahin, *Rebellion to Integration*, pp. 204–5; Burhan Magenda, "Peranan Bapak M. Natsir Sebagai Politisi dan Negarawan" (typescript, 2008), pp. 19–21. The young people were lodged in an *asrama* close to the Tjikini school.

[69] General Sukendro apparently ordered this arrest, and Natsir's nephew was held in jail for a year and a half. Interview with Natsir, June 24, 1967. Mohamad Roem, "The P.R.R.I. Rebellion and its Background," II (typescript, January–February 1959), p. 2.

[70] Interview with Sjafruddin Prawiranegara, Jakarta, February 21, 1971. For Sjafruddin's account of the meeting, see Letter from Sjafruddin Prawiranegara to President Soekarno (typescript), January 15, 1958.

[71] See Ajip Rosidi, *Sjafruddin Prawiranegara: Lebih Takut kepada Allah SWT.* (Jakarta: Inti Idayu Press, 1986), pp. 197–8.

[72] According to Mohamad Roem, there were also articles attacking Natsir in *Bintang Timur*, *Merdeka* and *Suluh Indonesia*. Roem, "The P.R.R. I. Rebellion and its Background," I, p. 2.

who informed him that only Soekarno could stop the harassment. Natsir then sent a letter to Soekarno asking for the protection due to an Indonesian citizen. Soekarno appeared to be sympathetic to this plea, for at the New Year's Day reception at the palace, Natsir recalled, the president "shook hands with me warmly and whispered in my ear that he had received my letter and was taking steps to regulate the matter."[73] Three days later, however, *Pemuda* reiterated its charges against him. Although Natsir and his family did not suffer any physical violence, both parents and children were intimidated by the phone calls and threats. Hatta advised him to leave the city and find refuge in Bandung. Instead, however, he decided to go to Medan, where he and Mohamad Roem had been invited to attend an anniversary celebration at the Islamic University. He arrived there on January 6, 1958 and three days later, together with Roem, went on to Padang, where he met with Sjafruddin and Burhanuddin.

Sjafruddin had left Jakarta in late December for the southern Sumatran city of Palembang, and Burhanuddin, hearing that he was slated for arrest, had fled even earlier.[74] At this time Natsir had not yet decided on his own course of action. He summoned his family to join him in Sumatra, and until they reached Padang and he had a chance to discuss the situation with his wife, Ummi, he was reluctant to decide whether or not to join the dissidents in Sumatra.

In Natsir's growing confrontations with the president as he moved toward rebellion, their long and ambiguous relationship still enabled him to make an insightful assessment of Soekarno's character and motivations, stating in an interview in Jakarta with a British journalist, James Mossman, in November 1957 shortly before he fled to Sumatra:

> Sukarno is no communist ... Not basically. He's a mixture of politician and artist, and he's not always governed by calm reason. He has a sort of psychological complex which seems to urge him to seek the most violent methods he can find, short of war, to represent his country to the outside world. Before 1955 it might have been possible for his gifts and prestige among the people to have been recruited on the side of moderation over New Guinea [West Irian], but once the Dutch refused to negotiate with him over sovereignty, Sukarno veered back to his favourite theme of the need to bang the table. Now he's temperamentally in his element, though he's tired and rather confused and has no plan whatsoever. He's just marking time in the hope that The Hague will make some move to which he could react.[75]

---

[73] Natsir interview, Jakarta, January 23, 1971.

[74] Roem, "P.R.R.I. Rebellion," p. 2.

[75] Mossman, *Rebels in Paradise*, pp. 39–40. In the same interview Natsir stressed that he, along with all the Indonesian parties, including the Masjumi, wanted the Dutch to cede West Irian to Indonesia "but we deplore the present irresponsible methods." Ibid.

By the time he joined his colleagues in Padang, Natsir's views had begun to harden and after the central government's forces retaliated against the regional rebellion and he and his family retreated into the jungle he increasingly viewed the struggle as one aimed directly at both Soekarno and the communists.

Natsir's flight and subsequent alliance with the rebels marked a sudden and drastic break with his long and frustrating efforts to find some sort of compromise that would enable him to harmonize his fundamental religious and political beliefs with the realities of post-independence Indonesia. In the years following his resignation as prime minister he had struggled with this issue, increasingly adopting a position advocating a larger place for religion in Indonesia's political life than he had appeared to champion when he was a member of the national government. In opposition, however, he still adhered strongly to his belief in representative government, arguing consistently that there was no contradiction between a Muslim nation and a democratic state. He steadfastly advocated the latter as the best form of government for Indonesia and a preferable alternative to the authoritarian order that Soekarno was moving toward. But in combating Soekarno's policies and in seeking a larger role for religion in Indonesia's political life, he was pushed into some untenable positions. Clearly in the Constituent Assembly debates he was contradicting some of his earlier arguments that the state philosophy of *pancasila* was consistent with a democratic order based on Islam. When he shifted to open rebellion in 1958 he moved onto a terrain where the problems of Indonesia could be viewed in much starker black-and-white terms.

6

In the Jungle, 1958–61

When he fled to Sumatra, Natsir was returning to his home region. Throughout his long sojourn on Java his upbringing in West Sumatra had exerted an influence on most aspects of his life, including his strong religious faith and his belief in the form of grass-roots democracy that characterized village government in the Minangkabau heartland. During his years in government, however, he had frequently needed to subordinate these beliefs to what he saw as the demands of his office, when either as minister of information, prime minister, or leader of the country's largest political party, his prime duty was as a representative of the national regime. Now back in West Sumatra his perspective changed and he could view the central government's actions in starker terms, no longer needing to adapt his opinions to those of the competing political forces represented by Soekarno, the army and the other political parties.

But he was also now faced with different choices, for the dissidents who launched the regional rebellion were united principally by their opposition to Soekarno, the Communist Party, and the army's central command, without any clear goals on which they could agree. Natsir joined a movement that had been developing for more than a year and was already displaying signs of discord and division.

Background to Rebellion

Behind the coups mounted by the Army colonels in December 1956 and March 1957 lay several years of growing unease among Indonesia's armed forces, especially in areas outside Java. In Sumatra, Sulawesi and Kalimantan disaffection toward the central government had been increasing since the transfer of sovereignty, especially among territorial commanders resentful at Army Chief of Staff A.H. Nasution's attempts to streamline the army and centralize its command structure. The military take-overs in Sumatra, however, were probably also sparked by Hatta's resignation from the vice-presidency in December 1956. People on Sumatra and the other islands outside Java had seen the vice president as their major representative in the central government, and his departure led to intensified dissatisfaction with the Soekarno regime throughout the archipelago. Among local military leaders in Sumatra and Sulawesi, this dissatisfaction combined with their disaffection toward the top army command.

It was less than three weeks after Hatta's resignation, that Colonels Ahmad Husein in Central Sumatra and Maludin Simbolon in North Sumatra took matters into their own hands and proclaimed autonomous governing councils in their territories. Chief of Staff Nasution was able to out-maneuver Simbolon by playing on rivalries within the North Sumatra command, forcing Simbolon to flee Medan and seek refuge in Central Sumatra. Colonel Husein and his Banteng Council in West Sumatra, however, were too strong and enjoyed too much local support for the top army leadership to displace them. Central Sumatra Governor Roeslan Moeljohardjo handed over his office to Husein, and throughout 1957 the Banteng Council succeeded in running an administration in the region largely independent of the Jakarta government. (Recognizing that the other component provinces of Central Sumatra — Riau and Jambi — would not willingly acknowledge dominance by the Minangkabau of West Sumatra, Husein promised to grant autonomy to those two regions.) Husein's take-over was soon followed, with considerably less success, by Colonel Barlian in South Sumatra and by Colonel Ventje Sumual in Sulawesi.

Faced with these regional challenges, political and military leaders in Jakarta with family or political ties to Sumatra and Sulawesi, especially former Vice President Hatta and leaders of the Masjumi and Socialist (PSI) parties, made efforts to mediate the crisis. They organized a series of meetings between the central government and the dissident colonels, the most important being the Munas (Musyawarah Nasional, National Consultation) held in Jakarta in September 1957, which was attended by most of the major contestants, including Cols Husein, Barlian and Sumual. (Simbolon did not participate, as he no longer held a military command.)

A few days prior to the opening of the Munas, however, the dissident colonels, together with Dr. Sumitro Djojohadikusumo (a member of Sjahrir's PSI, who had left Jakarta under threat of arrest for corruption), had met in Palembang on September 7–8, to coordinate their plans, and reach their own consensus as to their future course of action.[1] As a result of these discussions they issued a declaration, the "Palembang Charter," which included demands for a restoration of the Soekarno-Hatta joint leadership; replacement of the existing central military leadership; and a ban on "internationally oriented Communism."[2]

Husein, Barlian and Sumual went straight from Palembang to Jakarta for the opening of the Munas conference on September 10. There the three colonels demanded a restoration of the joint leadership (*dwi tunggal*) of Soekarno and Hatta, and all made speeches outlining their grievances. They did not, however, forcefully press their demands, perhaps because they were overawed at the collection of national leaders attending the meetings. Nevertheless, after the conference closed they initially expressed the opinion that they had received a fair hearing and believed progress had been made toward easing the center-regional tension.[3]

The conference did not result in a restoration of the joint Soekarno/Hatta leadership, known as the *dwitunggal*, though the president and former vice-president did pledge to "cooperate with the entire Indonesian people" for the good of the country and made a symbolic gesture of unity. Hatta was disillusioned by what he saw as the emptiness of this gesture and the unwillingness of the dissident colonels to press for more concrete changes to emerge from the conference. He was particularly disappointed that the regional participants had not insisted on the formation of a presidential cabinet or even that Hatta be assigned an important governmental position. Two months later, in November 1957, as the situation deteriorated further, he wrote to Col. Dahlan Djambek, one of the rebel leaders in West Sumatra: "If some of the regions now feel dissatisfied, this is a result of their having participated in the unanimous acceptance of the imprecise formula presented to them" at the Munas.[4] Immediately after the conference, Hatta left Jakarta and departed for a six-week trip to China, apparently dismissing any chance of playing any further role in the dispute.

* * *

The Masjumi leaders Sjafruddin Prawiranegara and Burhanuddin Harahap, who had both fled Jakarta in early December 1957, met early the following month in

---

[1] In addition to Husein, Barlian and Sumual, Colonels Simbolon, Djambek and Lubis also participated.

[2] See Audrey and George Kahin, *Subversion as Foreign Policy* (New York: New Press, 1995), p. 72, for a full list of their demands.

[3] Interview with Ahmad Husein, Jakarta, May 9, 1991.

[4] Hatta letter to Col. Dahlan Djambek, November 2, 1957, cited in Deliar Noer, *Mohammad Hatta: Biografi Politik* (Jakarta: LP3ES, 1990), p. 522.

Palembang with three of the dissident colonels: Zulkifli Lubis, who had evaded arrest over the Tjikini affair and had fled to Sumatra; Husein who now headed the government in Central Sumatra; and Dahlan Djambek, a former deputy to General Nasution, who had resigned his post and fled Jakarta in late August.[5] The two Masjumi politicians also met with the South Sumatra commander, Barlian, within whose territory lay the oil facilities and other strategic resources on which any open challenge to the central government would rely.[6]

Several of the colonels were determined to push ahead to challenge the Soekarno government, and they had obtained some economic and military support for their actions from the United States.[7] Former finance minister Professor Sumitro Djojohadikusumo, who had now joined the dissidents, also hoped to attract the Masjumi civilian leaders to their side. The colonels still, however, differed among themselves as to the course of action they should pursue. Probably most radical was Colonel Zulkifli Lubis who was reportedly pressing for the dissidents to proclaim a separatist state of Sumatra, a view that was apparently shared, at least initially, by Colonel Barlian.[8] He received the strongest support from Colonel Simbolon, the former commander in North Sumatra, who had been ousted by Nasution and was now residing in Padang, dependent on the good will of Colonel Husein, "a position that seemed to irk him considerably."[9] Husein, who had achieved his major objective in now

---

[5] A strong Muslim and vocal anti-communist, Djambek, too, had been subject to harassment. Grenades had been thrown at his house in mid-August, and the press in Jakarta had been publishing charges of corruption against him. The son of Syeikh Mohammad Djamil Djambek, a prominent Islamic leader in West Sumatra, Dahlan Djambek had been the first commander of the Republic's Banteng Division there during the Revolution and had been a close aide to Nasution after the transfer of sovereignty from the Dutch, also serving as ambassador to the United Kingdom. He had been a student of Natsir in Bandung in the 1930s and remained close to him.

[6] Mohamad Roem, "The P.R.R.I Rebellion and its Background, I–IV" (typescript, Jakarta, January–February 1959), I, p. 3.

[7] For the American involvement in the rebellion, see Kahin and Kahin, *Subversion as Foreign Policy*, passim.

[8] It should be noted that Lubis firmly denied that he had proposed a separate state of Sumatra (interview Jakarta, January 24, 1971). In a later interview (May 10, 1991) he said: "Since 1945 all the regions had wanted a federal government. No-one wanted a separate Sumatra, just a federation." His version of events, however, is contradicted by most other versions of the events. See, for example, Mohamad Roem, "The PRRI Rebellion, II," p. 2. On Barlian's advocacy of a Sumatra state, see Ajip Rosidi, *Sjafruddin Prawiranegara: Lebih Takut kepada Allah SWT: Sebuah Biografi* (Jakarta: Inti Idayu Press, 1986), p. 201.

[9] James Mossman, *Rebels in Paradise: Indonesia's Civil War* (London: Cape, 1961), p. 66. Simbolon considerably outranked Husein and had headed the South Sumatra command during the Revolution before succeeding Kawilarang as North Sumatra commander in 1950.

heading the government in Central Sumatra, was less eager to proceed to more drastic action, while South Sumatra commander Barlian was even more hesitant.

Natsir Joins the Dissidents

In talking with the colonels, Sjafruddin and Burhanuddin had become aware of the disagreements within the group, and they were particularly worried over the advocacy by some of the colonels of a separate Sumatran state. Returning to Padang, they met up on January 8 with Natsir, who had flown in from Medan, and they persuaded him to accompany them to a further meeting with the military leaders two days later in Sungai Dareh, a small town on the border between south and central Sumatra. By participating in the meeting, the three Masjumi leaders hoped to block any moves by the colonels to proclaim a separate state on Sumatra. They also hoped to create a rallying point to prevent other regions such as Aceh (on the north-west tip of Sumatra) and Menado (in North Sulawesi) from splitting off from the Republic of Indonesia.

When the three civilian politicians arrived at Sungai Dareh, the Sumatran colonels, together with Sulawesi colonel Ventje Sumual, were already holding discussions.[10] In the subsequent talks, Simbolon and Lubis continued to press for drastic action, while Barlian hung back and the civilian leaders argued that whatever course of action was pursued, there should be no movement toward a separatist solution. Thus, the outcome of the Sungai Dareh conference was inconclusive. An American journalist, James Bell of *Time* magazine, who was present at the meetings, summed up the position of the civilian politicians:

> Unlike the military leaders, Sjafruddin and Natsir wish to move slowly. Forming an emergency government would not be easy since it must be broad enough to represent all of Indonesia and not just Sumatra since it must not appear to be a separate government ... civil war must be prevented and nothing rash should be done until all possible steps have been taken to replace Djuanda [the current prime minister] with Hatta.[11]

Along with Sjafruddin and Burhanuddin, however, Natsir realized that by attending the meetings at Sungai Dareh the Masjumi leaders had taken a

---

[10] Natsir interview, Jakarta, May 31, 1971. For Sjafruddin's view see Ajip Rosidi, *Sjafruddin Prawiranegara*, pp. 202–5.

[11] "*Time* Correspondent Interviews," p. 4, as reported by the American Embassy in Foreign Service Dispatch 343, January 24, 1958 (National Archives, College Park, MD).

decisive step, and from that time on they had, at least in the eyes of the central government, thrown in their lot with the dissidents.[12]

Despite its inconclusiveness, the January 9–10, 1958 meeting at Sungai Dareh marked the beginning of a series of events that rapidly led to all-out civil war. Immediately after the conference, several of the participants went abroad to raise support for their cause: Dr. Sumitro Djojohadikusumo left for Singapore, accompanied by Colonels Husein and Sumual. There the three met with their foreign backers from the CIA and US military.[13] Then Sumitro went on to Europe, while Sumual traveled first to Japan and later to Taiwan and Hong Kong to seek aid from other Asian countries. Husein, however, returned to West Sumatra where he faced the misgivings of his supporters. The civilian politicians were also facing opposition, as emissaries from Masjumi headquarters in Jakarta came to Padang to try to persuade their colleagues against taking any irrevocable steps that would split the country.

Dissident civilian and military leaders later accused each other of following the wrong strategy to forward their aims. It appears that the key member of the Masjumi group in Padang was Sjafruddin Prawiranegara, still officially governor of the Bank of Indonesia. Ever outspoken, he sent an open letter to Soekarno in mid-January, explaining his own actions, calling on the president to abandon his "fascist concept of guided democracy," and stating:

> If your Excellency still has the interests of our Fatherland at heart Your Excellency will cease to exceed the limitations of presidential authority stipulated in the Constitution, and, again in accordance with the terms of the Constitution, hand over the powers of government to a Cabinet of which the members will be truly national leaders such as Hatta and Hamengkubuwono [the Sultan of Yogyakarta], respected and trusted by the overwhelming majority of the Indonesian people.[14]

All the Masjumi leaders shared this position, which was strikingly close to the one Natsir had long espoused, namely that Soekarno's role as president should

---

[12] According to Mohamad Roem, who was still in Padang, on their return from the meeting they told him that "we knew that once having participated in Sungei Dareh it was not possible to return to Djakarta." Roem, "The PRRI Rebellion II," p. 2.

[13] Sumitro and Simbolon had been in touch with the CIA stations in Singapore and elsewhere, as well as with British diplomats, since at least October 1957. Throughout these months the Americans had been discreetly supplying the dissidents with funds, arms and training, both in West Sumatra and in American facilities overseas. Interview with Ahmad Husein, Jakarta, May 9, 1991. For details of this period of American involvement, see Kahin and Kahin, *Subversion*, pp. 102–6 and 120–4.

[14] "Letter from Sjafruddin Prawiranegara to President Soekarno," January 15, 1958 (typescript of translation).

be largely ceremonial, with real power resting with a presidential cabinet headed by former vice president Hatta. The principal problem, however, was how best to achieve that result.

Most of the military leaders, while equally supportive of changing the power structure in Jakarta, had less confidence in Hatta and were pushing to achieve a change of government through an immediate military confrontation with Soekarno. In part, it seems, this was because of promises they had made to their overseas backers.[15] Sumitro broadcast bellicose statements from Geneva forecasting the imminent collapse of the Jakarta government, while Sumual and Warouw[16] met with Soekarno in Tokyo and made press statements anticipating that the rebels would soon issue an ultimatum on Jakarta. In Padang, Simbolon and Djambek were pushing Husein to issue such an ultimatum.

Colonel Barlian, the South Sumatra commander, still, however, opposed such a move. At the Sungai Dareh conference, he had expressed his lack of enthusiasm at the prospect of militarily confronting Jakarta, complaining that should he join in such an action the central government was in a position to cut off food supplies to Palembang. Although "Sumual tried to encourage him and offered to have food and funds provided to offset" any shortages, this did not seem to relieve his misgivings.[17] Barlian was in a much more vulnerable position than his colleagues, not only because of his greater proximity to Jakarta, but also because of the large number of Javanese resident in the province of South Sumatra — both laborers and soldiers, as well as members of the Indonesian air-force who were stationed around the Palembang airfield. Both of Barlian's predecessors as commander of South Sumatra had been Javanese and many of his subordinate officers still owed more loyalty to these Javanese commanders than to Barlian himself.[18]

Immediately after the meetings at Sungai Dareh, Sjafruddin visited Barlian in Palembang and became convinced that indeed the South Sumatra commander would never agree to challenge Jakarta directly. Sjafruddin had always believed that Barlian's support was crucial to the dissidents' success, for he saw the oil fields in Jambi and Palembang, which lay within the South Sumatra

---

[15] On the pressure being exerted from Washington, see Kahin and Kahin, *Subversion*, pp. 132–3.

[16] Col. J.F. Warouw, a native of the Minahasan region of Sulawesi, had been territorial commander in East Indonesia before being replaced in 1956 by Sumual and transferred as military attaché to Beijing. After the Sungai Dareh conference, Sumual had met him in Hong Kong and persuaded him to join the dissident colonels.

[17] Natsir interview, Jakarta, May 31, 1971.

[18] See Kahin and Kahin, *Subversion*, pp. 130–2.

military command, as vital assets in the struggle with Jakarta. With these in their hands the dissidents could deny the government's air force its source of petrol, while at the same time their sympathizers abroad could prevent other countries from providing alternative supplies. In Natsir's words: "We thought that thereby we could apply a squeeze on the government both in terms of necessary petrol supplies and economically that would produce effective pressure in the long run."[19] Sjafruddin was now certain, however, that Barlian's support would not be forthcoming, at least in the immediate future.

During the early days of February, conflicting pressures bore down on Husein, the dissidents' nominal leader. Soekarno at the time was abroad and the more belligerent of Husein's colleagues — Sumitro, Sumual, Simbolon, Djambek and Warouw— were eager to take action while the president was out of the country. Sjafruddin, however, after he returned from his meeting with Barlian, urged that any ultimatum be delayed for at least a month, during which he and his colleagues could try to persuade the South Sumatra commander to their point of view. Faced with the reluctance of both the Masjumi politicians and some of his local commanders in West Sumatra, who had never envisaged that the course they had been following would result in actual warfare, Husein hesitated. He broadcast a speech on February 6 in which he denied that the dissidents were going to establish a Sumatran state and expressed their determination to find a way out of the difficulties facing the country.

Husein's more bellicose colleagues were not willing to accept this prevarication. At a public meeting in Padang three days later, Simbolon and Djambek made fiery speeches in favor of issuing an immediate ultimatum on Jakarta. Sjafruddin, however, told Husein that he would not sign any such document and that if the colonels wished to issue a direct challenge to Jakarta it would have to be above Husein's signature alone. Natsir later stated that he himself was uncertain whether Sjafruddin was correct in urging restraint. He agreed that Barlian's position had to be taken into account but he was not clear as to whether a postponement would work to the dissidents' advantage or to that of the government, as he thought there was a possibility that Barlian would rally once an ultimatum had been proclaimed.[20]

Reluctant to pull back, Husein on February 10 finally issued the ultimatum, without Sjafruddin's supporting signature but with the backing of all the military leaders. The ultimatum demanded that the Djuanda cabinet return its mandate, that Hatta and the Sultan of Yogyakarta form a transitional cabinet

---

[19] Natsir interview, Jakarta, January 23, 1971.
[20] Natsir interview, Jakarta, May 31, 1971.

until a new general election could be held, and that Soekarno return to his constitutional position. If these demands were not met within five days "we hereby declare that from that moment we will consider ourselves free of any obligation to obey Dr. Ir Soekarno as Head of State."[21]

After the expiration of the five days and with no response coming from Jakarta, Husein on February 15, 1958 proclaimed the Revolutionary Government of the Republic of Indonesia (PRRI, Pemerintah Revolusioner Republik Indonesia), with Sjafruddin as its prime minister.[22] The central government in Jakarta responded immediately. On February 16 Prime Minister Djuanda ordered the arrest of the dissident politicians (Sumitro, Sjafruddin, and Burhanuddin — Natsir had not yet joined the rebel cabinet, so he was not slated for arrest at this time) and Nasution discharged all the rebel colonels on Sumatra and Sulawesi. Government planes attacked the West Sumatran towns of Painan, Padang and Bukittinggi on February 21 and 22, knocking out their radio equipment and severing their principal communications.[23]

Into Rebellion

Despite the apparently irrevocable nature of the actions the dissidents took in issuing the ultimatum and declaring a Revolutionary Government, Natsir later insisted that they had been willing to extend the ultimatum if necessary, as they were aware that Hatta and other politicians in Jakarta were trying to work out some sort of compromise.[24] "There was a general expectation that Jakarta would accommodate, and we knew at the time of the ultimatum that discussions were still going on there."[25]

Indeed, over the previous month, members of both the Masjumi and the PSI had been conducting increasingly frantic efforts to forge an agreement between the rebels and the central government. On his return to Jakarta on

---

[21] "Piagam Perdjuangan"/"Menjelamatkan Negara" [Struggle Charter/Saving the State] signed by Lt. Col. Ahmad Husein Padang, February 10, 1958 (typescript). See also *Waspada*, February 12, 1958. This account is in accord with information given by Natsir in an interview on February 24, 1971 and by Sjafruddin, in an interview on February 21, 1971.

[22] Sjafruddin was also named minister of finance. Other cabinet members were Simbolon as foreign minister, Dahlan Djambek as internal affairs minister and minister of defense, Warouw as minister of development, Burhanuddin Harahap as minister of security and justice, and Sumitro as minister of trade and communications.

[23] Makmum Salim, *Sedjarah Operasi2 Gabungan terhadap PRRI-Permesta* (Jakarta: Pusat Sedjarah ABRI, 1971), p. 20.

[24] Natsir interview, Jakarta, January 23, 1971.

[25] Natsir interview, Jakarta, May 31, 1971.

January 11, Mohamad Roem had reported to the Masjumi council on the results of the Sungai Dareh meeting, and had met with Hatta, Djuanda and other political leaders, as well as with Nasution, in an effort to head off the crisis. He returned to Padang a few days later, at Natsir's request, and for the rest of the month acted as liaison between the Masjumi leaders in Padang and the Jakarta government. In Jakarta, Djuanda had indicated that he was willing to resign in the hope that Hatta would replace him, but that nothing could be done until Soekarno returned from his trip abroad.[26]

Two leading members of the PSI, Djoeir Moehamad and Djohan Sjahruzah, also came to Padang and met with Husein to inform him that while they sympathized with the regional movements he should not proclaim any alternative government. Djoeir gave the same message to Natsir and Assaat, who told him that, despite the fact that both of them were native to the region, they had no influence with the military group there. Natsir added that "it was just because he had been terrorized in Jakarta that he had escaped to Sumatra," implying that he was ambivalent regarding the dissidents' actions and played no role in their decisions.[27]

The Masjumi party in Jakarta had been in an unenviable position ever since Natsir, Sjafruddin and Burhanuddin, three of the party's foremost leaders, had fled to Sumatra. Masjumi members were aware that, unless they could broker some kind of compromise between these leaders and the central government, their party would find it difficult to survive. The Masjumi's position became even worse after the Revolutionary Government was proclaimed in mid-February with Sjafruddin at its head. Defection of so much of its leadership to the rebels, led the Jakarta party to split over the attitude it should adopt, both toward the rebellion and toward the three Masjumi leaders participating in it. Many Masjumi members, particularly those from the Sukiman faction, argued that the party had to condemn the rebellion and expel Natsir, Sjafruddin and Burhanuddin if it hoped to survive. But the loyalty to Natsir of a large section of the party, notably the faction now headed by second vice-chairman Prawoto Mangkusasmito, stymied efforts to free Masjumi from the taint of its ties to the rebellion. In the event, Natsir remained as the Masjumi chairman *in absentia* until April 1959, when Prawoto was elected to the position. The party's controversial stance opened it to criticism and provided good reason for Soekarno to marginalize and eventually ban it in 1960.[28]

---

[26] Mohamad Roem "PRRI Rebellion III," pp. 1–2.

[27] Interview with Djoeir Moehamad, Jakarta, July 24, 1995.

[28] For a full discussion of the Masjumi's quandary and the course it adopted, see Daniel S. Lev, *The Transition to Guided Democracy: Indonesian Politics 1957–1959* (Ithaca: Cornell Modern Indonesia Project, 1966), pp. 135–40.

Though Natsir later blamed Jakarta's bombing of the West Sumatra cities for forcing the rebels to establish a competing government, these bombings did not in fact occur until February 20, 1958, five days after the proclamation of the PRRI. It is, therefore, difficult to understand why the three civilian leaders were willing to go along with their military colleagues in so promptly proclaiming the Revolutionary Government on February 15 — they must have known that this was an action that most of their sympathizers in Jakarta, especially the legalistic Hatta, could never countenance and their parliamentary colleagues from both the PSI and Masjumi had warned them against. Sjafruddin had earlier been willing to stand up to the colonels when he refused to sign the ultimatum on Jakarta, and had Natsir backed him strongly at that time it seems possible that proclamation of the rival government could at least have been delayed. Indeed, the PRRI proclamation seemed to go against Natsir's own political instincts up to that point, for he had already displayed misgivings toward the actions of his colleagues, and he had always been scrupulous in observing legal norms.[29] It seems likely that it was this reluctance to cross legal boundaries that initially made him hesitant to enter the rebel cabinet with the other Masjumi leaders.

Natsir was certainly an unlikely rebel. Although he would later deny any hesitation, he certainly seemed to be hanging back for some time from fully committing himself to the PRRI movement.[30] Apparently, however, he was unable to see any alternative course of action. The journalist James Mossman put a sympathetic gloss on his actions at this time, writing:

> I doubt whether anyone with his sense of honour would have been capable
> of climbing on to the fence beside Hatta and Sharir [*sic*] while his principles
> were being trampled down by Sukarno and the communists.[31]

Natsir shared this "sense of honour" with Sjafruddin, for whom he retained great admiration. But Sjafruddin was more willing to act decisively and fitted much more easily into the role of rebel, not questioning the rightness of his cause and not hesitating to speak out or to take a stance of open confrontation against Soekarno and his supporters, especially the Communist party. Throughout this period, Natsir subordinated himself to Sjafruddin, deferring to him

---

[29] For example, in his dealings a few years earlier with Daud Beureu'eh over Aceh and with Soekarno over the West Irian issue. See Chapter 4.

[30] Dan Jahya, for example, a former commander of the Siliwangi division and a PSI sympathizer who participated in the Sungai Dareh meetings, had the clear impression that Natsir was passive and hung back from offering clear-cut support. Interview Jakarta, May 30, 1971.

[31] James Mossman, *Rebels in Paradise* (London: Cape, 1961), p. 41.

and, apparently uncertain as to the course they should pursue, clearly reluctant to step into a leadership role. He, too, strongly opposed Soekarno and the actions he was taking that, in Natsir's view, betrayed the ideals of the nationalist struggle they had earlier shared. But, in part perhaps because of their earlier friendship, he seems to have shrunk from direct confrontation.

Indeed, he was not alone in this stance, for, even after the proclamation of the PRRI government, most of the civilian political leaders in Padang apparently continued to believe that they could still pressure Jakarta into an accommodation, thus avoiding a military confrontation.[32] At the same time, should military action become inevitable, they retained a misguided faith in the fighting qualities of the rebels' armed forces.

In doubting Jakarta's willingness to launch an attack against the dissidents, Natsir and his colleagues were probably relying on their awareness of Soekarno's inherent reluctance to employ military force. But they underestimated Chief of Staff A.H. Nasution and put too much faith in Hatta's support and his willingness and ability to defend their cause, ignoring the fact that the former vice president could never countenance the illegal step they had taken in proclaiming a competing government to that in Jakarta.[33] Hatta had indeed tried to negotiate with Soekarno and draw the crisis back from the brink, but he had been out-maneuvered by the president, who went along with Chief of Staff Nasution's determination not to compromise with the rebels.

By this time Nasution was in a strong political position. After being ousted from his post as Army Chief of Staff in 1952 he had spent three years outside the military structure, studying and writing influential books on military strategy and eventually forming a political party, the IPKI,[34] which had run

---

[32] By now, the three Masjumi politicians had been joined by Dr. Assaat, a respected non-party leader, close to Hatta, as well as by most members of the local Masjumi and PSI.

[33] In a letter of February 1, 1963, to the journalist Solichin Salam, Hatta expressed his disappointment at the actions of the Masjumi leaders, stating: "I stressed [to the people in the regions] that their step [in forming the PRRI] would achieve the opposite of what they intended, and would destroy what we had built up with our own efforts, making West Sumatra into a field trampled by elephants, and *last but not least* strengthening the dictator's spirit in government circles." Cited in Deliar Noer, *Mohammad Hatta: Biografi Politik* (Jakarta: LP3ES, 1990), pp. 532–3. Noer added that Hatta was disappointed that Natsir had ignored his earlier advice to seek refuge in Bandung, and in a later interview Noer repeated this opinion, stating: "Hatta of course blamed them [the Masjumi leaders]. I can understand Hatta's view because it made it impossible for him to come forward to defend them. He could not express sympathy." Interview, Jakarta, January 10, 2004.

[34] Ikatan Pendukung Kemerdekaan Indonesia, League of the Supporters of Indonesian Independence.

unsuccessfully in the 1955 elections. Under the Burhanuddin cabinet and with Masjumi encouragement, Soekarno had reappointed him as Chief of Staff in November 1955. At that time Natsir saw Nasution as a sincere Muslim and supported his candidacy.[35] Indeed the two had known each other since the Japanese occupation when Nasution had headed the Youth Militia (Barisan Pemuda) in Bandung and had been responsible to Natsir as Head of the Education Division (Kepala Jawatan Pengajaran) there.[36]

But when he became chief of staff, Nasution dashed the hopes of his Masjumi supporters and worked closely with Soekarno, helping the president pursue his aim of Guided Democracy in March of 1957 and successfully urging the introduction of martial law throughout Indonesia at the same time.[37] Aware that one of the major goals of the military rebels in the PRRI had been to challenge his policies and authority, Nasution knew that his future depended on defeating them decisively while keeping the army structure intact.

Nasution feared too that, if he did not move swiftly and decisively against the insurgents, some of the colonels' outside supporters might enter the conflict in their behalf. He was well aware that ships of the US 7th Fleet were stationed not far from the east coast of Sumatra and he feared that they would make use of any pretext to land marines near Pekanbaru "with the announced objective of protecting American lives and properties at the Caltex operation."[38] The Army Chief of Staff thus moved swiftly to secure the Pekanbaru oil fields, dispatching five battalions of marines to the area on March 12, with two companies of government paratroops landing directly on the Pekanbaru airfield and setting the defending rebel soldiers to flight. Jakarta's forces rapidly extended their control over much of the eastern coastal regions of Sumatra against virtually

---

[35] Ulf Sundhaussen, *The Road to Power: Indonesian Military Politics 1945–1967* (Kuala Lumpur: Oxford University Press, 1982), p. 93. Sundhaussen also states that "Prime Minister Burhanuddin Harahap, a South Tapanuli Batak like Nasution, was so well disposed to him that he had already offered him the portfolio of Minister of Veterans Affairs."

[36] A.H. Nasution, "Bung Natsir 80 Tahun," in *Mohammad Natsir Pemandu Ummat: Pesan dan Kesan Tayakkur 80 Tahun Mohammad Natsir*, ed. Moch. Lukman Fatahullah Rais, *et al.* (Jakarta: Bulan Bintang, 1989), p. 33.

[37] Thus he acted more in accord with Mochtar Lubis's more cynical view of him, expressed in an interview in 1971, when according to Lubis: "Nasution came back to power by convincing the Masjumi, in particular Natsir, that he was supportive of democratic government, with views close to Natsir's," but then worked closely with Soekarno and was instrumental in the fall of the Harahap cabinet. Interview (Jakarta), January 24, 1971.

[38] Gen. A.H. Nasution interview, Jakarta May 27, 1971. For a full discussion of Nasution's strategy and the American involvement, see Kahin and Kahin, *Subversion*, pp. 151–5 and passim. On Nasution's strategy and operations, see also Salim, *Sejarah Operasi2*, passim.

no resistance. Only in Medan was there any actual fighting, when, on March 16, a PRRI sympathizer, Major W.F. Nainggolan, launched a coup against the pro-Jakarta command and took over the city. After a brief firefight, however, he was forced to withdraw and ultimately join with the remaining PRRI forces in Central Sumatra.[39]

The rapid collapse of the rebel troops surprised the Masjumi politicians, but they took heart from Nainggolan's courageous if ultimately unsuccessful coup attempt in Medan. Despite the initial setbacks, Natsir and his colleagues all retained strong confidence in the ability of Colonel Husein's forces to repel any invasion Jakarta might launch against the rebel heartland in West Sumatra, and they were unaware that Husein had already determined that, possessing no heavy weapons with which to confront the invaders, his only realistic course would be to pursue a strategy of withdrawal and guerrilla war.[40] The political leaders were shocked and incredulous when, less than a month later, on April 13, Jakarta's invading troops, under command of Colonel Ahmad Yani, in their so-called 17th August Operation, succeeded in occupying Padang in less than a day against practically no resistance.

The invading force consisted of units from the Diponegoro and Brawijaya divisions of Central and East Java, together with paratroop units and air and sea forces. Indonesian naval warships began a systematic bombardment of the coast and the air force bombed the town of Padang, as well as Padang Hill where Husein's units were concentrated. At the same time, Javanese troops made an amphibious landing north of the town, meeting virtually no resistance, and succeeded in occupying Padang before the end of the day. The following day they secured the seaport of Teluk Bayur south of Padang, and landed reinforcements at Tabing airfield a few miles north of the town. They then concentrated on cutting the rebels' supply lines to South Sumatra and at the same time advanced east to Solok, to where Husein had withdrawn and established his major headquarters. Government troops occupied the town on April 21.

Only in their advance up the narrow and precipitous Anai Valley, the major entryway to the Minangkabau Highlands, did Jakarta's army face any real resistance. Units headed by Major Johan (who had been a battalion commander in Husein's Banteng division) were able to mount a successful defense of the road until government planes were brought in to strafe the rebel troops and set them to flight. Government ground forces reached Padang Panjang at the head of the valley on May 1, proceeding from there to Bukittinggi ten miles to the

---

[39] For more on this incident, see Kahin and Kahin, *Subversion*, pp. 154–5.
[40] Interview with Ahmad Husein, Jakarta, May 9, 1991.

north. They arrived in Bukittinggi three days later and joined up with other government units advancing from Medan and Tapanuli.[41]

For several weeks, Natsir, Sjafruddin and Burhanuddin, had felt secure in Bukittinggi, the largest city in the highlands and the site of the former Dutch fortress, Fort de Kock, where the Masjumi leaders had established their headquarters. Natsir's wife and five children had joined them there after being forced to flee Padang when Jakarta's air force bombed the coastal town in late February.[42] The rapid and disastrous collapse of Husein's forces in Padang came as a devastating shock to Natsir and his colleagues, compelling them to evacuate their refuge in Bukittinggi to escape the government troops making their way up from the coastal lowlands.

James Mossman, the British journalist reporting on the conflict, met Sjafruddin and Natsir as they emerged from the cabinet meeting in Bukittinggi where they had learned of the rebel collapse in Padang. Mossman reported that Sjafruddin strode out of the meeting, angrily stating that he was going to seek out Husein "to find out why our soldiers did not fight," vowing that he himself would "stay here in the jungle" to continue the resistance, as he had done ten years earlier in the struggle against the Dutch.[43] On entering the conference room, Mossman found Natsir wearing an old tweed coat, sitting alone at the table, with his face "twisted with misery." When asked what he would do, he replied: "What can I do? My wife and my children are all here. Any day now they might be captured. I've given everything to these people. And now this. It's all over. I don't care. Let them capture us. Let them come. What more is there?"[44]

Natsir and his colleagues, however, soon recovered their determination to continue the struggle. They gathered their families together and accompanied them to more defensible positions away from the major towns. After they were forced to evacuate Bukittinggi, Natsir and Burhanuddin escorted their wives and children to a village, Sungai Batang on the banks of Lake Maninjau, about 7 kms from the town of the same name, where their families were

---

[41] A full account of the military operations against the PRRI can be found in Salim, *Sedjarah Operasi2*, ch. 2, pp. 20–60.

[42] Immediately after the bombing Ummi and her children withdrew to their grandmother's house in Batu Sangkar, but shortly afterward moved again, this time to the house of a Masjumi supporter in Koto Tuo, Bukittinggi, where they were joined by the families of Sjafruddin and Burhanuddin. *Aba: M. Natsir sebagai Cahaya Keluarga* (Jakarta: Yayasan Capita Selecta, 2008), p. 40.

[43] Mossman, *Rebels in Paradise*, p. 165.

[44] Ibid., pp. 165–6.

able to live quietly and peacefully for the next eighteen months. Sjafruddin's family accompanied him to Kototinggi, where the PRRI leaders set up their headquarters.

Natsir's younger three children (his son Fauzie and two younger daughters) soon were attending school in Maninjau while their elder sisters helped their mother at home, leading a life they recalled as very different from the one they'd been accustomed to in the city. Living as villagers, the girls no longer wore short skirts, but instead, whenever they left the house they adopted the traditional long garments (*baju kurung, sarung*) and veil worn in the rural areas. In the early months, too, they washed their clothes and bathed in the lake, until they were able to fix up a way to bring water to the house.[45] During this period they felt safe as government forces were unable to penetrate the area because local villagers had blocked the road from Bukittinggi to Maninjau.

The PRRI troops in West Sumatra regrouped, dividing into a northern and a southern sector, and for much of the ensuing rebellion those in the northern sector were headed by Colonel Dahlan Djambek, who maintained his base in Kamang, near Bukittinggi, while Husein established his headquarters a few miles outside Solok, and commanded PRRI forces in the center and south. Natsir remained in the northern sector, based in Kototinggi, but traveled widely round the region, relying on Djambek's forces for protection.

Guerrilla War

In most parts of central Sumatra for nearly the first two years of the insurgency the rebels were able to conduct a much more successful guerrilla war than had seemed possible during their initial ignominious flight. During these months, government forces were generally restricted to the larger towns, while the rebels controlled the villages and rural areas. Until late in 1959, Jakarta was not even able to extend its control to Kamang, a few kilometers outside Bukittinggi, where Dahlan Djambek had his headquarters and from where he and his troops frequently launched forays against the town. The insurgents' success was in large part, however, due to the region's hospitable terrain. The jungle-clad upland valleys, with their cluster of volcanic peaks and crater lakes, offered many places of sanctuary to the guerrillas and their followers and provided secure bases from which they could attack the invading forces. The guerrillas were also helped by the fact that most of the people of West Sumatra, with the exception of members of the Communist Party, initially supported the struggle, and during

---

[45] *Aba*, pp. 41–3 and interviews with Natsir's children, Jakarta, October 28, 2008.

the first months after their invasion government forces did not pursue a very aggressive policy, for the soldiers, particularly those from East Java's Brawijaya division, were reluctant to fight fellow Indonesians and fellow Muslims.

But as the months wore on the fight became increasingly bitter, as more radical soldiers of Central Java's Diponegoro division largely replaced the strongly Islamic Brawijaya troops from East Java and began to challenge the rebels' grip on the countryside.

In the weeks immediately following the Javanese landings, antagonism had already intensified between the Revolutionary Government and the local Communists. The Communist Party (PKI) had been the only party in West Sumatra to oppose Colonel Husein's Banteng Council after its establishment in December 1956,[46] and as it consolidated its authority during 1957 the Council had detained many PKI members and their sympathizers in Padang and other large towns. After landing in Padang, Javanese troops released a number of these imprisoned communist and other leftist officials, and many of the bureaucrats accompanied Jakarta's forces as they advanced into the highlands.[47] These officials were then appointed to administrative positions previously held by PRRI supporters who had now left their posts to join the rebels in the jungle.[48]

As the Jakarta forces advanced, PRRI authorities rounded up many additional members of the Communist Party, together with other leftists and opponents of the Banteng Council on whom they felt they could not rely, including members of Sjahrir's Socialist Party (PSI).[49] Most of those considered communist sympathizers were detained in Suliki and Situjuh Padang Kuning, a small town high in the hills overlooking Payakumbuh and the Harau valley. In Situjuh they were held in the local schoolhouse.

Government troops occupied Payakumbuh on May 20, 1958, and before retreating from the area, the PRRI soldiers burned down the schoolhouse with

---

[46] Initially, the traditional Muslim party Perti also opposed the Banteng Council, but they were persuaded to switch their stance.

[47] Interview with Anwar Z.A., Guguk, Payakumbuh, February 16, 1991.

[48] Interview with Jalal Ibrahim, Lintau, February 3, 1991.

[49] About 400 of those detained, including the PSI members, some TNI officers and some from the Murba party, were held in a jail in Muara Labuh for several weeks, but were then released. Interview with Djoeir Moehamad (Jakarta), January 14, 1991, who was among the Socialist Party members who were detained. See also Saafroedin Bahar, "Peranan Elite Sipil dan Elite Militer dalam Dinamika Integrasi Nasional di Indonesia: Kasus Etnik Minangkabau di Daerah Sumatera Barat, 1945–1984," PhD dissertation, Gadjah Mada University, Yogyakarta, 1996, p. 212.

the prisoners inside, killing 143 of them.[50] This massacre was only the most blatant example of the growing brutality on both sides that was enflaming the hostility between the contending forces.

After withdrawing from Bukittinggi, the Masjumi leaders had established the PRRI government's headquarters in Kototinggi, a small town north of Payakumbuh, deep in the jungle highlands, where during the Republic's struggle against the Dutch in the 1940s, Sjafruddin's Emergency Government of Indonesia (PDRI) had also had a headquarters. This town initially was Natsir's major base, though he spent time in Kamang and Lintau, and traveled widely by car through much of the rebel-controlled area, meeting with the local people, reassuring them and rallying them to the PRRI cause.[51] Remaining in their refuge on the shores of Lake Maninjau, Natsir's wife and children were able to maintain contact with their father only via courier, until they too were forced to flee to even more remote villages as government forces penetrated the Maninjau area.

As the months passed, the conflict spread to the jungle and rural areas outside the towns and villages. In mounting a defense against the invading troops, the PRRI had mobilized young people in the countryside, who maintained communications and security in the villages under their control, establishing an organization, the Perlaras (Perlawanan Rakyat Semesta, Total People's Resistance) which had a structure stretching from the district to the village level.[52] This was modeled on the militias that the local Republican government had organized during the struggle against the Dutch ten years earlier.[53]

In 1959, however, largely because of the ever-widening fissures that had developed in Minangkabau society over the previous decade, this strategy was no longer so successful as during the independence struggle. Government troops were able to respond by creating a parallel organization, recruiting members of the local Communist youth branch (Pemuda Rakyat), to form a People's Defense Organization (OPR, Organisasi Perlawanan Rakjat), which assisted

---

[50] Visit to Situjuh, June 17, 1985 and discussions with residents there. Also interviews with Nizur Dt. Marajo (Situjuh Padang Kuning), June 17, 1985, Zulkifli Lubis (Jakarta) May 10, 1991 and Anwar ZA (Guguk, Payakumbuh), February 16, 1991.

[51] Interview with Nasrullah (Guci, Kamang, November 15, 2008), who acted as Natsir's driver and secretary (*juru tulis*) and traveled with him throughout the three years.

[52] Interview with Mansoer Sani, Padang, August 20, 1995.

[53] During the Revolution, the most important element in these local security forces had been the BPNK (Badan Pengawal Nagari dan Kota, Body for Guarding the Villages and Towns), which all young men between 17 and 35 who were not members of the armed forces had to join, and where they received military training from regular army officers.

the local military authority.[54] The over six thousand members of the OPR were charged with security and development functions in the countryside, as well as identifying and arresting suspected PRRI adherents.[55] The OPR eventually succeeded in undermining PRRI efforts to consolidate their control over many of the rural areas. Natsir later described the effectiveness of the members of this radical youth organization:

> As long as we were fighting just Javanese troops there was no problem about maintaining our guerrilla bases and controlling areas just outside towns such as Padang and Bukittinggi. While I was in the jungle we got food every day from the market in Bukittinggi.... But the situation was drastically altered when the Javanese troops developed a technique for using members of the local PKI's Pemuda Rakjat as scouts to trace down the guerrillas in the jungle. Being local lads they knew every creek and path just as our people did and could guide the Javanese forces.[56]

* * *

As they moved further from the political realities of compromise and accommodation that had marked life in Jakarta, Natsir and his colleagues and followers became more fixed in the belief that their cause was completely just and in tune with God's will. They began to portray the struggle as one largely between good and evil and made open religious appeals. With the PRRI coming under direct attack from Soekarno's forces, Natsir had certainly begun to perceive the situation in less nuanced terms than previously, viewing his opponents as guilty of destroying the ideals for which he and his fellow Indonesians had fought in the independence struggle. He soon adopted Sjafruddin's opinion that Soekarno and his government were merely acting as tools for the Communists. This attitude was strengthened by the polarization that was growing ever more rigid within West Sumatra between the Communists and the PRRI as members of the PKI took over most administrative positions in the local government from the previous office holders.

As we saw at the end of the previous chapter, on the eve of his flight from Jakarta, Natsir had acknowledged that Soekarno was no communist, and that it was his hunger for power rather than any ideological belief that was endangering his country. Now, in the immediate aftermath of Jakarta's invasion of West Sumatra Natsir altered his position, giving vent to his bitterness as the

---

[54] Salim, *Sedjarah Operasi*, pp. 52–3.
[55] See Audrey Kahin, *Rebellion to Integration: West Sumatra and the Indonesian Polity* (Amsterdam: University of Amsterdam Press, 1999), pp. 221, 339.
[56] Natsir interview, Jakarta, January 23, 1971.

regime's planes and land forces attacked and destroyed his people and region. In a radio broadcast on May 19, 1958, which he titled "The Sukarno regime has reached the height of its pride and arrogance," he charged that Soekarno was accusing the Western powers of aiding the rebels in order to hide his own reliance on Soviet military assistance and the fact that Russian influence had spread to the Independence Palace. He portrayed Russian influence as in part responsible for Soekarno's policy of "burying the political parties."[57] He seemed to be accusing the Soekarno regime of being the sole recipient of foreign assistance, despite the fact that by this time he was well aware that the rebels were indeed receiving substantial support from the Western powers.[58] In a speech four days later, Natsir went further, stating:

> Even if the Head of State is not a Communist, as has been proclaimed to left and right, it is no longer in doubt that he is, at least, international communism's strongest instrument in Southeast Asia, and possibly in the whole world, to be used up to the present day to implement its program in Southeast Asia.[59]

In these speeches, Natsir portrayed Soekarno as being used by the Communists until "the time when they are strong and no longer need Soekarno or when he has become an impediment to their aims" when they will in turn destroy him. Natsir described the president as a potential dictator intent on removing all elements of democracy in Indonesia, an aim that was in line with those of the Soviet Union.

For the balance of 1958 Natsir's speeches concentrated on the future of democracy in Indonesia. While directing most of his anger against Soekarno, he also took aim at other arms of the government, accusing members of Parliament of refusing to accept their responsibility to protect true democracy

---

[57] "Regime Sukarno telah sampai kepada puntjak ketjongkakan dan Kesombongnja," *Capita Selecta III*, p. 116.

[58] In a later interview, he disclosed that he had become aware of American assistance prior to the February ultimatum and stated: "We were willing to get whatever support we could from outside and were not ashamed of it. However, there is no doubt that in terms of marshalling support in Java the fact that we were getting outside support played into the hands of Soekarno, and his information ministry kept hammering on this theme with good effect." Interview, January 23, 1971.

[59] Radio speech by Natsir, "Satu Pertanjaan kepada para anggota parlemen," May 23, 1958, in *Capita Selecta III*, p. 120. [Kalaulah Kepala Negara itu bukan seorang komunis, sebagaimana berulang2 diteriakkannja kiri-kanan, maka tidak sjak lagi, sekurang-2nja ia adalah satu alat jang paling besar di Asia-Tenggara, bahkan mungkin diseluruh dunia, jang pernah dipakai oleh komunisme internasional sampai sekarang untuk melaksanakan programnja di Asia Tenggara ini.]

and prevent Soekarno from introducing his concept of "guided democracy." He attacked, in particular, Head of Parliament Sartono who was openly supporting Guided Democracy and was calling on Parliament to change the Constitution to accord with it: "Doesn't he realize that Guided Democracy transgresses the Constitution and is 'enslaved democracy' [*demokrasi terkungkung*] or disguised dictatorship [*diktatuur terselimut*]?"[60]

The following month Natsir tied Soekarno's ability to move toward a dictatorial form of government to the fact that political power was centralized in Jakarta, which "has led to a monopoly of power in the hands of a clique that exercises this power in the center of the administration." He accused the people's representatives in Parliament of failing to fight against both these evils and argued that they must return to the "basis of unqualified democracy ... a balance between the executive and legislative, and between politics, economics, society and culture, together with a balance among the regions and between them and the center."[61] Throughout this long speech there is no mention of the role of communism or the Communist Party.

A few weeks later, however, he was again tying international communism to Soekarno's efforts to usurp any form of democratic government and concentrate all power in his own hands. He accused the president of attempting "to kill the democratic parliamentary system in Indonesia gradually and in a systematic manner ... with the help of the Communist International." In destroying the political system, he contended, Soekarno wished to substitute a "state's party" with himself at its head.[62] And as the months proceeded Natsir's speeches assumed an ever-more open religious cast.

Sjafruddin too was outspoken in presenting his perception of the situation. In a speech he gave in February 1959, to mark the first anniversary of the formation of the PRRI, his words were initially reminiscent of some of Natsir's previous writings. In these Sjafruddin emphasized the desire of the peoples of the many ethnic groups and diverse regions that make up Indonesia to remain one, symbolized in the Indonesian motto: Bhineka Tunggal Ika, or Unity in Diversity. But he then went on to consider the *Pancasila* and charged that the Soekarno government was seeking to wipe out the principles on which Indonesia had been established:

> Moreover, the Indonesian symbol shows us the five principles that form the
> basis of our Provisional Constitution. But it is already clear that the Soekarno

---

[60] "Jalan jang Bersimpang Dua," Speech, August 20, 1958, in *Capita Selecta III*, p. 141.
[61] "Apa Inti Persoalan jang kita hadapi," Speech, September 20, 1958, in ibid., pp. 148, 149.
[62] "Pidato pada Dies Natalis Darul Hikmah," October 10, 1958, ibid., pp. 157–67.

regime is acting to remove the first principle [i.e. the belief in God] from the five principles. What is clear in Central Sumatra, where the administration is critically helped by the Communists, is that the government now being established is nearly completely staffed with Communist Party people or with people belonging to the same family as the Communists.

Previously we removed the color blue from the tricolor flag so that it became the Red and White [*Merah-Putih*], but now the Soekarno regime is trying to remove the white so that all that remains is the red flag.[63]

In a speech in January 1959, commemorating along with Sjafruddin the first anniversary of the declaration of the PRRI, Natsir's words remained in keeping with the arguments he had been making throughout the 1950s. He stressed what he perceived as Soekarno's pursuit of a dictatorship and disregard of the fact

> that Indonesia, comprising thousands of islands stretching over an area as extensive as western Europe, and the Indonesian people, comprising dozens of distinct ethnic groups, each with a different way of thinking different traditions and customs, and differing stages of development, cannot be governed in a dictatorial manner from one place by one man or one group.[64]

He urged the Indonesian people to "return to democracy based on belief in God Almighty," and warned the elected members of Parliament that Soekarno was moving to separate them from the people who elected them, changing "the parliament elected by the people into an instrument designed to serve the ends of the dictator."[65]

In these speeches, then, are elements that Natsir had stressed throughout his career, namely that the government of Indonesia had to accord with the diversity of its people, and should be in the form of a decentralized democracy. He also continued to argue that Soekarno's attempts to move toward authoritarianism had to be consistently opposed. But these arguments were now combined with much more strident attacks on Soekarno personally and as a potential dictator, and charges that the president's actions were bringing Indonesia under the influence of the international communist system. He no longer accorded Soekarno any of the understanding and sympathy he had earlier evidenced.

Sjafruddin had never had the type of relationship with Soekarno that Natsir had enjoyed, which, despite its tensions and antagonisms, had been

---

[63] Speech by Sjafruddin over Radio PRRI, February 15, 1959 (PRRI Document #13). These statements do reflect the situation as it was in West Sumatra.

[64] "Sukarno is looking for New Victims," monitored transmission from Radio PRRI, January 15, 1959 (typescript).

[65] Ibid.

forged in the recognition that the two men had shared a common struggle in achieving Indonesia's independence. Sjafruddin, on the other hand, despised the president and felt that Soekarno had betrayed him and his country at the end of the Revolution by ignoring the Emergency Government Sjafruddin headed and being willing to settle for less than full political and economic sovereignty. Ten years later, Sjafruddin was determined that this time the struggle would not end on Soekarno's terms. He renounced any allegiance to the unitary Republic and went beyond calls for decentralization and autonomy to embrace the goal of a federal Indonesia.

By early 1959 Natsir had joined Sjafruddin in urging formation of a federal Indonesia incorporating all the regions in Sumatra and Sulawesi that were currently under rebel control and eventually embracing the whole archipelago. This argument fitted well with his previous advocacy of decentralization and his attacks on a Jakarta-centered monopoly of power. Both he and Sjafruddin envisaged that the center's role in a federal system would be largely limited to foreign relations, defense and communications. They were also making more openly religious appeals and discussing an alliance with the major Darul Islam leaders, particularly Daud Beureu'eh in Aceh and Kahar Muzzakar in South Sulawesi.[66]

During the second half of 1959, PRRI leaders held meetings to draw up a Constitution for this proposed federal state, which they called the Federal Republic of Indonesia, or the United Republic of Indonesia (RPI, *Republik Persatuan Indonesia*). For the time being the RPI, with Sjafruddin Prawiranegara as its president, would consist of ten component states, all outside Java, each of which would choose a form of government to accord with the culture and wishes of its people.[67]

One cannot help but think that in discussing and formulating their ideas for a new state, the Masjumi leaders were now in their element. Despite being evicted from all major cities and being confined to the isolated interior

---

[66] It is interesting that there seems to have been little effort to enroll Kartosuwirjo's Darul Islam in their ranks and West Java does not appear among the component states of the RPI. Perhaps communications with Kartosuwirjo were too difficult at the time, though Dengel notes that DI strength at the beginning of 1959 was about 4,200 "and there were efforts by the Darul Islam movement to establish contact with the rebels in West Sumatra via Banten and the Sunda Strait." Dengel, *Darul Islam dan Kartosuwirjo*, p. 186. Apparently nothing came of these efforts.

[67] These were the State of the Islamic Republic of Aceh; Tapanuli/East Sumatra [North Sumatra]; West Sumatra; Riau; Jambi; South Sumatra; North Sulawesi; Islamic Republic of South Sulawesi; North Maluku; and South Maluku. "Undang-Undang Dasar Republik Persatuan Indonesia" (typescript), paragraph 179, p. 62.

highlands of Sumatra, they behaved as if they were working in the center of a governmental structure. Able to maintain radio communications with their sympathizers on Sulawesi and other regions of Sumatra, as well as their representatives in other parts of the world, they devoted their time and efforts to discussing, drawing up and typing out a detailed Constitution for the federal state they now envisaged establishing.[68] This was a process with which they felt completely at home. After twelve months spent in drawing up the Constitution, the civilian leadership then proclaimed formation of the Republik Persatuan Indonesia (RPI) at a meeting held in Bonjol on February 8, 1960.

Growing Civilian-Military Dissension

The moves toward forming the RPI, especially approaches by Sjafruddin, Natsir and Burhanuddin to leaders of the Darul Islam and the inclusion of these DI territories within the proposed federal order, aggravated tensions within rebel ranks. Religion had always been a sensitive issue amongst the PRRI leaders, for two of the regions that supported them — North Sumatra and North Sulawesi — were predominantly Christian, and feared as much as did the Soekarno government a rapprochement with proponents of an Islamic state. This fear does not seem to have been alleviated by the provision in the RPI Constitution allowing each of the component states to choose its own form of government.

Proclamation of the federal government also further exacerbated a growing rift between the civilian and military leaders, for non-Muslim commanders, such as Simbolon on Sumatra and Kawilarang in Sulawesi, together with the former minister of finance, Sumitro Djojohadikusumo, not only opposed any cooperation with the Darul Islam but also still favored a unitary state and saw the establishment of a new federal state as "in conflict with the Independence Proclamation of August 17, 1945."[69]

Civilian-military tensions amongst the insurgents had already been reinforced by events in Jakarta, where President Soekarno on July 5, 1959 had proclaimed a return to the 1945 Constitution and abolished the Constituent Assembly. Nasution and the military leadership supported this move, for

---

[68] The typescript of the RPI Constitution consists of 113 single-spaced typewritten pages, with a further 41 pages of appendices made up of proclamation documents. The date of the document is February 8, 1960.

[69] Payung Bangun, *Kolonel Maludin Simbolon: Liku-liku Perjuangannya dalam Pembangunan Bangsa* (Jakarta: Sinar Harapan, 1996), p. 310. See also Salim, *Sedjarah Operasi2*, p. 54 for Husein's attitude. On the attitude of Sumual and other colonels in Permesta, see Harvey, *Permesta*, pp. 128–9.

it strengthened the army's role in the country's affairs, as well as that of the president. Most of the rebel colonels saw these developments as opening up the possibility of a government being established in Jakarta more in accord with their own aims. Rebel sources overseas described the 1945 Constitution as "compatible with our goal of forming a stable Government in Indonesia, which … would not provide maneuvering room for communism because it would be controlled by a single executive body."[70] With Nasution now appointed minister of defense and almost a quarter of the cabinet in Jakarta consisting of members of the armed forces, the rebel colonels began to perceive that the goals they had been pursuing were in closer accord with those of the military leadership in Jakarta, even with their earlier opponent General Nasution, than with the path that their fellow rebels were now following. According to Natsir, they "began to have second thoughts" and "there began something of a rift, a sort of undercurrent whereby the military began to think in terms of how to make the best of things."[71]

Over the three years since proclamation of the PRRI, then, fissures within the rebel government had grown ever wider. While all elements within the rebel forces were still united in their opposition to communism and Soekarno's alliance with the PKI, they disagreed on most other issues. Nearly all the military officers, especially those from Christian areas, opposed the Masjumi leaders' concept of a federal Indonesia and their willingness to cooperate with the Darul Islam in establishing it. On this matter, Sumitro and perhaps others from the Socialist Party (PSI) were in accord with the military's position. But these politicians sided with their Masjumi colleagues in opposing the efforts of Simbolon and Husein to seek an accommodation with the central army leadership as the army's power and influence grew in Jakarta. These disagreements were played out against the background of a long and consistent string of military defeats in both Sumatra and Sulawesi, as the territory the rebels controlled diminished and they were forced to retreat ever further into the hills.

---

[70] Foreign Service Despatch [841], Amembassy Jakarta to Department of State, April 5, 1959 (756D.00/4-559), citing the Jakarta daily newspaper *Merdeka*.
[71] Natsir interview, Jakarta, May 31, 1971.

7

Surrender and Imprisonment, 1961-67

End of the Rebellion

By the end of 1959 government forces had pushed ever further into the interior of Central Sumatra. They had advanced into the regions of Pariaman and Tanah Datar early in the year, taking over several of the major rebel strongholds.[1] The rebels had attempted to regroup, but their proclamation of the Federal Government (RPI) in February 1960 marked the beginning of the end.

Natsir and Sjafruddin had never lost the belief that their struggle would ultimately be successful. Both were intensely devout and retained a strong faith in the justice of their cause. Even this late, they felt that time was on their side and they still anticipated that eventually the government in Jakarta would collapse, though as the months proceeded this became an ever more remote possibility. In the meantime, during the first half of 1960 they were still able to maintain their centers in the jungles and hills surrounding some of the region's more isolated small towns and villages, where their administration and educational system functioned smoothly. Most of their followers were able to live within these small centers, only withdrawing to the surrounding hills whenever government troops came in to attack.

But Jakarta's forces were being increasingly aggressive and successful on both Sumatra and Sulawesi. Their advances on Sumatra culminated in July 1960

---

[1] For the official government account of these operations, see Makmum Salim, *Sedjarah Operasi2 Gabungan terhadap PRRI-Permesta* (Departemen Pertahanan-Keamanan Pusat Sedjarah ABRI, 1971), pp. 46–9.

139

with their occupation of the rebel stronghold of Kototinggi, when government troops were able to destroy the transmitters that had been the rebels' major connection to the outside world. Until then the civilian leadership of the PRRI had been able to maintain an administration in this mountain redoubt and keep up relatively sophisticated communication with their main pockets of support in Sumatra and Sulawesi, as well as with their sympathizers overseas. Forced to flee from Kototinggi, Natsir split from Sjafruddin and Burhanuddin and joined his family and close colleagues in an area near Palembayan (Desa Sitalang, Lubuk Basung).[2] But once Sjafruddin, Natsir, Burhanuddin and Assaat separated from one another, they were no longer able to act effectively as leaders of the rebel government. Rather, they were now reduced to the status of refugees dependent on the strength and goodwill of their military commanders, several of whom were by now questioning the utility of further action.

Gradually both the PRRI military and civilian leaders and their families retreated to more remote areas of the countryside. According to Nasrullah, a local Masjumi member who acted as Natsir's secretary and driver, by the end of 1960 Natsir, his family and his colleagues had finally been forced out of the villages and into the jungle itself.[3] Government troops continued to advance, forcing the group to retreat further into the interior of Pasaman, in the northern part of West Sumatra. As they made their way deeper into the jungle, Natsir's wife Ummi was so weak that she had sometimes to be carried. When the small band reached the Batang Masang, a wide and fast-flowing river barring their retreat, they saw it could only be crossed if they constructed a makeshift ferryboat. One of Natsir's daughters recalled:

> To cross the river we made a rattan basket big enough for two people. Because there was a telcom official in our group he was able to fashion posts from tree trunks on each side of the river, attach a telephone cable and install a pulley, so that the rattan basket could be suspended from the pulley. We were then able to cross the river by pulling on the basket.[4]

Once they had crossed, the river provided an effective deterrent to pursuit by government troops.

After climbing into an even more inaccessible area they finally felt secure. Close to a small stream the group of about twenty built themselves a couple

---

[2] Interview with Nasrullah, Guci, Kamang, November 15, 2008; also interview with Dt. Tan Kabasaran, Bukittinggi, January 8, 2009.

[3] Interview with Nasrullah, November 15, 2008.

[4] Raja Juli Antoni, ed., *Aba sebagai Cahaya Keluarga* (Jakarta: Yayasan Capita Selecta, 2008), pp. 46–7.

of huts, one for sleeping and eating and one for Natsir's office, with a small kitchen close by. Though now connected to the outside world only by courier, Natsir and his staff continued to work as if still in their Jakarta office, while the children studied and sought ways to make use of whatever food they could find to cook their meals. The months of hardship, however, did seem to take a toll on the health of both their father and mother.

Despite the increasing hopelessness of their cause, many of those who had accompanied Natsir into the jungle, when recalling these months, give an idyllic picture of the life they had led then. Natsir's children remembered it as a period when they were closer to their father than at any other time in their lives. Ibu Asma Malim, who had been active in the Masjumi since she was a young girl and had been a colleague of Ratna Sari and Rahmah El Junusiah,[5] accompanied Natsir and his family to the jungle. She portrayed their life there as in tune with "the will of Allah," where even the animals were peaceful and did not attack them. She recalled that once settled in their retreat, they planted

Natsir (standing second from L) and his companions outside their
huts in the jungle.

---

[5] Ratna Sari had been a leading member of the pre-war Permi party and Rahmah El Junusiah had founded and headed the innovative and influential school for girls, Diniyyah Putri. During both the Revolution against the Dutch and the PRRI Rahmah accompanied the guerrillas into the jungle.

Resting on the bank of the Sianok river (Natsir is seated at the extreme R).

their own crops and built their own shelters.[6] Photographs from that time reflect this bucolic picture of life in the jungle, with Natsir and his family and friends standing outside thatched huts or sitting at plank tables typing out their speeches, orders and copies of the RPI Constitution.[7] Despite their tenuous communications with the outside, they still had a battery radio that was strong enough to receive BBC and VOA broadcasts, so they remained aware of international developments, one of the daughters recalling that they had been able to follow the election of President Kennedy in the United States.

* * *

After the proclamation of the RPI federal order and especially after Jakarta's forces occupied Kototinggi, and the rebel leadership split up, rifts between the remaining civilian politicians and the rebel colonels had further widened. From Sulawesi came news of even greater disintegration there. As Kawilarang, the most respected of the rebel officers in the Permesta, described the worsening situation on Sulawesi:

---

[6] Interview with Ibu Asma Malim, Padang, November 16, 2008.

[7] In addition to the photos above, see those in Lukman Hakiem, *70 tahun H. Buchari Tamam: Menjawab Panggilan Risalah* (Jakarta: Media Da'wah, 1992), pp. 81–2. Buchari Tamam, a close friend and colleague of Natsir in both the Masjumi and Dewan Da'wah, accompanied him throughout his years in the jungle.

By 1960 the forces of the rebels were very badly disunited. They had incorporated many robber gangs and these groups asserted much independence. The country was ruined by the fighting. Almost every battalion was on its own, many of them fighting each other. When a battalion commander moved from one place to another he would need an escort of at least 60 men to protect him, Sumual generally had a whole company.[8]

As the year progressed the situation worsened further, with two of the rebel commanders, Timbuleng and Warouw, murdered, one allegedly by Sumual.[9] This internecine warfare on Sulawesi probably had an effect on the Sumatran colonels, making them more receptive to the pleas from Jakarta that they should abandon their rebellion and return to "the arms of the motherland."

Nasution later stated that, in dealing with the insurgency, he employed a strategy

> of using the right and left hand both — the right hand to strike at the rebels, while at the same time with the left hand inviting them to come back to the fold of the Republic and accept amnesty. This was essentially the same tactic we had used with the Darul Islam.

He said that Soekarno had initially agreed with this strategy, but later reversed himself and jailed many of those who had been granted amnesty.[10]

In late 1960, Nasution intensified his attempts to detach less fervent rebel leaders from their colleagues and attract them back to the government's side, focusing especially on the Permesta military commanders on Sulawesi, such as Kawilarang and Sumual. He renewed these appeals in early 1961, and at the end of March Kawilarang authorized their forces to surrender. By April all Permesta troops had laid down their arms, and only Sumual among the officers had not yet surrendered. Nasution also sent emissaries to officers on Sumatra, especially to Simbolon and also to Husein, accompanying these feelers with an intensification of Jakarta's military operations against the Sumatran rebels.

By this time both the civilian and military rebels on Sumatra were also contemplating abandoning the struggle. Sjafruddin and the other RPI leaders appointed Simbolon to represent them in negotiating an end to the conflict with the central government. Simbolon and Husein, however, clearly felt they could obtain better terms if they negotiated directly with their counterparts

---

[8] Interview with A.E. Kawilarang, Jakarta, May 26, 1971.

[9] On the complicated series of events in Sulawesi, see Barbara Harvey, *Permesta: Half a Rebellion* (Ithaca: Cornell Modern Indonesia Project, 1977), pp. 130–3. She does not believe that the allegation against Sumual was correct.

[10] Interview with Gen. A.H. Nasution, Jakarta, May 27, 1971.

in the Indonesian army on behalf of the military rebels alone. Ignoring their agreement with Sjafruddin and Natsir, the two colonels disavowed the RPI government and established their own Emergency Military Government (Pemerintah Darurat Militer), headed again by Husein, which opened independent negotiations with Jakarta's military authorities.[11]

During April and May, pockets of rebel troops began surrendering individually in Aceh and North, Central and South Sumatra. In late spring Nasution apparently approached both Husein in the southern sector and Djambek in the northern to urge them to give up the struggle. Husein was the more amenable. He started talks with Jakarta's commander in West Sumatra, Col. Soerjosoempeno, and officially surrendered in Solok on June 21, bringing with him about 600 men. During the balance of June and July nearly all the rebel units gave themselves up, with Simbolon negotiating his own terms and returning to the Republic in Balige on August 12, together with Nainggolan and about 4,000 of their soldiers.[12]

Djambek, however, held back. He had not joined with his fellow officers in disavowing the RPI, and felt that Sjafruddin, as the official head of the Federal Government, had to be consulted before any agreements were reached with Jakarta. He had also been hoping that through further negotiations with Nasution he could obtain better terms for the rebel forces. The two men had retained their respect for each other and, as a former adjutant to Nasution, Djambek still felt close ties to the army chief of staff. He had drawn up a plan whereby the central government would allow the PRRI forces to evacuate most regions of Sumatra and consolidate all their troops in Riau. He apparently hoped that, should they achieve this, they would then be in a stronger position to take negotiations with Nasution to a new level, and, if these negotiations broke down, at least the rebels would have an easy avenue of escape to Malaysia. On hearing of Husein's surrender, however, Djambek realized that whatever slim chance his plan may have had, it was no longer viable. He therefore ordered his

---

[11] During interviews with Dan Lev in Medan on September 7 and 8, 1961, Simbolon described his action as "a coup from within," during which he instructed Husein to stop using the RPI name so that "from now on they should simply name the rebellion 'pemerintah darurat militer [emergency military government]'." According to Dan Lev's notes on the interview, "Husein asked what about the civilian leaders? Simbolon replied 'tinggalkan sadja mereka [just leave them behind]' and that's what happened. The civilian leaders came in alone. There was nothing else they could do." Dan Lev kindly gave us copies of his interview notes.

[12] According to Feith and Lev, Husein brought with him 13,500 men and Simbolon 11,000 men. Herbert Feith and Daniel S. Lev, "The End of the Indonesian Rebellion," *Pacific Affairs* 36, 1 (Spring 1963): 43, but these numbers seem too high.

officers to go down with their troops, while he remained alone in the highlands of Palupuh with a few followers and his adjutant, Yussari.[13]

Without any military protection, the civilian leaders of the RPI felt they had no alternative but to follow the example of Husein and Simbolon. After an exchange of letters with Nasution, Sjafruddin on August 17 made a radio broadcast calling on all RPI forces "to cease hostilities." That same day President Soekarno announced a general amnesty for all rebels "who surrendered unconditionally by October 5, 1961" and swore loyalty to the Constitution, the state, and the "Great Leader of the Revolution." The following day Zulkifli Lubis surrendered and a week later Sjafruddin, Assaat and Burhanuddin Harahap came down from the jungle in the southeastern corner of Tapanuli, having first written to Nasution to ensure that their surrender went smoothly. A lieutenant met them with a bus and jeep and transported them to Padang Sidempuan, where units of the Siliwangi Division of West Java were in control.[14]

On hearing the news of the order to surrender and the promise of amnesty and pardon (*amnesti dan abolisi*), Natsir gathered his family and staff together to discuss the situation. He told his wife and children to go down to Bukittinggi, urging his younger children to return to school. He himself was unwilling to give up yet, in part because of mistrust of the government soldiers to whom he would have to surrender, and in part because of the belief he shared with Col. Dahlan Djambek that a Muslim was forbidden from swearing an oath to anyone other than God. Before deciding on his course of action he wanted to meet with Djambek, who was in hiding a few miles away at Laring Palupuh. The whole group climbed back down the mountains and again crossed the Masang River before they separated, with Ummi and her children scrambling along the riverbank toward the nearest hamlet, while Natsir and a few followers went off in the direction of Bonjol.

Natsir's wife and children arrived at the nearest village, where they were detained by the military authorities and taken first to Palembayan where they were interrogated as to Natsir's whereabouts. They were then transported to Bukittinggi and the children were housed in army barracks while Ummi was taken away for further questioning. The children had to swear a loyalty oath, be photographed, and have their fingerprints taken before they were reunited with

---

[13] This account is largely based on that given by Nizar (a member of the Pasukan Dahlan Djambek and very close to Djambek himself) in the presence of Djambek's sister and other close followers of Djambek. Bukittinggi, March 27, 1999.

[14] Ajip Rosidi, *Sjafruddin Prawiranegara: Lebih Takut kepada Allah SWT* (Jakarta: Inti Idayu Press, 1986), p. 216. They were all fearful of surrendering to Diponegoro troops, who occupied most of West Sumatra and who were more likely to treat them harshly.

their mother, who had spent the past two days "in the women's prison, being treated as a common criminal." Finally the family was released and allowed to resume a normal life in Bukittinggi, although still having to report regularly to the local military authorities.[15]

During this period Natsir, with six companions, stayed in the hills above the Masang River, not far from where Col Djambek was hiding. A few weeks later, after his surrender, Natsir recalled his ambivalence at the time, writing:

> From the end of July we had no support whatsoever. All our forces had gone down. Both civilians and [military] leaders. From the end of August there remained in all of West Sumatra only the late Col. M. Dahlan Djambek, myself, together with a few friends (+/− 10 people). Finally we were faced with only two alternatives: to go down, which meant falling into the hands of APRI [Government army]. But on the other hand we were surrounded by the 3rd force (PKI activists), uniformed and armed, who were carrying out their activities around us.

He was convinced that when it became clear that he was unwilling to take the oath to the head of state, the army would immediately put him in jail.[16]

While pondering his course of action, Natsir expressed his feelings in a piece written from the "Battlefield" [*Medan Djihad*] on August 24, 1961, portraying the struggle he had been waging in purely religious terms as a Holy War. He later included the piece in his *Capita Selecta III*.

Pemimpin Pulang (A Leader Comes Home)

There are four ways for a Leader to come home from the Struggle:

He can return with his head held high, bearing the fruits of battle

He can return with his head held high, but his hands shackled by the enemy, destined for jail or worse. His tale will become fertilizer to enrich the battlefield for the Mudjahidin who come after him.

He can come home. But only his name returns. His body is left on the battlefield. In truth, along with his name, his living soul will also return to restore the spirit of the *Ummat* until the seasons change, bringing new leaders to take his place.

He can return with his hands up, his head bowed, his heart abandoned to fear of the enemy – the enemy who is fighting against Allah and his Prophet. What returns is his body, which once again will be destroyed. His life will kill the *Ummat's* spirit for ages to come. Who knows when the *Ummat* will

---

[15] *Aba*, pp. 52–6.
[16] PRRI document # 6: Natsir to Taher Karim Lubis, Padang Sidempuan, October 15, 1961.

live again. Perhaps God will later supplant it with another *Ummat,* one that
is more worthy.

He is a "leader" in quotation marks.

At times there is the captain, tacking his ship to run against the tide. But
forbidden from changing direction, from taking another course.

He has not yet come home.[17]

Like Natsir, Djambek was unwilling to surrender and take an oath of
loyalty to President Soekarno.[18] He sent a message to Natsir stating that he was
going to contact the TNI commander in Bukittinggi, Col. R. Soerjosoempeno,

---

[17] *Pemimpin Pulang*

Empat tjara-pulang bagi seorang Pemimpin dari Perdjuangan

Dia pulang dengan kepala tegak, membawa hasil perdjuangan.

Dia pulang dengan kepala tegak, tapi tangan dibelenggu musuh
untuk tjalon penghuni terungku, atau lebih dari itu. Riwajatnja akan
mendjadi pupuk penjuburkan tanah perdjuangan bagi para Mudjahidin
seterusnja.

Dia pulang. Tapi jang pulang hanja namanja. Djasadnja sudah
tinggal dimedan djihad. Sebenarnja, disamping namanja, djuga turut
pulang ruhnja jang hidup, dan menghidupkan ruh Ummat sampai tahun
berganti musim, serta meng-ilhami para-pemimpin jang akan timbul
debelakangnja.

Dia pulang dengan tangan keatas. Kepalanja terkulai, hatinja
menjerah ketjut kepada musuh jang memusuhi Allah dan Rasul.
Jang pulang itu djasadnja, jang satu kali djuga akan hantjur. Njawanja
mematikan ruh Ummat buat zaman jang pandjang. Entah pabila pula
Ummat itu akan hidup kembali. Mungkin akan ditukar oleh Ilahi
dengan Ummat jang lain, jang lebih baik, nanti.

Ia "Pemimpin" dengan tanda-kutip.

Adakalanja ada nachoda berpirau melawan arus. Tapi berpantang ia bertukar haluan,
berbalik arah.

Ia belum pulang.

Capita Selecta III (typescript, unpaginated, last page). After his arrest Natsir was able to
send the manuscript of this volume to Singapore, and, at his request, it was sent out to a
few people abroad, including my husband. After Natsir's death, the editors of his memorial
volume used:"Pemimpin Pulang" as its title.

[18] The following account is based largely on that given in an interview with Dt. Tan
Kabasaran (Bukittinggi), January 8, 2009. Dt. Tan Kabasaran was one of the few followers
who accompanied Natsir during the surrender. It also draws on interviews with members
of Dahlan Djambek's family and some of his followers in Bukittinggi (including Dt. Tan
Kabasaran) and a visit with them to Laring where Djambek was killed (Bukittinggi, Laring,
March 27, 29, 1999), and upon *Aba,* pp. 52–9.

a former friend and colleague, to inform him that instead of surrendering he was willing to be arrested and brought to trial to contest the charges of corruption that had been brought against him four years earlier. He wrote that, according to his understanding of Islam, it forbids its adherents from taking an oath of loyalty to any human being, so he "refused the amnesty and pardon offered by President Soekarno," which entailed taking such an oath, but he was "willing to be arrested and brought before a court of justice."[19]

Natsir himself was now ready to surrender, and he moved east with his companions[20] to Air Kijang, a hamlet near the border of Agam district, where one of his group had a house, which was only an hour's walk away from Djambek's hiding place at Laring. Hearing of Djambek's plans, Natsir sent him a message, asking him not to contact Soerjosoempeno until he and Natsir had a chance to talk. Natsir was fearful that Djambek's letter could fall into the hands of their enemies in the Communist youth militia, the OPR. But Natsir's courier was delayed at a guard post and by the time he reached Djambek the letter had already gone off. Now aware of Natsir's concern, Djambek came to Air Kijang to meet with him. He told Natsir that the letter would reach Soerjosoempeno the following day and he feared that, if he were not in Laring waiting to be arrested, the government army would attack the village and might also search out Natsir. According to some of the onlookers at the meeting the two men wept as they took leave of each other and Djambek returned to Laring.

As Natsir had feared, Djambek's letter was leaked and passed on to the communist militia (OPR). Villagers in Laring later recounted how in the early morning of September 13, while Djambek and his adjutant were still asleep, an OPR platoon of about thirteen men, under command of a young radical called Gandi, climbed the long, rocky path from the road to the village. They knocked loudly on the outside wall of the hut where Djambek and his adjutant were sleeping. Seeing the intruders were not in uniform, Djambek realized they were not members of the TNI and that they intended to kill him. He asked permission to go down to wash before praying, but as he went down the bank toward the stream, the militia members shot his adjutant and then gunned him down, killing him with bullets to his leg and body.

Members of the OPR unit, fearing the reactions of the Minangkabau people to Djambek's murder, threatened the villagers with reprisals if they

---

[19] Letter dated September 10, 1961 from Dahlan Djambek to "Saudara Panglima Kodam III/17 Agustus Kolonel R. Soerjosoempeno." I am grateful to Col Djambek's sister, Ibu Naimah Djambek, for giving me a copy of this letter.
[20] These were all Masjumi members: Buchari Tamam, Tasman Mansur, Sahidin Dt. Dilangit, Lahmuddin Masri, Ridwan and Dt. Tan Kabasaran himself.

told anyone what had happened. So in the months and years that followed, in the absence of any definite reports, rumors spread that Djambek had fled to Malaysia or was living under an alias in another part of Indonesia.[21] When the intruders left, the villagers buried the two men.

The next morning in Air Kijang Natsir received news of Djambek's death. He knew he would have to surrender but was fearful that any formal approach to the authorities would have the same outcome and lead to his own death. For, according to a courier who came from Kumpulan, Gandi, Djambek's murderer, had been heard boasting that he had killed Djambek and that Natsir was to be next. Leaving their hiding place on the morning of September 20, Natsir and his four or five companions finally reached a small village, Lubuk Gadang, before nightfall, and there they surrendered to the sector commander.[22] They were taken by car first to Palembayan, the commander's headquarters, and from there to Bukittinggi, where they arrived before midnight that same night.

Here Natsir was treated much better than he had anticipated. He refused to take the oath, but this did not result in his being arrested and put in the notorious jail in Bukittinggi. Instead he was taken to a hotel where he met with Brawijaya commander, Captain Sitompul, who, on Nasution's orders, had come down from Padang Sidempuan, in southern Tapanuli, together with Haji Damanik, to take charge of Natsir and his companions.[23] After being questioned and meeting briefly with his family, Natsir was escorted to Sidempuan, where Sjafruddin, Burhanuddin and Assaat were already in detention. Ummi and their older children were allowed to join him there the following February. A few weeks later, Natsir and the other Masjumi leaders were flown to Jakarta, while his family followed by sea.

---

[21] Interviews with Laring villagers, including Usman and Khatib Suleiman, Laring, March 29, 1999. One of these villagers had himself fled to Negeri Sembilan in Malaysia, together with many other PRRI members, and had returned only about a couple of months before my visit. Members of Djambek's family were insistent on disproving another rumor that Djambek's head had been severed in the murder.

[22] Interview with Dt. Tan Kabasaran, who was one of the group, Bukittinggi, January 8, 2009. According to him, Natsir was hurt in fording a stream, which delayed their progress. The commander informed them that, had they arrived earlier, he would have shot Natsir, for the orders he had received had been to shoot on sight anyone who emerged from the jungle without questioning them first. But because the group had been delayed, his unit had left the immediate area before Natsir and his companions came out of the jungle.

[23] Natsir's letter to Taher Karim Lubis, Padang Sidempuan, October 15, 1961. In this letter he noted that several months previously Dahlan Djambek's elder brother, Gafar Djambek, had "disappeared" while being held in this jail and they did not know whether he was dead or alive.

Imprisonment

The president's order of August 17 had granted the rebels "amnesty and pardon,"[24] but despite this declaration the government kept Natsir and the other civilian politicians, as well as many of the military leaders, under house arrest or in jail for several years. After being flown to Jakarta, Natsir was kept in detention either there or in the hilly region (*puncak*) near Bogor before being sent by rail, together with Ummi, to East Java. There they were quarantined in a bungalow at Kota Batu south of Malang for more than a year.[25] Then on September 9, 1963, the government separated Natsir from his wife and transferred him to the Jakarta military prison (RTM, Rumah Tahanan Militer), the same jail where his fellow rebels Husein, Sumual, Simbolon, and Zulkifli Lubis were being held.

During his time in detention, Natsir continued writing, with his children carrying his essays and articles to his friends in Jakarta. Some of these pieces were later gathered into a short publication, *Dibawah Naungan Risalah*, which was brought out several years later.[26] In these essays, Natsir examines the reactions of the Prophet Mohammad to the behavior of those around him, both friends and enemies, and how through his words and teachings the Prophet was able to raise the community to a new and higher stage of development. In these pieces Natsir is clearly seeking the relevance of this history to the situation he and his colleagues were facing in Indonesia, examining the role that *da'wah* (missionary activity) could play in improving the society around them. He concludes:

> "*Da'wah* means moving the community (*ummat*) from one state to another."
> Moving the community from a situation of atheism (*kekufuran*) to one of
> belief (*keimanan*). For this reason, *da'wah* has the meaning of cultivating the
> individual, cultivating the community and developing the society. *Da'wah*
> is an effort to change a negative into a positive situation. A deliverer of

---

[24] Keputusan Presiden Republik No 449 Tahun 1961, August 17, 1961, states: "1) With the granting of amnesty, all criminal measures against the people concerned in sections 1 & 2 [which spell out the rebels involved] are erased; and 2) with the granting of pardon all procedures are canceled against these people." See Audrey Kahin, *Rebellion to Integration*, pp. 341–2.

[25] According to the Natsir children's account, Ummi soon fell sick, and Natsir and she were allowed to return to Jakarta for a time while Ummi underwent an appendicitis operation. They were also allowed to return briefly when Natsir's mother died. *Aba*, pp. 60–2; interview, Jakarta, January 20, 2004.

[26] M. Natsir, *Dibawah Naungan Risalah* [In the form of (lit, under the aegis or shelter of) a letter] (Jakarta: Sinar Hudaya & Documenta, 1971).

da'wah or a *Da'i* is a person who believes in an idea that he conveys through sermons, daily discussions, even through his charitable activities, either personal or social, by every *da'wah* path he can pursue.[27]

According to Natsir, he himself underwent no serious interrogations during his detention, just one pro-forma meeting in the office of the attorney general. He was allowed to have books, write, and occasionally receive newspapers, and he joined the other prisoners every week in a big hall where their families visited them and brought them food and clothing.[28] But he was apparently granted no special concessions. One of his daughters, Aisha Faridah Natsir, recalled that when her elder sister was getting married in 1964, her mother and other members of the family kept asking the attorney general for permission for her father to attend the wedding. Aisha was told to go to the jail on the wedding day, and when she got there she found her father sitting in his cell, weeping. He had been denied permission to be present at the ceremony. "It was the only time I ever saw him cry."[29]

In 1960 Soekarno had banned both the Socialist Party (PSI) and the Masjumi because of their alleged support of the PRRI rebellion. Two years later, on January 7, 1962, the president was the target of another assassination attempt, this time in Makassar, when a grenade was thrown at his car. Although he was not hurt three others were killed.[30] Again, suspicion immediately fell on the Masjumi and PSI leaders, and there were rumors that plans for the assassination attempt had been hatched at a meeting in Bali the previous August, when several of these politicians had attended the cremation ceremony of Anak Agung's father, the Raja of Gianyar.[31] So on January 16, 1962 Prawoto Mangkusasmito, Isa Anshari, Mohamad Roem and other Masjumi leaders, none of whom had been involved in the PRRI rebellion, were arrested, along with Sjahrir, Subadio Sastrosatomo and Anak Agung of the PSI and other Jakarta

---

[27] Ibid., p. 59. It seems likely, however, that this conclusion was written shortly before the essays were published, rather than while he was in detention, for it is clearly relevant to the foundation of the Dewan Da'wah (see Chapter 8).

[28] Natsir interview, Jakarta, February 24, 1971. He noted that, in contrast to the other prisoners Zulkifli Lubis was kept in solitary confinement in a windowless cell. For Sjafruddin's account, see Ajip Rosidi, *Sjafruddin Prawiranegara: Lebih Takut kepada Allah SWT* (Jakarta: Inti Idayu Press, 1986), pp. 222–3, also p. 237 for the prisoners' release from jail.

[29] Interview with Aisha Faridah Natsir and her siblings, Jakarta, January 20, 2004.

[30] Rudolf Mrazek, *Sjahrir: Politics and Exile in Indonesia* (Ithaca: Cornell Southeast Asia Program, 1994), p. 463.

[31] Ibid., pp. 461–2.

politicians.[32] When Natsir was brought to Jakarta many of these friends and colleagues were already in the same military jail that housed the PRRI rebels. Natsir's old Masjumi colleague, Prawoto Mangkusasmito, who had been transferred there from Madiun, shared Natsir's cell.

In early September 1965, Natsir was transferred from the political prisoners' section to the more securely guarded military section and his family, together with those of the other prisoners, was no longer allowed to visit. Shortly thereafter Jakarta was shaken by the coup that transformed the political order in Indonesia and the lives of all Indonesians, including Natsir and his fellow detainees.

Transition to the New Order

Soekarno's rule essentially came to an end on the night of September 30, 1965, when a group of military officers, calling themselves the "September 30 Movement" (Gerakan Tiga Puluh September) and headed by Lt. Col. Untung, a battalion commander in President Soekarno's Palace Guard (Cakrabirawa), kidnapped and murdered six of Indonesia's top military leaders whom they accused of belonging to a "Council of Generals" that was planning to carry out a "counter-revolutionary coup" against the Soekarno government.[33] The kidnapped officers were transported to Halim air base, where those who were still alive were killed and all were buried. Early on the morning of October 1, Col. Untung made a radio broadcast to the nation from Halim declaring that his movement had acted to protect Soekarno from the threat posed by the Council of Generals. He gave no indication that the president had backed their actions, but that afternoon a statement was issued from Halim air base in Soekarno's name, declaring that he was safe and that the leadership of the army was directly in his hands. He appointed General Pranoto Reksosamudro to a position of temporary leadership of the army.

By the evening of October 1, however, General Suharto, head of the Army's Strategic Reserve Command (Kostrad), had mustered his forces to crush the Untung group, and his soldiers had seized their few footholds in or near Jakarta,

---

[32] Leon Salim, *Bung Sjahrir: Pahlawan Nasional* (Medan: Masadepan, 1966), p. 73. Sjahrir fell ill in jail in 1962 and suffered a series of strokes in the next two years, dying in 1966, after he had finally been allowed to seek medical treatment in Switzerland in July 1965.

[33] "Statements of the September 30th Movement: Initial Statement of Lieutenant Colonel Untung," broadcast at approximately 7.15 a.m. on the morning of October 1, 1965, *Indonesia* (April 1966): 134. The original texts appeared in *Antara* (*Warta Berita*), October 1, and *Harian Rakjat*, October 2, 1965.

including the broadcasting station and Halim air base. (Soekarno by that time had driven to his palace at Bogor.) Almost immediately General Suharto and his supporters began to accuse the Communist Party of responsibility for the attempted coup and the murder of the generals. Over the next months they launched a campaign to exterminate the PKI and its adherents throughout the archipelago while gradually easing Soekarno from power.

These events marked yet another major upheaval not only in the life of the Indonesian nation but also in that of Natsir himself. Throughout his adult life, his stormy relations with Soekarno had largely determined the course of his career, both in and outside government. During the first years of the Soekarno regime he had stood in the forefront of the Republic's leadership, and enjoyed a favored relationship with the president, but, as the two gradually became alienated over the path along which Soekarno was leading the country, Natsir was ultimately pushed into rebellion and eventually jail. He had seen no alternative to violent opposition to the Soekarno regime, which he perceived as violating his political and religious values. Now that a new regime was coming to power he was bound to hope that this course would be reversed.

8

Return to the Jakarta Political Scene

The New Regime

After Suharto crushed the Untung group, Soekarno spent months trying to shore up his power and protect the Communist Party from the pogrom that had been unleashed against it, but he was out-maneuvered by Suharto. On March 11, 1966, Soekarno was compelled to delegate to General Suharto the authority "to take all necessary steps to guarantee security and calm and the stability of the running of the government and the course of the Revolution." Though he officially continued to hold the titles of president and prime minister, Soekarno's authority was steadily eroded over the next year until he was ultimately persuaded to surrender his administrative powers to Suharto in February 1967. A year later, in March 1968, the MPRS proclaimed Suharto president. Subsequently, Soekarno was held under house arrest for more than two years, until his death, on June 22, 1970, at the age of 69.[1]

Natsir was initially relieved at Soekarno's fall from power and the defeat of the Untung movement. Along with most other Muslim politicians, he hoped that the Suharto government would reverse the increasingly authoritarian actions of its predecessor. But for several months after the coup the new military authorities continued to keep Natsir and his fellows in detention. Only in February 1966, were they transferred from prison to a detention house in Jakarta and five months after that were allowed to return to their homes, though still confined to Jakarta. This delay was the first indication of any antipathy

---

[1] John Legge, *Sukarno: A Political Biography* [1972] (Singapore: Archipelago Press, 2003), pp. 451–8.

154

toward them on the part of the new regime. As Robert Hefner has written, "it was no secret that the effort [to release them] had been impeded by opposition from high-ranking members of the military."[2] Finally, in July of 1967 they were granted complete freedom.[3]

Their release was delayed despite the fact that, while still in jail, Natsir had already been of assistance to Suharto's "New Order" government. At that time Indonesia was still in a state of "confrontation" with Malaysia.[4] Even after the fall of Soekarno, Malaysia's prime minister, Tunku Abdul Rahman, continued to regard Indonesia as an enemy and refused even to meet with General Suharto's emissary, Brigadier General Sofyar. In doing so, the Malaysian premier ignored the advice of Tan Sri Ghazali Shafi, an influential minister in his cabinet who had close ties to some of the Indonesian military leaders and had long been attempting to broker an agreement between the two countries. Faced with Kuala Lumpur's adamant stand, some of Suharto's advisers turned to Natsir, who wrote a letter to the Malaysian prime minister, whom he knew well, urging him to receive an envoy from General Suharto in an effort to normalize Indonesian-Malaysian relations. Because of his respect for Natsir, Tunku Abdul Rahman acceded to his request and received the envoy.[5] Shortly thereafter, in May 1966, negotiations began between Kuala Lumpur and Jakarta and relations were normalized in August of that year.

Nevertheless, the new regime disregarded Natsir's assistance in smoothing the path to renewed relations with Malaysia and consistently blocked his efforts to return to political life. Suharto adopted as strong a stand against him and his Masjumi party (and also against the Socialist Party [PSI]) as had his predecessor, Soekarno.

The new government's attitude came as a severe blow not only to Natsir but also to other Masjumi leaders who had hoped that they and their party would be rehabilitated "on the assumption that they were the very people who had resisted Soekarno's Guided Democracy,"[6] and had shared with the new regime a common enemy in the Indonesian Communist Party (PKI).

---

[2] Robert W. Hefner, *Civil Islam* (Princeton, NJ: Princeton University Press, 2000), p. 97.

[3] Natsir interview, Jakarta, February 24, 1971.

[4] Indonesia's policy of "confrontation," inaugurated in 1963, was an expression of Jakarta's opposition to the British creation of the Federation of Malaysia through uniting its former colonies of Sarawak and North Borneo with Malaya and Singapore.

[5] Natsir interview, Jakarta, January 18, 1971, and with Natsir's children, January 20, 2004; Deliar Noer, "Kedudukan Natsir Masa Kini," *Panji Masyarakat* 691 (August 1–20, 1991): 26.

[6] B.J. Boland, *The Struggle of Islam in Modern Indonesia* (The Hague: Martinus Nijhoff, 1971), p. 151.

Natsir and his wife Ummi (to his R) return to West Sumatra, June 15, 1968.

Realignment of Muslim Politics

For several years after the advent of the Suharto regime, the Masjumi leaders were not willing to accept their continued exclusion from political activity. They set up a Committee for the Rehabilitation of Masjumi in 1966, which established contacts with some key generals, as well as with Suharto's close adviser, Colonel Ali Moertopo. They were joined by a number of other organizations also expressing support for the rehabilitation of both the Masjumi and the PSI. The government, however, rejected these pleas and the Army's regional commanders issued a statement in December 1966, which made clear their enmity toward the Muslim party. It coupled the Masjumi with the PKI as "having once deviated from the 1945 Constitution,"[7] labeling it "extreme right" as against the "extreme left" PKI.[8] Acting as spokesman for the Masjumi, Prawoto Mangkusasmito protested the commanders' statements and pleaded

---

[7] K.E. Ward, *The Foundation of the Partai Muslimin Indonesia* (Ithaca: Cornell Modern Indonesia Project, 1970), pp. 23–5.

[8] Deliar Noer, *Aku Bagian Ummat Aku Bagian Bangsa: Otobiografi* (Bandung: Penerbit Mizan, 1996), p. 600. According to Ken Ward, district army officers "were inclined to view PKI and Masjumi as equally subversive." Ken Ward, *The 1971 Election in Indonesia.* Monash Papers on Southeast Asia – Number Two (Victoria, Australia: Monash University, 1974), p. 117.

directly to Suharto to disavow them, as they could be "misused by elements who wish to fish in troubled waters and thereby seriously endanger the consolidation of the New Order."[9] Suharto's response was unequivocal. He declared that the soldiers and their families who had suffered in quelling the PRRI and Darul Islam rebellions would be completely unwilling to see the Masjumi return, and that "Juridical, constitutional and psychological considerations have brought the Armed Forces [ABRI, Angkatan Bersenjata Republik Indonesia] to one viewpoint, that is, that the party cannot be rehabilitated."[10]

Thus, by mid-1967 it was obvious that there was little hope of resurrecting the Masjumi as such, but it was not yet certain that another reformist Muslim party could not be established espousing the same principles. At that time Natsir was still waiting for the government to indicate whether it would agree to such a party being formed under the tentative name of Pamusi (Partai Muslimini Indonesia). He and his colleagues had submitted a list of proposed leaders to the government, "as well as its platform, but permission to establish it has still not been granted."[11]

By then, however, Natsir was coming to the realization that, whether or not the new government allowed another reformist Muslim party to be established, he would not be permitted to head it. In addition to the stigma of his open participation in the PRRI rebellion, he recognized that there was widespread suspicion in government and particularly military circles of the Masjumi party under his leadership during the 1950s. During that decade, he acknowledged, the government had increasingly viewed the Masjumi as a radical Islamic party: "The trouble was that the [Masjumi] party leadership was beset by pressures from two sides": on the government side, there was a widespread perception that the Masjumi leaders maintained close ties with the Darul Islam, which had drawn much of its membership from Masjumi ranks; on the other side, the Darul Islam was similarly convinced that the Masjumi leadership's moderate stance regarding an Islamic state was merely "tactical expediency" and that the party actually supported this goal. Natsir maintained that the Masjumi had not harbored plans to impose an Islamic state, and, regretting speeches made a decade earlier by such extremist members of the party as Isa Anshari, stated: "This time there must be an effort made to ensure that extremist leaders in the

---

[9] Ward, *Foundation*, p. 26. See also Hefner, *Civil Islam*, p. 98.

[10] Ward, *Foundation*, p. 26.

[11] Natsir interview, Jakarta, June 24, 1967. Former Vice President Hatta was also trying at the time to establish his own political party based on Muslim principles, the Partai Demokrasi Islam Indonesia (PDII), but, with the excuse of the need to "simplify" the parties, Suharto forbade its formation as well.

Natsir and Mohamad Roem.

party do not make radical statements on this subject at variance with those held by the central leadership."[12] He was aware that suspicion stemming from the 1950s clouded the possibility of any Masjumi leaders playing a meaningful future political role in Suharto's Indonesia.

Nevertheless, some of the Muslim leaders were still confident that the government would countenance formation of a new modernist Islamic party, and they held a meeting on May 7, 1967 in which they declared their intention to establish the Partai Muslimin Indonesia (PMI, later Parmusi), and formed a "Committee of Seven" to implement their decision. Leaders of the committee wrote to Suharto to inform him of their move. Recognizing that no Masjumi leaders who had participated in the PRRI rebellion would be acceptable to Suharto, they suggested that former foreign minister Mohamad Roem and Faqih Usman, both respected party leaders from the 1940s and 1950s who had not joined the rebellion, could head the new party. Initially army circles objected principally to Mohamad Roem and his name was dropped.

Extensive discussions continued over months between members of the Committee of Seven and government representatives, during which Suharto made it even clearer that he would not countenance the PMI emerging as

---

[12] Natsir interview, Jakarta, May 19, 1967.

"Masjumi in a new coat." To ensure that this did not occur, he stipulated that "for the time being no Masjumi leaders who had been prominent either in Djakarta or in regional branches at the time of Masjumi's dissolution could assume leadership of the Partai Muslimin Indonesia," thus definitively excluding such leaders as Roem.[13] Eventually all the government's wishes were met, and the Partai Muslimin Indonesia (PMI) was legalized on February 20, 1968, with a Muhammadiyah leader, Djarnawi Hadikusuma, at its head and no prominent Masjumi members among its central leadership. (Natsir himself resigned from any leadership position within the PMI on October 24, 1967.[14])

In contrast to the new military regime's antipathy toward the Masjumi, the Muhammadiyah had remained in the government's good graces so its leaders were acceptable as heads of the new Muslim party. Muhammadiyah had distanced itself from the Masjumi since 1958 when the PRRI rebellion broke out,[15] and when Soekarno banned the party in 1960, Muhammadiyah officially withdrew as a "corporate member," because any association with Masjumi could "endanger its [Muhammadiyah's] organizational independence and encumber the future development of modernist Islam." During the closing years of Guided Democracy, as Allan Samson has written:

> … the group that had led Muhammadijah out of Masjumi grew ever more powerful, benefiting from a political ambience in which Masjumi ties were an embarrassment and accommodation to secular organizations and institutions and to Sukarno seemed to be the sine qua non of survival. Muhammadijah, the rank and file were told, must act from its own imperatives as an autonomous entity within the Ummat Islam, sympathetic to Masjumi but impelled by different needs and ends.[16]

Thus, Muhammadiyah remained acceptable to Soekarno, and after his fall its cautious approach and desire not to antagonize non-Islamic groups ensured

---

[13] Ward, *Foundation of the Partai Muslimin Indonesia*, p. 36. Ward deals at length with these negotiations in ibid., pp. 30–9. In his monograph on the elections, Ward cites a radiogram from Kopkamtib [Komando Operasi Pemulihan Keamanan dan Ketertiban, Operation Command for the Restoration of Security and Order], which "stipulated several categories of members of dissolved parties who would be forbidden to stand: members who had held executive positions on the national or provincial councils, members with wide influence and those who were the 'brains of the party.'" Ward, *The 1971 Election*, p. 15.

[14] Boland, *Struggle of Islam*, p. 152.

[15] Deliar Noer, *Partai Islam di Pentas Nasional 1945–1965* (Jakarta: Grafiti, 1987), p. 372.

[16] Allan Samson, "Religious Belief and Political Action in Indonesian Islamic Modernism," in *Political Participation in Modern Indonesia*, ed. R. William Liddle (New Haven: Yale University Southeast Asia Studies, 1973), p. 133.

that in the early months of the New Order regime it was also acceptable to the military.

Shortly before agreeing to the legalization of the Partai Muslimin Indonesia, Suharto met with some of its supporting organizations, and spelled out his position on establishing a new Islamic party, stating:

> … in order to speed up the birth of this party, prominent Masjumi leaders, in the capital as well as in the regions, namely those who were the party leaders at the time of the dissolution of the party, should not appear now. They may lead from behind the scene. As for the future, if the party convenes its Congress and Masjumi leaders are elected, this is the internal affair of the party. It is a matter of the people's sovereignty. At such time I will not interfere. But now I am the one who is responsible.[17]

By this time there were two ill-defined factions within the Partai Muslimin, what Ward described as the "idealists," including most of the former Masjumi members, and the "realists," drawn in large part from other, less political Muslim organizations, most notably the Muhammadiyah. In considering the new party's future, the "idealists" focused on Suharto's use of the phrase "for the time being" in his speech, and his concession that the former Masjumi leaders could lead "from behind the scene," and that, after it held its congress, choice of the party's leadership would be an "internal affair." In light of these statements, they hoped that in a few months Suharto would lift the Masjumi prohibition.

On the eve of the Party Congress in November 1968, however, Suharto hardened his position, informing the PMI's Executive Board, made up almost completely of Muhammadiyah members, that any return of Masjumi leaders would have to await the outcome of the future general elections. The Executive Board was unwilling, or perhaps afraid to inform the rest of the party of Suharto's new stance, and the Party Congress enthusiastically elected a new leadership council, with Mohamad Roem again its General Chairman. In line with Suharto's warnings, the government refused to accept this new council, reiterating Suharto's recent statement that any transfer of leadership would have to await the holding of general elections, after which the party would be free to choose its own leaders. This option, however, was long delayed for elections did not take place until over two years later, in July 1971.

In preparing for the elections, the PMI drew up a list of candidates, among whom it again included former members of the Masjumi, who now began to

---

[17] Allan Samson, "Army and Islam in Indonesia," *Pacific Affairs* 44, 4 (Winter 1971–2): 553, citing a Report of the Committee of Seven to the PMI Executive Board Session in Jakarta, August 21, 1968, appearing in *Operasi*, November 25, 1968.

campaign in behalf of the new party. They were greeted with joy and excitement throughout the country. As Natsir described the situation:

> With the reappearance of the old party symbol there was an upsurge of enthusiasm on the part of not only people where the old infrastructure of Masjumi had been previously developed but also surprisingly in areas of East Java where Masjumi had previously not had branches.[18]

Allan Samson recalled a North Sumatran youth leader stating: "When Natsir or Prawoto come up here to speak, the devotion in which they are held by young and old alike is unbelievable. It's their names that make the PMI. No one else is comparable."[19]

The government, according to Natsir, then became "so alarmed at the response to the party" that it "set about to wreck the whole organization."[20] It instigated a split in the leadership of Partai Muslimin Indonesia, now generally known under the acronym of Parmusi. In early October 1970, it encouraged two of the party's leaders, John Naro and Ali Imran Kadir, to set up their own competing headquarters to the party's head, Djanarwi, who had by this time established a working relationship with the former Masjumi leaders. Suharto then announced that he was appointing a new party head, Muhammad Safaat Mintaredja, a Muhammadiyah member with no ties to the Masjumi, to "heal the split" within the party.[21] After the government had thus shaped and manipulated the leadership of Parmusi, inserting government loyalists at its head, the party lost much of its support.[22]

In the approach to the 1971 elections, the government's emasculation of Parmusi moved beyond its top leadership, and in March of that year names of known Masjumi supporters were removed from the party lists of candidates throughout the country, reflecting "ABRI's determination to separate the PMI from even the most tenuous identification with Masjumi, thereby ensuring that it would be easily manipulable."[23] By the time the elections were finally

---

[18] Natsir interview, Jakarta, January 18, 1971.

[19] Samson, "Army and Islam," pp. 554–5.

[20] Natsir interview, Jakarta, January 18, 1971.

[21] Natsir interviews, Jakarta, January 18, 23, 1971. On Mintaredja, see Ward, *The 1971 Election*, pp. 118–9, where he notes that Mintaredja directly attacked Natsir, Burhanuddin, and Sjafruddin for their PRRI involvement, arguing that they were "responsible for the disunity of the Islamic community."

[22] For Mohamad Roem's account of these machinations, see his *Bunga Rampai dari Sejarah Buku Keempat* (Jakarta: Bulan Bintang, 1988), pp. 38–40.

[23] Samson, "Army and Islam," p. 560. Ward spells out how the party electoral committee in Jakarta made sure that nominees from the districts [regencies] were distributed, for "otherwise the name of Mohammad Natsir would be first in every regency throughout Indonesia." Ward, *The 1971 Election*, pp. 115–6.

held, Parmusi's backing within the Muslim community had plummeted, and it came in as a weak fourth to Golkar, NU and the PNI, with under 6 per cent of the vote.[24]

Even before the elections Natsir expressed the opinion that it would be "quixotic" for him to try to play any further political role. After Mintaredja was appointed to head the Parmusi he thought there was no further scope for any useful political activity: "To compromise with such army interference and control would be a disappointment to former Masjumi supporters. Perhaps later, sometime after the elections things will change and there will be better possibilities for playing a political role again."[25]

The Renewal Movement

In the early years of the Suharto regime Natsir's influence among sections of the modernist Muslim community was less dominant than during the period before he joined the Sumatran rebels. Many Muslims in the modernist camp, especially members of the Muhammadiyah, did not feel the same ties of loyalty to Natsir and the other Masjumi leaders who had gone into rebellion as had been the case in the early 1950s. Some younger Masjumi members too were unwilling to accept their exclusion from a political role and influence within the New Order government of Indonesia because of the sins of their elders. These modernists openly embraced cooperation with the Suharto regime and accepted leadership positions within the Parmusi party. As bitterness arose within the Muslim community over the perceived lack of loyalty demonstrated by those former Masjumi members who now accepted government-sanctioned positions within the new Muslim party, Natsir acted as a moderating influence. He urged Masjumi adherents not to accuse those who entered the Parmusi of being motivated by personal ambition, writing:

> Stop, stop the dispute about joining or not joining [Parmusi]. In differences we must honor the right of each person to reason independently.... Only in this manner can we ensure that differences do not result in antipathy.[26]

As Samson perceived, in many ways the divisions within the modernist Muslim community in the post-1965 years reflected those that had existed

---

[24] It received 2,930,746 votes (out of nearly 54,700,000 cast), and gained 24 seats in the 351-member Parliament.

[25] Natsir interview, Jakarta, March 1, 1971.

[26] Mohammad Natsir, "Letter to the Djama'ah Bulan Bintang," in *Dari Medan Djihad* (Surabaya: S.U. Bajasut, 1968), pp. 78–82, cited in Samson "Religious Belief and Political Action," p. 124.

within the Masjumi ten years earlier. We have seen that, since its inception, the party had always been a loose alliance among Muslims with often-contradictory views, what Samson described as the fundamentalists, the reformists and the accommodationists.[27] A similar division still existed within the modernist Muslim community in the early years of the New Order, with the Muhammadiyah leaders who now headed the new Parmusi party clearly among the accommodationists. Most former Masjumi members could still be classified within the reformist faction, though frustration with the impediments consistently thrown in their way when they tried to influence the new political structure was pushing many of them toward the fundamentalist group.

A majority of these reformists belonged to what was often called the Keluarga [or Keluarga Besar] Bulan Bintang (Family [or Large Family] of the Crescent and Star), which saw Mohammad Natsir as its political and spiritual leader. Ties among its members were unusually close, involving long-standing friendships and family relationships, and also "a solidarity based on the spirit of Islamic reformism and the years of shared suffering during the period of Sukarno's Guided Democracy."[28] Most members of the "family" remained distinct from the fundamentalists who saw the struggle of the Muslim community (*perjuangan ummat Islam*) as one aimed at establishment of an Islamic state. Natsir and his fellows, rather, "interpret *perjuangan* [struggle] in a religio-political sense, as a striving to achieve an Islamic society (though not necessarily an Islamic state) and an influential role for Islamic parties."[29]

There was, however, another group within the reformist faction, drawn mostly from the younger generation, who, though unwilling to accept positions within the discredited Parmusi party, "sought to strike a balance between criticism and constructive engagement."[30] Members of this group had become impatient with the methods of their seniors, viewing the ideological struggles of the 1950s over such issues as the Jakarta Charter and creation of an Islamic state as no longer relevant under the New Order. Impatient with their elders' perceived adherence to these outmoded ideas, these young people chose to moderate their stance to adapt to the new political situation and seek a place for themselves and their ideas within the political constellation of the New Order. From this group sprang the ideas of the "Renewal Movement (Gerakan

---

[27] Samson, "Conception of Politics," p. 215.

[28] Ibid., p. 208. See also Bernhard Platzdasch, *Islamism in Indonesia: Politics in the Emerging Democracy* (Singapore: ISEAS, 2009), pp. 39–40.

[29] Samson, "Conception of Politics," p. 209.

[30] Hefner, *Civil Islam*, p. 113.

Pembaharuan)," which seized the initiative in providing a moral and intellectual basis for reformist Muslims to cooperate with the Suharto regime.

While generally tolerant toward the various and often contradictory stances within the modernist Islamic community, Natsir was, nevertheless, deeply disappointed by the attitude of many of these educated young people who had been his pupils and whom he had counted among his followers, yet who now headed up the new movement. He saw their actions as springing from a "desire to disengage themselves 'from Islamic ideals, creed and community.'"[31] The Renewal Movement included several members of the Muslim Students' Organization HMI (Himpunan Mahasiswa Islam), which in earlier years had been closely allied to the Masjumi party. In the closing years of Soekarno's rule, in contrast to the majority of the Muhammadiyah who had accommodated with Guided Democracy, members of the HMI had formed common cause with the opposition. They had made alliances with elements within the armed forces, and in 1965–6 had cooperated with Suharto and other military leaders in the demonstrations that led to the overthrow of the Old Order. Once Suharto came to power they allied with the new regime and continued to support it even when it became clear that the government was not fulfilling most of the hopes they had entertained at its inception. In the words of Martin van Bruinessen, these educated young people

> created a new liberal Muslim discourse that was highly compatible with the depoliticization of Islam considered necessary by Suharto's advisers.... Throughout the New Order period, these people received much favourable press coverage, giving them a disproportionate influence, whereas Muslim thinkers and politicians of a less accommodating approach were virtually ignored.[32]

The foremost leader of this renewal movement was Nurcholish Madjid, who was General Chairman of the HMI from 1966 to 1971. Born into a strongly Islamic family in Jombang, East Java,[33] Madjid was an intelligent young man, who had received a religious education in the Gontor *pesantren* and at the State Institute of Islam in Jakarta and was later to receive his doctorate at the University of Chicago. During the final months of Guided Democracy,

---

[31] Muhammad Kamal Hassan, *Muslim Intellectual Responses to "New Order" Modernization in Indonesia* (Kuala Lumpur: Dewan Bahasa dan Pustaka, 1980), p. 121.

[32] Martin van Bruinessen, "Genealogies of Islamic radicalism in post-Suharto Indonesia," *South East Asia Research* 10, 2 (July 2002): 124.

[33] His family was NU, but his father had remained with the Masjumi at the time of the 1952 split.

he was one of the members of HMI who worked with the military in the demonstrations leading to the President Soekarno's overthrow. In the early years of the New Order, many Muslims saw Madjid as the "new Mohammad Natsir," and Natsir himself viewed him "like my own son."[34]

During the mid- and late 1960s Madjid's arguments regarding religion and politics seemed to mirror those of Natsir, as both tried to harmonize an appreciation of modern science and technology with their Islamic beliefs. In their acceptance of the *Pancasila*, both contended that modernization in Indonesia should build on the twin bases of religion and what Madjid termed "rationalization," which relates to concrete and material matters. According to Madjid, modernization should consist of: "rationalization supported by moral dimensions arising from the principal basis of faith in the One Supreme God [the first principle of *Pantja Sila*]."[35] He saw this first principle as not only underlying but also giving meaning to the rest of the *Pancasila* principles, i.e. nationalism, democracy, humanitarianism and social welfare. Like Natsir, Madjid in 1968 argued that modernization did not mean Westernization or secularism, and both men, while praising the idea of individual freedom, did not extend this to "unbridled freedom," because they recognized the "potentially disastrous social consequences" of allowing freedom free rein. Madjid contended that "Islam upholds individual freedom but teaches that freedom is limited by the freedom of other individuals."[36]

As the 1960s drew to an end, however, it became clear that the stance of the old Masjumi leadership was not helping the Muslim community adapt to the current situation and was impeding the younger Muslim generation's participation in the new government's efforts toward national reconstruction and modernization. Madjid, then, along with other young Muslim intellectuals, began to tailor his views to the new political situation. In 1964 in the closing years of Guided Democracy the army had established a "Joint Secretariat of Functional Groups" (Sekber Golkar) to counter Communist influence within the Soekarno government.[37] The Himpunan Mahasiswa Islam (HMI), now under Madjid's chairmanship, had always been one of Golkar's component organizations. Increasingly Madjid, along with many other younger members of

---

[34] "Revolusi Nurcholis Madjid," *Tempo*, July 29, 1972, pp. 46–7; Hassan, *Muslim Intellectual Responses*, p. 120.

[35] Nurcholish Madjid, *Modernisasi Adalah Rationalisasi Bukan Westernisasi* (Bandung: Mimbar Demokrasi, 1968), cited in Hassan, *Muslim Intellectual Responses*, p. 25.

[36] Ibid., p. 26.

[37] Sekber Golkar = Sekretariat Bersama Golongan Karya [Joint Secretariat of Functional Groups].

HMI, began to distance himself from the older generation of modernist Muslim leaders and embrace the principles of Golkar, which the Suharto government was now shaping into its prime political instrument. In a conversation with the Malaysian scholar, Muhammad Kamal Hassan, in 1972, Natsir recalled asking Madjid about what HMI's attitude would be toward Golkar in the run-up to the 1971 elections. Madjid responded that HMI would remain in Golkar because, if it left, many of its alumni in the provincial legislative assemblies would have to leave their posts and thus lose HMI influence.

> Natsir inquired as to how HMI leaders would explain its attitude to the *ummat* because the latter expected it to promote its cause, not the secular groups'. Madjid replied that at the time of the elections, HMI would issue instructions to its members to quit Golkar. Natsir said that such political ethics reminded him of Machiavelli and he did not expect HMI to display such traits.[38]

Madjid was clearly restless under the restrictions he felt had been imposed on young educated Muslims by the old Masjumi leadership whom he now viewed as unnecessarily narrow in interpreting Islamic teachings, and he began to seek "a middle ground between Islamic piety and the exigencies of modern life."[39] Believing that the strategy of modernist leaders such as Natsir had left Muslims "unprepared to compete with more modernized groups in Indonesian society,"[40] Madjid issued an open challenge to the former Masjumi in January 1970 with the publication of his paper, "The Necessity of Renewing Islamic Thought and the Problem of the Integration of the *Ummat*,"[41] wherein he proposed "liberating the *ummat* from 'traditional values' in favor of 'future-oriented' values." He advocated adopting "secularization, the promotion of intellectual freedom, the pursuit of the 'idea of progress' and the cultivation of open attitudes," contending that: "Islam is essentially a personal religion ... that ... provides a place for the secularization required for Indonesian modernization."[42] Such a position ran directly counter to the beliefs that Natsir had held since

---

[38] Hassan, *Muslim Intellectual Responses*, p. 121.

[39] Robert Pringle, *Understanding Islam in Indonesia: Politics and Diversity* (Honolulu: University of Hawaii Press, 2010), p. 102.

[40] Hefner, *Civil Islam*, p. 117.

[41] "Keharusan Pembaharuan Pemikiran Islam dan Masalah Integrasi Ummat," in *Pembaharuan Pemikiran Islam*, ed. Utomo Danandjaja (Jakarta: Islamic Research Centre, 1970), pp. 1–12. An English translation appears as Appendix A in Hassan, *Muslim Intellectual Responses*, pp. 188–98.

[42] Hassan, *Muslim Intellectual Responses*, p. xi. See also "Pembaharu '70 pada sebuah Tebing," *Tempo*, July 29, 1972, pp. 44–9.

the 1930s, namely that Islam was "a philosophy of life, an ideology, a system of living,"[43] a belief that was expounded by the Muslim newspaper *Abadi*:

> Islam embraces the spiritual *and* the material; it does not separate the two. Islam is a system of beliefs and a set of principles which regulate all aspects of life — man's relationship with God, his fellow men, and nature.[44]

The positions Madjid laid out in his 1970 paper and in the other articles he wrote spelling out the principles of his "Renewal Movement" can be viewed either as an effort to make religion "a force in public life without degenerating into the simplistic idealizations of the 1950s," as contended by Robert Hefner,[45] or as a plea to his fellow Muslims "for an intellectual adjustment and acceptance of the secularist socio-political *status quo*," as the Malaysian writer Muhammad Kamal Hassan, described it.[46] Either way, Golkar was able to make use of these "Renewal" ideas, which were congruent with its own political perspective.[47]

The disagreements of Natsir and the older Masjumi generation with Madjid and other leaders of the Renewal Movement were reminiscent of polemics carried out in the late years of colonial rule regarding Islam's place in the state. It has frequently been noted that the Suharto regime's policy regarding Islam's place in Indonesia's political life resembled that advocated by Snouck Hurgronje, namely that Islam should be excluded from politics while being fostered in the social and cultural fields. This too appears to have been the stance of Madjid and his followers, who argued strongly against the idea of any political party being founded on religion and advocated the "compartmentalization of religious belief from political affairs."[48] The question as to whether Islam was an individual matter or provided a guide and basis for ordering society and the state had also been the nub of Natsir's disagreements with Soekarno in the 1930s.

Formation of the Dewan Da'wah Islamiyah Indonesia

Within a year of his release from detention, when Natsir had been forced into awareness that the government would not allow him to resume his place as a Muslim political leader, he began to search for the future path he should

---

[43] Samson, "Conception of Politics," p. 214.

[44] *Abadi*, May 5, 1970, cited in Hassan, *Muslim Intellectual Responses*, p. 5.

[45] See Hefner, *Civil Islam*, p. 116. For an extensive treatment and defense of Madjid's stance and arguments, see ibid., pp. 115–9.

[46] Hassan, *Muslim Intellectual Responses*, p. 114.

[47] Ibid., pp. 89–99.

[48] Samson, "Conception of Politics," pp. 225–6.

follow. In our interview with him in May 1967 he revealed something of the direction in which his mind was turning. Since the 1930s, Natsir had always enjoyed friendly relations with Christians of all stripes and had been able to cooperate with them both when he held positions in government and when he was in rebellion. But ever since his schooldays in Bandung in the early 1930s, and even during his childhood in West Sumatra, when he had witnessed Dutch efforts to use education to convert their Indonesian pupils to Christianity, he had harbored deep suspicions of Christian missionaries, especially when they were proselytizing in actual or nominal Muslim areas.

Viewing the situation in Indonesia in the aftermath of Soekarno's overthrow and the subsequent massacres of communists and their alleged sympathizers in 1965-66, especially in central and east Java, Natsir expressed his consciousness of the "great bitterness that must have been engendered" among former PKI members and their relatives and "the political dangers in the long run arising from this." He recognized that many of those targeted because of their ties to the Communist Party were "not logically communist but for a variety of reasons members of mass organizations," and he viewed them still as part of the Muslim community. He saw that Christian groups — both members of the World Council of Churches and the Catholics — were putting considerable effort into winning support and conversions among these needy people by bringing them medicine and food, something that the Muslim community should have been doing. He criticized Muslim organizations for not fulfilling this role, complaining that "the Muhammadiyah should be the logical instrument for working with the people in the formerly strongly PKI areas of Java, but its leaders show no inclination to do this." He said that he had discussed the problem with the State Secretary, General Alamsjah Ratuprawiranegara, who generally acted as liaison between the Suharto regime and the Muslim politicians, and urged him to give Masjumi leaders a chance to work among the former communists. Alamsjah, however, rejected the plea, accusing Natsir of "just trying to rehabilitate the Masjumi as a party."[49]

Worries about these Christian conversions were clearly among the principal motivations behind Natsir's founding of the Dewan Da'wah Islamiyah Indonesia (DDII, Islamic Propagation Council of Indonesia) on May 9, 1967. But it was also tied to his frustration at all political paths being blocked to him. According to one account, he acknowledged his strategy openly, saying: "Before we used politics as a way to preach, now we are using preaching as a way to engage in politics."[50]

---

[49] Natsir interview, Jakarta, May 19, 1967.

[50] "Dulu berdakwah lewat jalur politik, sekarang berpolitik lewat jalur dakwah," ICG Report No. 83, September 13, 2002, citing Lukman Hakiem and Tansil Linrung, "Menunaikan

The government, too, was conscious of the Christian-Muslim tensions stemming from the conversion of many former PKI adherents to Christianity, and on November 30, 1967 it convened an Inter-Religious Consultation in Jakarta in an attempt to smooth relationships among the religious communities. Two days before the Consultation, a few of the top religious leaders met in closed session, and Natsir and A.M. Tambunan, one of the foremost leaders of the Protestant Christian faction, apparently came to an agreement regarding the ground rules for missionary activity that both sides should observe. At the open meeting, Tambunan praised the understanding Natsir had displayed regarding the duty of Christians to obey Christ's injunction for his followers to spread the gospel throughout the world. Following the Protestant leader's speech, however, Natsir laid down the limitations of this understanding, stating that he realized that religions "of the book" have to proselytize their own religion, but, in so doing, both Muslims and Christians have to respect each other's faith and concentrate on preaching to those without faith: "So recognize that we are not a heathen or animistic group. We are people who already embrace religion, the Islamic religion. Do not make us a target for your Christianization activities." A few years later, in 1973, Natsir further spelled out his views of Christian-Islam relations in Indonesia, writing:

> Thus in Indonesia we have close ties of friendship between many Christians and many Muslims, both in the struggle to achieve independence and now after independence. And I myself have many such friends. But the situation is different when a Muslim individual or the Muslim community feels, or even sees the reality, that their religion has become a target for sabotage by Christians or other religions.[51]

Nevertheless, Natsir drew hope from the history of Protestant-Catholic hostility, noting that after centuries of antagonism the two groups no longer strove to impose their brand of Christianity on each other, and asked: "Why could not this development also take place in the relationship between Muslims and Christians?"[52]

This attitude is in line with the advice he gave in the early 1970s to Anwar Ibrahim, at the time a Muslim youth leader in Malaysia. According to Anwar:

Panggilan Risalah: Dokumentasi Perjalan 30 Tahun DDII," Jakarta, 1997. However, even while he was under detention, his writings reveal that he was already thinking about the role of *da'wah* in Indonesian society. See Chapter 7, pp. 150–1.

[51] Mohammad Natsir, "Kerukunan Hidup antar Agama," in *Dari Masa ke Masa* 1 (Jakarta: Fajar Shadiq, 1974), pp. 24–35, esp. p. 26.

[52] Yusuf Abdullah Puar, *Muhammad Natsir: 70 Tahun Kenang-kenangan Kehidupan dan Perjuangan* (Jakarta: Pustaka Antara, 1978), pp. 282–6; Boland, *Struggle of Islam*, p. 236.

> When I formed Angkatan Belia Islam Malaysia [ABIM, Body to Defend
> Malaysian Islam] he [Natsir] always reminded me of the social reality in
> Malaysia, and the substantial presence there of Chinese, Indians and others.
> He was very positive and always encouraged interaction and dialogue between
> Islamic organization and non-Muslim society.[53]

At the end of the Jakarta conference a draft joint declaration was prepared,
but the various groups could not agree on its final wording and both Protestants and Catholics rejected it.[54] In the view of the Muslim participants, the
Christians "refused to accept the formula that one religious community should
not address its propaganda to adherents of another religious community."[55] So
instead of bringing the religious groups together, the conference ended with
their further alienation.

In large part, the disagreement between Christians and Muslims stemmed
from their conflicting views of what constituted the Islamic community in
Indonesia. Natsir and most other Muslim leaders believed that Indonesia was
a 90 per cent Muslim country and they saw all nominal Muslims, particularly
those in Java known as *abangan*, as part of the Muslim *ummat*. Others,
including the Christian groups, saw these Javanese not as part of the devout
or *santri* community, but as syncretists, blending their Islam with elements of
Hinduism, Buddhism and animism.[56] As such, they were, in missionary eyes,
candidates for conversion to Christianity.

When he founded the Dewan Da'wah Natsir did not see it as a movement
to carry out missionary activities among Indonesians of other faiths, but as
one that would strengthen and educate members of the Muslim community
who were apathetic or ignorant of their own religion. In his "Ethical Code of
the Da'wah Islam" published in 1975, he spelled out the duty of the group's
members to practice tolerance and not to attempt to convert people from other

---

[53] Anwar Ibrahim continued that when he became finance minister in Malaysia, he always
repeated Mohammad Natsir's message "that we should not build while destroying …
develop industry while oppressing workers, develop the infrastructure while destroying
the environment." Anwar Ibrahim, "Natsir, Politikus Intelektual," in *Mohammad Natsir,
Berdakwah di Jalur Politik Berpolitik di Jalur Dakwah*, ed. Mohd. Asri Abdul, *et al.* (Selangor:
Lembaga Zakat Selangor, 2009), p. 28.

[54] Puar, *Muhammad Natsir*, pp. 287–8.

[55] Boland, *Struggle of Islam*, p. 237. For a translation of one of Natsir's most important
speeches in 1967 on the subject of Christian-Muslim relations, see "The Code of Religious
Tolerance," in *Voices of Islam in Southeast Asia*, ed. Greg Fealy and Virginia Hooker
(Singapore: ISEAS, 2006), pp. 433–5.

[56] The classic analysis of this group appears, of course, in Clifford Geertz, *The Religion of Java*
(Glencoe, Ill: Free Press, 1960).

religions.[57] He declared that God's decree was clear: that people of different faiths should live together not merely with passive but with positive tolerance toward one another:

> doing good and *behaving justly*, toward one another, we the Islamic community, are instructed that religious differences should *not* obstruct us ... but we should behave toward the Human Community without discrimination of religion and faith.... Even though the Islamic Community in one time and in one place form the majority, they *are forbidden* by the Ethical Code of Islam, to force their faith and religious conviction on the minority that has a faith other than Islam.[58]

With respect to the DDII's mission, Natsir laid particular stress on its educational and social aims and those of the *da'wah* movement in general. He concentrated on its role in education, where the council

> helped the building and equipping of libraries in mosques, universities and *da'wah* institutes. In an effort to standardize the curriculum of rural Islamic seminaries (*pesantrens*), it cooperated with a number of reformist-oriented *pesantren* associations in Java and other areas.[59]

The Dewan Da'wah also stressed its mission of improving medical care and hygiene, working closely with the Islamic Hospital Foundation in Jakarta (Jajasan Rumah Sakit Tinggi Islam [JARSI]) and founding hospitals in other areas, notably the Ibnu Sina Islamic Hospital in Bukittinggi.[60] B.J. Boland summarized Natsir's aims in establishing the Dewan Da'wah as they were laid out in one of his speeches:

(1) Methods and techniques must be evolved to make the *da'wa* work more effectively, e.g. by improving the training of the *da'is*.

---

[57] M.Natsir, "Isyhadu bi Anna Muslimun: Saksikanlah! Kami ini adalah Muslimin," in M. Natsir, *Dari Masa ke Masa* 3 (Jakarta: Yayasan Fajar Shadiq, 1975), pp. 25–32.

[58] Ibid., pp. 25–6, italics and capitalization as in the original. Natsir here is probably referring back to the Medina concordat, where the "religious and material rights of Jewish (and Christian) populations were formalized." Bernhard Platzdasch translates paragraph 25 of the concordat as: "To the Jews their religion and to the Muslims their religion," and notes: "The Medina concordat remains a significant symbol for Muslim unity in a pluralist society under the guidance of Islam." Platzdasch, *Islamism in Indonesia*, p. 23. Hefner contends, however, that the DDII "chose to work in regions where it competed directly with Christian missionaries" (Hefner, *Civil Islam*, p. 109), presumably areas inhabited by *abangan* communities.

[59] Hassan, *Muslim Intellectual Responses*, p. 71.

[60] Ibid., pp. 70–1.

(2) *Da'wa* must be intensified with tangible contributions in the socio-economic field, particularly for the relief of poverty.

(3) Close co-operation between traditional Islamic institutions such as *pesantrens* and *madrasas* must be achieved in order to raise the level of education.

(4) Co-operation must be stimulated between all kinds of Islamic institutions and organizations as well as between Muslims personally.[61]

With respect to the Council's educational aims, as with his Pendis school in Bandung in the 1930s, Natsir again saw a marriage between basic education, religious instruction and practical skills as the right path for training students. This was demonstrated in an "agricultural pesantren," which he supported, called *Darul Fallah* [house of the farmer] in Tjiampea, a village close to Bogor. The school had been opened in 1956 but closed during the final years of the Soekarno regime. Reopened in 1967, it had eighty pupils four years later, and offered five years of post-primary school education, stressing at the same time agricultural training.[62] Boland noted that the pupils, "young men about 14–20 years old receive the usual religious instruction as well as a training in cattle-breeding, poultry-keeping, the use of a small motor-plough, the use of a sickle for cutting rice, and so on."[63] Through this instruction, the school aimed to give the young people skills that would keep them in the villages rather than being forced to migrate to the towns without a job and ending up either unemployed or working as *becak* drivers. By 1971 Natsir thought that the school had achieved some very good results and he was thinking of establishing similar schools, perhaps in Bandung and in Payakumbuh in West Sumatra.[64]

At least during its early years when Natsir was by far its dominant influence, the Dewan Da'wah, while being active in the social and educational field, embraced what Martin van Bruinessen describes as "an unlikely combination of attitudes." In van Bruinessen's view, these included:

A belief in the superiority of Western-style democracy over the neo-patrimonial forms of rule adopted by both Sukarno and Suharto, an almost paranoid obsession with Christian missionary efforts as a threat to Islam, and an increasingly strong orientation towards the Middle East, notably Saudi Arabia.[65]

---

[61] Boland, *Struggle of Islam*, p. 194. A *da'i* is one who practices *da'wah*.

[62] Natsir interview, Jakarta, January 30, 1971.

[63] Boland, *Struggle of Islam*, p. 195. The school is still in existence, with one of Natsir's daughters active in its operations.

[64] Natsir, interview, Jakarta, January 30, 1971.

[65] van Bruinessen, "Genealogies of Islamic radicalism," p. 123.

These three preoccupations were equally dominant in Natsir's thinking and would remain so through the final decades of his life.

The Dewan Da'wah's "unlikely" embrace of democracy reflected Natsir's life-long fight against an authoritarian form of government and his contention that some sort of representative democracy was the system best suited to a diverse, extensive, multicultural country such as Indonesia. He never, however, actually embraced "Western" democracy as such, usually arguing for either "Islamic democracy" or some less clearly defined representative system, though he always believed in the need for a division of powers between the different branches of government and their duty to protect the rights of minorities. Discussing the role of the legislature in an interview in 1971, he gave some idea of how he perceived an Islamic democracy operating, stating: "the art of legislation in a country is to make Islamic principles as universal as possible, trying to make them apply to and acceptable to the non-Islamic part of the community."[66] As shown earlier, he often drew a line between liberal democracy (what both he and Soekarno criticized as 50 + 1 democracy) and Islamic democracy, but, as we have also seen, he rejected the distinctions that Soekarno and others drew between "Western" and "Eastern" democracy, asserting that there was only "democracy" and "no democracy." He never wavered in his allegiance to a form of government wherein its members were representative of the electorate and answerable to them. We will see that during the final phase of his life Natsir continued to adhere strongly to this principle, although, again, it would lead to further government restrictions against him personally.

I thus feel that Robert Hefner is being unfair when he denigrates Natsir's positions in this regard by stating: "Natsir himself *claimed* to be a supporter of democracy but qualified his endorsement by insisting that Islamic democracy differs from what he called liberal democracy [Emphasis added]."[67] Natsir did indeed make this distinction, but he was also explicit in defining what he considered the basic characteristics of the democracy he supported, where those in power responded and were responsible to the various peoples making up the society they governed, whatever their religion or ethnicity. If anything, his adherence to, arguments for, and defense of democracy strengthened during the last few years of his life.[68]

With respect to the two other characteristics of the Dewan Da'wah posited by van Bruinessen, we have seen how Natsir's childhood experiences with Christian missionaries in West Sumatra and Bandung and the conversions

---

[66] Interview with Natsir, February 24, 1971.
[67] Hefner, *Civil Islam*, p. 102.
[68] See Chapter 9.

in Java in the aftermath of the 1965 coup influenced Natsir's attitude toward missionary activity. This attitude he passed on to the organization he founded, though in the Dewan Da'wah it frequently appeared in much more extreme forms.

The "strong orientation toward the Middle East" only became manifest under the New Order, when Natsir's exclusion from the political scene in Indonesia led him to be more active in the international sphere. Although in his study of Islam during the 1930s, he had drawn on the work of Middle Eastern thinkers, he did not visit the area until after Indonesia achieved its independence. During the 1950s, he had developed close ties with scholars and rulers in the Arab world, especially with the king of Saudi Arabia, and enjoyed enormous respect in the region. After founding the Dewan Da'wah he and the organization grew ever more reliant on leaders and institutions in the Middle East for support of their activities.

Post-election Politics

The Suharto government's manipulation of the leadership of both the secular and religion-based political parties and the parties' subsequent failure in the 1971 elections was followed over the next two years by further pressure and the ultimate amalgamation in 1973 of the nine political parties into two omnibus parties. The new Indonesian Democratic Party (PDI) incorporated the major secular and Christian-based parties,[69] and the Partai Persatuan Pembangunan (PPP, United Development Party) incorporated the former Muslim parties.[70] All party activity was forbidden in the rural areas in the years between elections, though Golkar, not technically a party, was free to act and campaign throughout the country at all times.

Largely because of the government's actions, during the early 1970s the Muslim community was divided and frustrated. Nevertheless it was able to come together once more in 1973, as it had done in 1937, to mobilize against the regime's attempts to introduce a marriage law that most Muslims felt "would have thoroughly secularized Indonesian marriage law and effectively abolished much of the country's Islamic court system."[71] The government in this instance

---

[69] It incorporated the Partai Nasional Indonesia (PNI), Partai Katolik, Partai Kristen Indonesia (Parkindo), Murba and Ikatan Pendukung Kemerdekaan Indonesia (IPKI).
[70] Parmusi, NU, PSII and Perti.
[71] See Mark Cammack, "Indonesia's 1989 Religious Judicature Act: Islamization of Indonesia or Indonesianization of Islam?" *Indonesia* 63 (April 1997): 143–68, esp. p. 151. See ibid., pp. 151–2 for a description of the proposed act's provisions.

was forced to back down. (It is perhaps worth noting that a couple of years earlier, when discussions of the marriage law had stalled in Parliament, Natsir expressed the opinion that it would be "more sensible and realistic simply to settle for the existing laws rather than to try to give them a more Islamic cast against the wishes of Christians and abangans."[72])

By this time disillusionment with the New Order was growing among many of the young activists who had participated in the demonstrations that had helped bring Suharto to power and had been attempting to cooperate with the regime. In addition, Indonesians of many ages and classes were increasingly resentful of the foreign investors, who were financing the government's economic policies and contributing to the rampant corruption that was enriching many of the top generals and other close advisers around Suharto.

This resentment came to a head with the visit to Jakarta of Japanese premier Kakuei Tanaka in January 1974. Students mounted a series of protest demonstrations against the prime minister, which deteriorated into riots, with cars burned and shops looted. The army responded with force, killing about a dozen looters, arresting close to 500 demonstrators and ultimately bringing the riots to an end.

This so-called "Malari" incident (*Malapetaka Limabelas Januari*, January 15 Disaster) led to a government crackdown on students and the press.[73] The riots had been in part encouraged by elements within the leadership of the armed forces,[74] but the regime again laid major blame on adherents of the banned Masjumi and Socialist Party (PSI). Several former PSI members, together with some Muslim activists and student and human rights leaders, were arrested and held in jail for several months.[75] Subsequent to Malari, the government began to exert an even stronger grip on Indonesia's intellectual and political life, closing newspapers and clamping down on student activity on the university campuses, though they were unable to quell outbursts of dissatisfaction at some of the government's policies that seemed to threaten religion.

---

[72] Natsir interview, Jakarta, February 24, 1971.

[73] Among the newspapers banned were *Nusantara*, *Harian Kami*, *Indonesia Raya*, *Abadi*, *Jakarta Times* and *Pedoman*. See Hamish McDonald, *Suharto's Indonesia* (Victoria, Australia: Fontana/Collins, 1980), p. 138.

[74] General Soemitro, deputy commander of the armed forces and head of its internal security agency (Kopkamtib) was widely believed to have encouraged the students, and he was relieved of his Kopkamtib post and later resigned as deputy armed forces chief. See Adam Schwarz, *A Nation in Waiting: Indonesia in the 1990s* (Boulder: Westview Press, 1994), pp. 33–5, and Harold Crouch, *The Army and Politics in Indonesia*, rev. ed. (Ithaca: Cornell University Press, 1988), pp. 314–5.

[75] For a list of those arrested see, Crouch, *Army and Politics*, p. 316, n. 16.

Struggle over the Pancasila

Facing real and perceived threats from human rights advocates and especially Muslim radicals, the Suharto government embarked on a program aimed at undermining these challenges and ensuring that the government organization Golkar would continue to emerge successful in future elections. Starting in the mid-1970s it introduced a program that involved the "ideologization" of the *pancasila*, using the state ideology as a weapon against its critics, especially those in the Islamic community. It made strenuous efforts to instill its interpretation of the *pancasila* throughout the society, including government and non-government organizations, the educational system and eventually, in the early 1980s, the remaining political parties and religious organizations.

In the field of education, as part of its nationwide program to expand primary education to all children between the ages of 7 and 12, the government introduced into the schools a curriculum that incorporated "*pancasila* principles." In 1978 it formulated the "Guide to Realizing and Experiencing the *Pancasila* (Pedoman Penghayatan dan Pengalaman Pancasila, P4)" which promoted the values of "hierarchy, harmony, and order." These became a compulsory part of the curriculum at all levels of education, affecting, in particular, the teaching of such subjects as history, language and literature, and religious education. In introducing this program, the Department of Education brought out a textbook on "Moral Education" based on *pancasila* principles. Beginning in October 1980, this textbook was to be taught at all school levels.[76]

Natsir publicly and strenuously opposed these government attempts to introduce *pancasila* principles as part of the school curriculum. He saw them as an effort both to consolidate the government's power and to undermine monotheistic religions and introduce Javanese traditional beliefs in their place. He criticized in particular the textbook's portrayal of the *pancasila* as the basis of "moral education," and essence of the Indonesian people's "spirit, identity, world view, *pegangan hidup*, awareness, moral ideals, and so on."[77] If it were indeed the case that *pancasila* formed the basis of moral education, he asked, what role did religion play in the spiritual life of the Indonesian people? He argued that the Ministry of Education should reverse its decision to replace civics textbooks

---

[76] Mohammad Natsir, "Jangan Meng-agamakan Pancasila dan sebaliknya, jangan mempancasilakan agama," in M. Natsir, *Agama dan Negara dalam Perspektif Islam* (Jakarta: Media Da'wah, 2001), pp. 285–90.

[77] Mohammad Natsir, "Pancasila akan hidup subur dalam pangkuan ajaran Islam" [speech given as member of Islamic Leaders delegation before DPR/MPR leadership concerning the PMP textbook]. Ibid. pp. 291–6, esp. p. 294. Originally published in *Media Dakwah*, No. 100, October 1982.

in the schools by the book entitled *Pendidikan Moral Pancasila* (*PMP*, *Pancasila* Moral Education). He also expressed his concern that the Ministry of Religion had been excluded from discussions regarding the portrayal of spiritual and moral issues in this textbook.

Calling on both houses of Parliament (DPR and MPR) to withdraw the *PMP* and replace it with a civics textbook, such as had previously been used in the schools, Natsir argued against civics classes including any religious or faith teachings, which, in his view, should be left to the teachers of the individual religions. He contended that the only way to prevent people of differing religious persuasions resenting the presentation of religious viewpoints in the children's textbooks "is to avoid, without exception, anything concerned with religion and faith appearing in the curriculum that is taught to pupils of all faiths. If not, this book will inevitably become a source of dissension." He suggested that a textbook on "*Pancasila* Citizenship" or "*Pancasila* Civics" should replace the "*Pancasila* Morals" textbook (*PMP*), and that the teaching of civics and citizenship should not be intermixed with the teaching of religion and morals.

In his address to Parliament Natsir again raised the problem of the relationship between religion and the *pancasila*, restating some of the positions he had put forward in the 1950s. He argued that, while not a single principle in the original formulation of the *pancasila* had been in conflict with Islamic teachings, this was no longer the case with the formulation propagated by the Suharto regime. For when the government introduced elements contrary to the teachings of Islam into the *pancasila*,

> then *Pancasila* is no longer fulfilling its prime function as Unifier of the Indonesian People to create what we mean by *Bhinneka Tunggal Ika* [Unity in Diversity (Indonesia's national motto)]. No longer can the *Pancasila* act as the meeting place for all the varied peoples of Indonesia. Rather it can become a continual source of conflict.[78]

This, in his view, was what the Department of Education had done in the *PMP* textbook, where syncretism had been introduced under the name of "*Pancasila* Morals." He saw the compulsory introduction of the *PMP* textbook into the schools, then, as a way of introducing elements of Javanese mystical beliefs (*kepercayaan*) into the curriculum:

> But if there is planted in the spirits of those students who belong to a revealed religion, Islam, Catholic/Protestant under the name of *Pancasila*

---

[78] Ibid., p. 292.

> Morals, then this means that *Pancasila* is among other things being used
> to promote Mystical Beliefs (*Aliran Kepercayaan*). Then if this is the case,
> the *Pancasila* that we have all accepted no longer forms a meeting point for
> Indonesians who adhere to different religions.[79]

He complained that when anyone objected to introducing the textbook into the schools they were told: "Whoever doesn't want to accept the *PMP* he is anti-*Pancasila*."[80]

At the same time as it was changing the curriculum in all the schools, the government was moving to stifle expressions of opinion and dissent in the universities, prohibiting students from playing an active role in politics. In 1978 it established a Normalization of Campus Life-Campus Coordination Board (NKK-BKK, Normalisasi Kehidupan Kampus/Badan Koordinasi Kampus) to enforce the policy. Actions by this Board essentially clamped down on open political life on the campuses.[81]

That the government's efforts were not more successful was due to a significant degree to the strategies of Natsir and several other Muslim leaders now excluded from politics, who in establishing the Dewan Da'wah (DDII) had shifted their emphasis from party politics to the social and education field. A few years earlier, in line with Natsir's conviction that "Indonesian politicians of both the Islamic and nationalist groups from the older generation must educate the new core of leaders through personal contact" and give them "necessary training and thinking,"[82] the Dewan Da'wah had initiated a campus-based program under the name of Bina Masjid Kampus (Campus Mosque-Building), in which many Muslim scholars and intellectuals took part. Natsir sent a stream of *dosen* to teach on the campuses, "where they received a very enthusiastic response."[83] When the Suharto government effectively closed down university political life in the late 1970s, the Bina Masjid Kampus program provided an alternative for the Muslim students, and "the campus mosques became a refuge for would-be activists."[84]

---

[79] Ibid., p. 288.

[80] Ibid., p. 293.

[81] Noorhaidi, "Laskar Jihad: Islam, Militancy and the Quest for Identity in Post-New Order Indonesia," PhD. Dissertation, University of Utrecht, 2005, p. 37.

[82] Natsir interview, Jakarta, May 31, 1971.

[83] Interview with H. Misbach Malim of the DDII, Jakarta, November 21, 2008.

[84] ICG Asia Report No. 83 (September 13, 2004), pp. 6–7. In my interview with H. Misbach Malim (November 21, 2008), when I raised the fact that the government discouraged political and religious activity on the campuses at this time, he said that the *dosen* sent by Natsir taught in the mosques, "and there was nothing the government could do about that."

Much of the inspiration for the movement came from the Middle East and drew in particular from the ideas of the Muslim Brotherhood in Egypt.[85] Since 1970 the Dewan Da'wah had been translating and publishing books and pamphlets by such authors as Sayid Qutb and Abu A'la Maududi. In reaching out to young people in the *pesantren*, mosques and universities Natsir and his colleagues in the DDII circulated these works on the campuses.[86] As van Bruinessen notes, however, Qutb's "more radical political ideas" did not have much impact on the DDII followers on the university campuses: "It was the non revolutionary Saudi-sponsored brand of Brotherhood materials that became most influential in former Masyumi circles in the 1980s and 1990s."[87] The Muslim Brotherhood also provided a model for organization with their example of "forming small, tight-knit cells (commonly referred to as *usrah*, literally 'family') as incubators of pious, professionally successful young Muslims."[88]

One of the foremost campuses where the DDII's Bina Masjid Kampus program was active among the students was the Bandung Institute of Technology (ITB). Most influential at the Salman Mosque on the ITB campus was Imaduddin Abdurrachim, a senior Dewan Da'wah leader, who had been appointed general secretary of the Kuwait-based International Islamic Federation of Student Organizations (IIFSO) and who would later become a founder of the ICMI.[89] Imaduddin, who was personally supported by Natsir, established a program called Latihan Mujahid Dakwah (Training for Islamic Propagation Warriors), which trained new cadres among university students prepared to undertake *da'wah* activities.[90] Some of Indonesia's best-known Muslim scholars and activists took part in this program. Most of the participants were not members of radical movements, but rather Muslim intellectuals, interested in international developments, such as Amien Rais, who later became chair of

---

[85] Solahudin, *NII Sampai JI: Salafy Jihadisme di Indonesia* (Jakarta: Komunitas Bambu, 2011), pp. 150–1.

[86] Ibid., pp. 125–6; Platzdasch, *Islamism in Indonesia*, pp. 52–3. On the Brotherhood and on Qutb and Maududi, see Chapter 9.

[87] Van Bruinessen, "Genealogies of Islamic Radicalism," p. 125.

[88] Fealy and Hooker, *Voices of Islam*, p. 48.

[89] Noorhaidi, *Laskar Jihad*, p. 63. ICMI = Ikatan Cendekiawan Muslim Indonesia, All Indonesia League of Muslim Intellectuals, a government-sponsored body set up in December 1990, and headed by then minister of research and technology, B.J. Habibie.

[90] Noorhaidi, *Laskar Jihad*, p. 36. Other universities that were active in the movement were the University of Indonesia, Surabaya's Airlangga University and the Gadjah Madah University in Yogyakarta, as well as Andalas in Padang, the Eleventh March State University in Solo and the Diponegoro University in Semarang. Ibid., and Platzdasch, *Islamism in Indonesia*, pp. 86–7.

Muhammadiyah and speaker of the People's Consultative Assembly. But the influence of these ideas in encouraging the students to be more active politically should not be underestimated.

In fact, the Suharto government's repression of political expression on university campuses "stimulated growing numbers of students to turn toward Islamic activism.[91] As Ruth McVey noted in 1983, the exclusion of Muslim political activity "from the vulnerable and by now pointless arena of party politics" did not lead to depoliticization of the society. Rather, by the late 1970s,

> inspired to some extent by the Islamic revival elsewhere but largely propelled by Indonesian circumstances — a religious militancy has been developing which radically challenges the socio-economic and cultural assumptions of the established Indonesian order and appears as the spokesman for the common man against an exploiting elite.[92]

---

[91] Noorhaidi, *Laskar Jihad*, p. 37.

[92] Ruth McVey, "Faith as the Outsider: Islam in Indonesian Politics," in *Islam in the Political Process*, ed. James P. Piscatori (Cambridge: Cambridge University Press, 1983), pp. 199–225, esp. p. 218.

9

The Closing Years

Activities in the International Arena

After the advent of the New Order regime, while Natsir was largely excluded from the domestic political scene in Indonesia he devoted increasing attention to developments in the international arena, and, through the Dewan Da'wah Islamiyah Indonesia (DDII), forged ties between the Islamic community in Indonesia and Muslim movements in the Middle East.

He was held in high esteem abroad, and leaders in other Islamic countries, especially Saudi Arabia, Pakistan and Malaysia, welcomed his perspective and insights. In 1967, shortly after his release from detention, he visited Jordan and other Middle Eastern countries. Together with religious leaders from Pakistan, Egypt, Lebanon, Tunisia and Kuwait, he was invited to view the impact of the Six-Day War and the occupation of Palestine. His visits to the Palestinian refugee camps made a deep impression on him. On his return home he told his countrymen "how ashamed he had felt at seeing relief coming from India and many other countries but not from Indonesia."[1] At a meeting in Amman during that same trip Natsir was appointed to head a delegation to discuss the Palestinian problem with the leaders of other Muslim countries in the Middle

---

[1] Martin van Bruinessen, "Modernism and Anti-Modernism in Indonesian Muslim Response to Globalisation." Paper presented at the Workshop "Islam and Development in Southeast Asia: Southeast Asian Muslim Responses to Globalization," organized by JICA (Japan International Cooperation Agency) Research Institute, Singapore, November 21–22, 2009, p. 2. Appearing on Dr. van Bruinessen's website.

Natsir with King Faisal on his visit to Indonesia in 1972.

East.[2] He was also chosen as vice-president of the Karachi-based World Muslim Congress (Mutamar al-Alam al-Islami), a position he held for most of the rest of his life.

The ties he established during this visit both with King Faisal of Saudi Arabia and with the World Muslim Congress were to have a strong influence over his activities and over the relationship between Indonesian Muslims and those in the Middle East during the next twenty years. His close friendship with the Saudi king was influential on the development of the DDII; in addition, the king's open expressions of respect for Natsir undoubtedly protected him against serious reprisals from the Suharto government when he was too outspoken in his criticism of its actions. His receipt of the "Faisal Award" for his services to Islam in 1980 provided an added protection.

*   *   *

Natsir's initial visit to Syria, Jordan and Saudi Arabia after his release from detention occurred at a time of Islamic resurgence in the Middle East in the aftermath of the defeat of Arab armies in the 1967 war against Israel, which had done much to discredit the nationalist regimes of the region. The resurgence drew on ideas first promulgated by Hassan al-Banna and the Muslim Brotherhood, the organization he had established in Egypt in 1928,

---

[2] These included Sudan, Lebanon, Iraq, Kuwait and Saudi Arabia.

"with the express goal of counteracting Western influences" in the region.[3] The ideas of the Brotherhood stressed the equality of all Muslims in their need to seek God's guidance through the Qu'ran and the example of the Prophet, as well as Islam's ability to provide the moral precepts for a just social order. By 1948 the organization "constituted a strong force in Egyptian politics,"[4] and numbered among its adherents Sayyid Qutb, "one of the original theorists of modern Islamism."[5]

During the inter-war years a *modus vivendi* had existed between the Brotherhood and Egypt's secular nationalists because of the conviction of both groups that their first task was to move toward political independence and bring an end to European dominance. Their cooperation came to an end, however, after the assassination of al-Banna in 1949 and Nasser's seizure of power in Egypt in 1952.[6] At first Nasser tried to co-opt the Brotherhood, but his ideas and those of other nationalists conflicted with the Muslim group's vision of the post-independence state. After an assassination attempt against him in 1954, which he blamed on the Brotherhood, Nasser banned the movement and over the subsequent decade tried to annihilate its members, jailing or exiling them and executing their leaders.[7] Many left the country. On August 29, 1966, the Nasser regime hanged Qutb, an act that symbolized, in Gilles Kepel's words, "the rift that had occurred between the then-dominant Arab Nationalists, as personified by President Gamal Abdel Nasser, and contemporary radical Islamists."[8] At Qutb's death many of his followers still in Egypt also fled the country.

It was in Saudi Arabia that many of the Egyptian Islamists sought refuge. The Saudi authorities understandably rejected their more violent and revolutionary ideas, seeing these ideas as a threat to their own power. Rather, the

---

[3] Ladan and Roya Boroumand, "Terror, Islam, and Democracy," in *Islam and Democracy in the Middle East*, ed. Larry Diamond, *et al.* (Baltimore: Johns Hopkins University Press, 2003), pp. 283–98, esp. p. 285.

[4] John Kelsay, *Arguing the Just War in Islam* (Cambridge, MA: Harvard University Press, 2007), pp. 90–2.

[5] Gilles Kepel, *Jihad: The Trail of Political Islam*, tr. Anthony F. Roberts (Cambridge, MA: Harvard University Press, 2002), p. 23.

[6] Reportedly, Egyptian government agents were responsible for Hassan al-Banna's 1949 murder in retaliation for the assassination of the Egyptian prime minister allegedly by a Muslim Brother. Ian Buruma, "Tariq Ramadan has an Identity Problem," *New York Times Magazine*, February 4, 2007. Ramadan is the grandson of Al-Banna.

[7] See Kepel, *Jihad*, pp. 27–30 for a summary history of the relationship between the Brothers and the Nasser government.

[8] Ibid., p. 23. See also Lawrence Wright, *The Looming Tower* (New York: Knopf, 2006), pp. 7–31 for an account of Qutb's life and his confrontations with the Nasser regime.

Saudi government favored the pursuit of what they called "Islamization from below" through distributing money to mosques and social and educational institutions, as well as funding *da'wah* activities.

At the time of Natsir's 1967 visit, Saudi Arabian influence was gaining momentum throughout the Islamic world, and it was soon spurred by the skyrocketing of oil prices in the early 1970s. As Noorhaidi noted, Saudi influence over cultural and religious activities had already been institutionalized by its sponsorship, in 1957, of the Organization of Islamic Conference "whose purpose was to formulate the foreign policy of the Muslim world."[9] Five years later it had set up the RAI (Muslim World League), based in Jiddah. Natsir became a member of the RAI in 1969 and was later appointed its vice chairman.[10] According to Martin van Bruinessen, the Saudis sponsored the RAI "as a vehicle for supporting the conservative Saudi regime against Nasser's revolutionary Arab nationalism."[11]

When asked in 1971 about which non-Indonesian religious leaders were most influential with him, Natsir indicated Mohammad Abduh and Rasjid Rida,[12] but when queried on current Islamic thinkers, said that Sayyid Qutb (1906–66) was influential[13] and that the Pakistani Abu A'la-Maududi (1903–79), although "more operational," exerted influence in the Middle East, though not yet in Indonesia. He cited in particular Maududi's opposition to Ajub Khan and the contribution he had made to the drafting of the first Pakistani constitution. Natsir does not seem to have met with Qutb, but about a decade earlier in 1956 he and Maududi had both attended a conference in Damascus, Syria, held to discuss the Palestinian problem, and they later met on several occasions.[14] Natsir recalled that when Maududi had been arrested and sentenced to death, Muslims in Jakarta, along with those from many other countries, had

---

[9] Noorhaidi, *Laskar Jihad: Islam Militancy and the Quest for Identity in Post-New Order Indonesia*, Dissertation, University of Utrecht, 2005, p. 30.

[10] ICG Asia Report No. 83 (September 13, 2004), "What is Salafism?" p. 6.

[11] Van Bruinessen, "Modernism," p. 5. Van Bruinessen notes that the Malaysian youth organization ABIM was also closely tied to the RAI. Ibid.

[12] Natsir interview, Jakarta, January 30, 1971; on these two, see Chapter 2.

[13] Natsir interview, Jakarta, February 24, 1971. He noted, in particular, Qutb's book *Social Justice in Islam*, a book that, according to Lawrence Wright, made Qutb's reputation as an important Islamic thinker. Wright, *Looming Tower*, p. 16.

[14] Yusuf Abdullah Puar, ed., *Muhammad Natsir: 70 tahun Kenang-kenangan Kehidupan dan Perjuangan* (Jakarta: Pustaka Antara, 1978), pp. 138–9. Natsir also made reference to meeting in Damascus with Maududi in a 1977 interview with Prof. Merle Ricklefs. Tape transcript of BBC interview of Merle Ricklefs with Mohammad Natsir, August 14, 1977. (I am grateful to Prof. Ricklefs for sending me a copy of the transcript.)

held demonstrations and sent a letter of protest to the Pakistani government. In the face of the furor in the Muslim world the government had felt compelled to release him.[15]

At the time of Natsir's visit to Saudi Arabia in 1967 the ideas of both Qutb and Maududi were increasing in popularity.[16] But whatever similarities may have existed between them and Natsir in the realm of religious thought, it would appear that Natsir's approach to politics and strategy deviated drastically from the path advocated by these two thinkers. Qutb in particular called for "a clean break with the established order," even when that order was Islamic, labeling all government that did not match his narrow interpretation of the Muslim religion as *jahiliyya*.[17] He rejected both egalitarianism and nationalism and insisted on the strict implementation of *syariah* (Islamic law). There was greater similarity between Natsir's views and those of Maududi, who "viewed the establishment of an Islamic republic as a task to be undertaken slowly, step by step," and believed in participating fully in the political system of Pakistan.[18] However, in contrast to Natsir, Maududi was a fierce foe of nationalism and a strong advocate of an Islamic state. According to Kelsay, Maududi, like Rasjid Rida and Hassan al-Banna, did believe that "Islamic government may involve a parliament or a consultative assembly. It may involve elections, so that the process of consultation, or *al-shura*, is more widely participatory than in the past." However, Maududi, and for that matter Rasjid Rida and Hassan al-Banna, did not advocate any real form of democracy, which they suggested was not well suited to the Muslim mission.[19] Maududi also argued that the political order "cannot compromise on Muslim leadership" for if the Muslim voice were only "one among many contributing to the making of policy" this would imply a "moral equivalence between Islam and other perspectives," which would be dangerous "not only for the standing of the Muslim community, but for the moral life of mankind."[20]

---

[15] Puar, *Muhammad Natsir*, pp. 138–9.

[16] Noorhaidi, *Laskar Jihad*, p. 30.

[17] That is pagan, "the name given to the state of things which obtained in Arabia before the promulgation of Islam" or "the time of ignorance." H.A.R. Gibb and J.H. Kramer, *Shorter Encyclopedia of Islam* (Ithaca: Cornell University Press, 1982), p. 82.

[18] Kepel, *Jihad*, pp. 24, 35. Natsir himself used the same wording when he described an Islamic state as an "ideal" that had to be approached "step by step," a process that would take decades. Natsir interview, January 30, 1971.

[19] Kelsay writes that in their view: "By separating religious and political institutions, and thus limiting the role of Islam in public life, democracy would inhibit the Muslim community's capacity to influence behavior." Kelsay, *Arguing the Just War*, p. 219.

[20] Ibid., p. 166.

Natsir's stance contrasted sharply with this position. Although, along with most Muslim Indonesians, he probably believed that the president should be a Muslim, he never restricted non-Muslims from occupying high ministerial positions, and in the governments that he headed or participated in, there were several Christian ministers.[21] No distinction appears to have been made between them and their colleagues on the basis of their religious affiliation.

Bernhard Platzdasch has seen a major source of difference between Natsir and the Middle Eastern Islamists lying in the fact that the ideological basis of Natsir and his Masjumi party was rooted in their country's independence struggle against the Christian Dutch colonizers, while that of Qutb, Maududi and the Muslim Brotherhood "was embedded in a sense of global Muslim defeat and suppression with the abolishment of the Ottoman caliphate in 1923 at its heart, and tied to the conviction in the glorious Islamic past."[22] It should be noted, however, that the ideas of Qutb and Al-Banna also were intermixed with their country's independence struggle and for several years they, like Natsir, were able to cooperate with the secular nationalist movement in pursuing Egyptian independence. Also Maududi, though opposed to the Pakistani nationalists and also to "the project for a circumscribed 'Muslim state,'" which would empower them, did found a political party, the Jamaat-e-Islami and participated fully in the political system of Pakistan.[23]

In the field of practical politics, both Natsir and Maududi developed their ideas against the background of the anti-colonial movements in their respective countries. But in pre-independence India the Muslim community felt threatened by the numerical dominance of the Hindu majority that would have certainly controlled the political structure in any state based on representative democracy, while in the Netherlands East Indies Natsir could see the majority Muslim population exerting major influence in any post-independence state. Thus, in contrast to Natsir's important role in the independence struggle in Indonesia, Maududi openly opposed the nationalist movement and the formation of Pakistan, and he and his Jamaat-e-Islami party refused to take part in the establishment of the new state in 1947 although repression and discrimination compelled him to leave India for Pakistan the following year.

---

[21] For example, Prof. Herman Johannes and Dr. J. Leimena, both Protestants, served in his 1950 cabinet as minister of public works and minister of health respectively, while F.S. Harjadi, a Catholic, served as minister of social affairs. In the PRRI and RPI cabinets S.J. Warouw and Maludin Simbolon, both Christians, held ministerial portfolios.

[22] Bernhard Platzdasch, *Islamism in Indonesia: Politics in the Emerging Democracy* (Singapore: ISEAS, 2009), p. 18.

[23] Kepel, *Jihad*, pp. 34–5.

In a conference on Natsir's thought and struggle held to commemorate the centennial of his birth, Yusril Ihza Mahendra, who was very close to Natsir in the final decades of his life, contrasted his ideas with those of Maududi with regard to the place of religion in contemporary society. In Mahendra's eyes, Natsir was a "modernist" and Maududi a "fundamentalist."[24] He noted that some of the differences between the two men lay in the fact that Maududi's party was always marginal in Pakistani politics, while during the early years of independence Natsir's Masjumi was Indonesia's largest party and a leading member of the country's governing coalitions.[25] Exercising power in such a situation, Natsir was compelled to seek real-world solutions rather than holding too firmly to inflexible ideas, realizing that Muslim teachings had to be implemented with a view to place and time. As a result, while Maududi appeared more consistent in that he never had to adapt his ideas to concrete situations, Natsir was generally more flexible and willing to compromise. Nevertheless, there were some practical issues on which Natsir was unwilling to seek common ground, as evidenced in his unwavering opposition both to Soekarno's introduction of Guided Democracy and to Suharto's later misuse of the *pancasila*. While Maududi always opposed the separation of powers, visualizing an ideal government order as based on a Caliphate where the Caliph was advised by a consultative council, Natsir saw the division of power among the executive, legislative and judicial branches of government as integral to a democratic state based on Islam.

In light of these views, while Natsir openly admired the writings of Qutb and Maududi, he is unlikely to have felt that their political ideas were relevant in the Indonesian context. Throughout his life he recognized the multi-ethnic and multi-cultural character of Indonesian society and the need for Muslims to adapt to this fact. In the atmosphere of colonial and post-colonial Indonesia, Natsir tended to be realistic and pragmatic, accepting and even welcoming the need to work with people of all religions and cultures to achieve a democratic and independent state based on religious values. Social pluralism for him was "a reality that can't be denied.... Religious pluralism forms a social reality that wont disappear so should be used as a basis for solving joint problems."[26]

As Platzdasch has written, Natsir and the Masjumi reflected "the ambiguities and contradictions inherent in Islamist politics ... the tension of practical

---

[24] See Yusril Ihza Mahendra, "Mohammad Natsir dan Sayyid Abul A'la Maududi," in *Pemikiran dan Perjuangan Mohammad Natsir*, ed. Anwar Harjono, *et al.* (Jakarta: Firdaus, 2001), pp. 98–113.

[25] Ibid., pp. 108–9.

[26] Ibid., p. 104.

and ideological concerns, which stands at the heart of constitutionalist Islamism," and thus they

> consented to a number of programmes and ideas that set them apart from Islamists such as Maududi or Qutb. Most importantly, Masyumi took on Western concepts such as a multiparty system, the separation of powers, and parliamentary rule. It deemed free speech and a formal opposition in parliament mandatory for a democracy.[27]

Although he never accepted the idea of a "liberal democracy" for Indonesia, and would frequently advocate instead an "Islamic democracy," for Natsir the only way for Islam to thrive there was in a democratic state, and his adherence to his concept of democracy in the political field was as strong as his adherence to Islam in the field of religion. He believed that Islamic values would necessarily exert major influence in a democratic state with a majority Muslim population.

He clearly differentiated in his own mind between the societies of the Middle East and Indonesia, and in contrasting Indonesian government with the authoritarian regimes of the Middle East in 1971, stated his belief in the essentially democratic nature of Indonesians:

> I don't think the political climate in Indonesia is as fertile for military dictatorship as in the countries of the Middle East. Traditionally and imbued in the hearts of the peasantry there is in village life, as Hatta has observed, a persisting democratic orientation.[28]

With such a democratic orientation, one can conclude, it would be as difficult for the society to accept a strict Islamic state. As another of his associates in the DDII noted, Natsir stressed that Indonesians "would not be free (*belum merdeka*) until two conditions had been met: freedom of assembly and freedom of speech. Everyone must be free to speak and express his/her opinion, and seek opportunity without hindrance."[29]

It has been argued that Natsir's involvement with international Islamic organizations and his deepening relationships with Muslims outside Indonesia influenced his attitudes toward Western societies.[30] In the 1930s and 1940s,

---

[27] Platzdasch, *Islamism in Indonesia*, pp. 19, 31.

[28] Natsir interview, Jakarta, May 31, 1971. It should be recalled, however, that both Hatta and Natsir were of Minangkabau origin, a society much more democratic in essence than that in Java.

[29] Interview with Mohammad Siddik, Jakarta, October 29, 2008.

[30] Robert W. Hefner, *Civil Islam: Muslims and Democratization in Indonesia* (Princeton: Princeton University Press, 2000), pp. 103–5.

while strongly opposing all forms of colonialism, he had been drawn to the ideals of democracy and human rights as expressed in Western thought. Even then, however, he had expressed wonderment at what he viewed as the belligerence of Europeans and the ease with which "they made use of bullets and bombs ... sacrificing the freedom of other peoples to ensure that their own freedom was not disturbed."[31] As he became involved in examining the Palestinian problem in the aftermath of the 1967 war, he was outraged at the Palestinians' plight, though it is unclear the extent to which he saw the United States and Europe as complicit in Israel's occupation of Arab lands. He was further alienated from Western secular societies by the growth in them of counter-culture movements in the late 1960s, which he saw as removing moral barriers in society and practicing behavior forbidden under Islam, such as pornography, violence and drugs.[32] Nevertheless, he continued to admire the basic concepts underlying Western political thought and to embrace the core democratic values of egalitarianism and social justice, together with belief in a multi-party system and separation of powers.[33] He made this clear even in the final three of years of his life (see below).

As we have seen earlier, while always criticizing the extreme nationalism of the "my country right or wrong" variety, Natsir recognized a love of country as being acceptable within Islam, a love that he himself had displayed throughout Indonesia's independence struggle, and his approach to politics had always laid great emphasis on the concepts of democracy and elections. Indeed after

---

[31] "Hakikat Agama Islam," in *Capita Selecta* [I], pp. 119–32, esp. p. 119.

[32] For Natsir's arguments against adoption of such aspects of Western societies, see his "Pembangunan Negara dan Tanggungjawab Ummat Islam," in *Dari Masa ke Masa* 1 (Jakarta: Fajar Shadiq, 1974), pp. 5–10. In a speech in 1969 Natsir had used the example of Western societies removing moral barriers, and the resulting spread of the five moral prohibitions in Islam (opium, robbery, gambling, drinking, adultery) as an argument against the 1969 proposal that gambling be legalized in Indonesia. See "Peranan dan tanggung jawab civitas Akademika dan Perguruan Tinggi" (August 4, 1969), in H. Mas'oed Abidin, *Taushiyah Dr. Mohamad Natsir: Pesan Dakwah Pemandu Umat* (unpublished manuscript 2001), pp. 36–62. Also in arguing against the activities of Christian missionaries in Java that same year he stated that, rather than attempting to convert Muslims, Christians would better work to combat "crime and sex" and permissiveness among their own people. *Muhammad Natsir: 70 Tahun*, p. 291. He expressed similar feelings in his interview with Merle Ricklefs in 1977, when he wondered why Christian missionary organizations were more concerned in the "de-Islamization of Islamic countries, than the de-Christianization of the Christian communities in Europe, and asked why they didn't "exert their efforts to prevent the de-Christianization of the Christian communities [than to] come in here to Christianize the Muslims."

[33] Natsir interview, Jakarta, May 31, 1971.

the founding of the DDII some Muslim purists apparently criticized the organization for espousing these values.[34]

Efforts at Cooperation

As shown in the previous chapter, the New Order regime's refusal to allow Natsir and other former Masjumi leaders to resume political activity was part of its general policy of marginalizing political Islam. By the late 1970s this policy had divided and disheartened much of the Muslim community and had led to dissatisfaction and some active opposition to the Suharto regime. Nevertheless, though Suharto was bent on excluding Natsir from politics and even seemed to bear some personal animus towards him, throughout these years Natsir frequently acted in support of the Jakarta government. While open in criticizing those policies of which he disapproved, he continued to make public statements urging Indonesians to support the New Order's development plans and frequently interceded for the regime on the international stage.[35]

As Natsir turned more of his attention to the world outside Indonesia, he made efforts to smooth Indonesia's international position especially in the Middle East. One early example occurred when he was in Saudi Arabia in 1967. For several years previously Jakarta had enjoyed poor relations with the Saudi government because of an incident that had occurred during the Soekarno period, when Indonesian police had raided the Saudi ambassador's house in the hilly *puncak* region of West Java between Bogor and Bandung. When the ambassador demanded an explanation, he received no reply and the Jakarta government offered no apology. The diplomat left Jakarta in protest, and thenceforth relations between the two countries were cool and remained at the *chargé d'affaires* level. On his 1967 visit to Saudi Arabia, when King Faisal granted him an audience, Natsir asked the king how relations between the two countries could be improved. According to Natsir, Faisal replied that he had no quarrel with the people of Indonesia and, as the incident in the *puncak* had occurred under the previous regime, the present government need offer no belated apology. Restoration of diplomatic relations, then, was just a matter of protocol. All that was required was for the Indonesian foreign minister to send a letter expressing Jakarta's desire to restore relations at the ambassadorial level. Natsir got in touch with Foreign Minister Adam Malik, who was an old friend,

---

[34] ICG Asia Report, No. 83 (September 13, 2004), p. 6, states: "It [DDII] is criticized by the purists for supporting the concepts of democracy and elections."

[35] Deliar Noer, "The Confrontational Natsir? A Commemorative Essay" (Jakarta: typescript, February 15, 1993), p. 5.

Natsir with Takeo Fukuda, Japan, September 1968.

and was able to ensure that the requested letter was sent. Within a few months the two countries resumed diplomatic relations.[36]

On a subsequent occasion, at the request of Ali Moertopo, Natsir wrote to the Kuwaiti government, asking them to invest in Indonesia, a request that resulted in Kuwaiti support of the Indonesian fishing industry.[37]

Natsir's intercessions on behalf of the Suharto regime were not limited to countries in the Middle East. In 1971, on a visit to Tokyo, he asked the Japanese finance minister, Takeo Fukuda, to help smooth relations between Tokyo and Jakarta and ensure Japanese financial support to the Suharto regime.[38] Over the next decades Natsir continued to enjoy close relations with Fukuda, who apparently often relied on his advice. The closeness of their friendship was manifested in a letter Fukuda wrote in reaction to Natsir's death in February 1993, where he said: "When we received this sad news [of

---

[36] Interview of August 1979 by *Media Dakwah* with Natsir, appearing in Mohammad Natsir, *Agama dan Negara dalam Perspektif Islam* (Jakarta: Media Da'wah, 2001), pp. 281–2. See also Puar, *Muhammad Natsir*, pp. 142–4.

[37] Lukman Hakiem, ed., *Pemimpin Pulang: Rekaman Peristiwa Wafatny M. Natsir* (Jakarta: Yayasan Piranti Ilmu, 1993), pp. 30–1.

[38] Ibid., pp. 29–30. On the tense relationship between the two countries at the time, see Franklin B. Weinstein, *Indonesian Foreign Policy and the Dilemma of Dependence* (Ithaca: Cornell University Press, 1976), pp. 234–7.

Natsir's death] it was more horrifying than the dropping of the atom bomb on Hiroshima, because we had lost a world leader, and a great leader of the Islamic world."[39]

Natsir was even willing to defend internationally the Indonesian invasion of East Timor in 1976. At the time he wrote to Saudi King Faisal to explain and justify the Suharto government's policies. And in an interview with the Pakistani press, he defended Indonesia's actions, arguing that: "what it was trying to prevent is the self-extermination by its population and a sort of second Angola."[40] Hamka, a leading Muslim scholar and close friend of Natsir, confirmed this account of Natsir's stance, stating that when the world was criticizing Indonesia for its actions in East Timor, Natsir approached various Islamic leaders in the Middle East and won their acquiescence to Indonesian actions. He repeated Natsir's statement that if a civil war had broken out in Portuguese Timor, "a second Angola will be born in the back yard of Indonesia, the majority of whose population is Muslim."[41]

In an interview we held with Natsir in January 1971, he voiced his frustration at the refusal of the Suharto regime to acknowledge any of the assistance he had rendered it in its early years, lamenting that

> The military refuses even to talk with us. It accuses us of being confrontative. When I talked with Alamsjah about a year and a half ago, he said if the party [Parmusi] is to have any future it is up to you. If you will stop being negative and not be confrontative there can be a future for the party. I tried to explain that I had done many things that had been positive, such as helping the government restore relations with Saudi Arabia and interesting the Japanese government in helping Indonesia economically (when a guest of the Secretary General of the Liberal Democratic Party, who was Minister of Finance).

---

[39] Facsimile of a letter from Takeo Fukuda dated February 8, 1993, appearing in Lukman Hakiem, *et al.*, *Pemimpin Pulang*, p. 144. Here Fukuda acknowledges Natsir's role in convincing the Japanese government to support the New Order regime. According to Anwar Harjono, ever since the 1950s Natsir had enjoyed close ties with Fukuda. Harjono spoke with Nakajima, the emissary sent by Fukuda to Natsir's funeral, who said that the minister had sent him 200 (!) times to meet with Natsir, when he wanted to consult him about international problems, etc. (ibid., p. 123). In his recollection "Kami Banyak Belajar dari Mohammad Natsir," in the same volume, Nakajima stressed Natsir's closeness to Fukuda and how dependent Fukuda was on his advice. Ibid., pp. 202–4. It is possible that the two first established a relationship during the PRRI rebellion, when Sumitro was close to Fukuda and the Japanese provided the rebels with financial support. See Masashi Nishihara, *The Japanese and Sukarno's Indonesia* (Honolulu: East West Center, 1975), pp. 192–4, 205.

[40] "Indonesia wants self-determination in East Timor: Natsir," article in *Dawn* and *Morning News*, Karachi, March 17, 1976, reproduced in *Muhammad Natsir: 70 Tahun*, p. 147.

[41] *Pemimpin Pulang*, pp. 29–30, citing an article by Hamka in *Panji Masyarakat*.

He recalled the letter he had written even when still in jail to Tunku Abdul Rahman in behalf of Suharto to help smooth the way for better relations with Malaysia, which was carried by a delegation of the military to Kuala Lumpur. Then he contrasted the Suharto regime with that of Soekarno. As he was to say on another occasion, Soekarno had displayed "no personal animosity" toward him and had never barred him from palace functions, whereas Suharto's treatment of him was "the action of a man with limited education and a limited world view."[42]

Growing Militancy and Government Response

From 1967 on Natsir performed a yearly *haj* to the holy sites in Saudi Arabia until in 1981, after he participated in the *Petisi 50* (see below), the Jakarta government forbade him from going abroad. Throughout these years, in line with his consistent emphasis on the importance of training the next generation of young people, he focused his efforts on the Dewan Da'wah's programs on university campuses, pressing on the students the idea that they could become cadre in the effort to raise the quality of Islam among the next generation. Thus, when King Faisal asked him in what way he could assist him in his work, Natsir reportedly replied merely that the king should "help my children," meaning his students. Responding to this request, the Saudi government awarded grants to Natsir's students to study at universities in Saudi Arabia and other educational institutions in the Middle East.[43]

From that time on, the DDII acted as the main channel in Indonesia for distributing scholarships from the Saudi-funded Muslim World League (Rabitat al-Alam al-Islam, RAI) for Indonesian young people to continue their education in Middle Eastern countries. In addition to providing numerous grants for Indonesians to study in Saudi Arabia, the League also provided Natsir with funds for building mosques and training preachers in Indonesia.[44] In the early 1970s the Indonesian Dewan Da'wah opened an office in Riyadh to facilitate its links with Saudi Arabia. Most of the students who studied in the

---

[42] David Jenkins reporting Natsir's remarks in *Suharto and his Generals*, p. 185. In our interview with him, Jakarta, January 18, 1971, he remarked, "The military in their repression are crude while Soekarno's style was at least elegant."

[43] Interview with H. Misbach Malim, Secretary of the Dewan Da'wah, Jakarta, November 21, 2008. Malim himself had studied in Medina, Saudi Arabia, from 1980 to 1986.

[44] Van Bruinessen, "Modernism & Anti-Modernism," p. 5. Van Bruinessen further notes: "Recipients of these grants were to play leading parts in the Islamist and Salafi movements that flourished in semi-legality in the 1990s and came to the surface after 1998."

Middle East under these grants eventually returned to teach in Indonesia.[45] In 1980 the Islamic University in Riyadh established an institution for teaching Arabic (LPBA, Lembaga Pendidikan Bahasa Arab) in Jakarta, which worked in conjunction with the DDII and with *pesantren* in other parts of Indonesia, including the Ngruki *pesantren* outside Solo. Saudi and other Arab members of the Muslim Brotherhood taught in the LPBA and introduced many of its books and organizational methods to the institutions in Java.[46]

The ties between Saudi Arabia and the Dewan Da'wah in Jakarta were expanded throughout the 1970s and 1980s apparently in part to counter the Suharto government's own program, "under which religious teachers were dispatched for their further education to Western universities (notably McGill University in Canada), rather than to venerable Islamic institutions in the Middle East."[47] As Robert Hefner has noted, after receiving their degree, many of these Western-trained students "went on to receive important appointments in the Department of Religion."[48]

In countering these Western influences, the graduates of institutions in the Middle East became influential in mosques and *pesantren* throughout Indonesia, especially Java, and were responsible for spreading Islamist ideas among Indonesian young people. This stream of radical Islam within the modernist community gained traction and adherents on and off Indonesian university campuses in part because of the Suharto regime's intransigence and its repression of legal means for expressing dissent. The young Islamists were increasingly described as *salafi* [lit. believers in a return to the practices of early Islamic times]),[49] and over the years *salafi* was frequently tied to the word *jihad*, and identified with the doctrine of "salafi jihadism" that had developed in the 1980s in Afghanistan, where Muslim forces were confronting the armies of the Soviet Union.[50]

In Indonesia, *salafi* was also often used to describe former members of the Darul Islam movement. As early as the late 1960s, only a few years after

---

[45] H. Misbach Malim interview, Jakarta, November 21, 2008.

[46] Solahudin, *NII sampai JI*, pp. 15, 17–8.

[47] R.E. Elson, *Suharto: A Political Biography* (Cambridge: Cambridge University Press, 2001), p. 240.

[48] Hefner, *Civil Islam*, p.110.

[49] The term is generally used to describe members of "an international movement that seeks to return to what is seen by its adherents as the purest form of Islam, that was practiced by the Prophet Mohammed and the two generations that followed him." ICG Asia Report No. 83, p. 2. Solahudin sees teachers and activities of the LPBA as major sources of introducing *salafi* ideas to Indonesia.

[50] Solahudin, *NII sampai JI*, pp. 1–2.

the capture and execution of its head, S.M. Kartosuwirjo, some leaders of the Darul Islam (DI) had begun to revive the organization and make contact with its former supporters in both Java and Sumatra. They formed the genesis of a movement, known as the *Komando Jihad* (Holy War Command), that emerged in the early 1970s, drawing its leadership and much of its following from former DI followers.[51] The violent activities associated with the *Komando Jihad* would later include the high-jacking of a Garuda DC9 aircraft and an attack on a police station near Bandung in 1981. Accusing perpetrators of these attacks of belonging to an organization that was "committed to following the ideals of Kartosuwirjo and establishing the Islamic State of Indonesia," the government at that time arrested 185 of its members.[52]

It is difficult to analyze the character and aims of the *Komando Jihad* and assess its strength in the 1970s and 1980s, as some of the Darul Islam leaders who headed it had, from the beginning, been in contact with, and were encouraged by General Ali Moertopo, head of Suharto's intelligence agency, Bakin (Badan Koordinasi Intelijen Negara, State Intelligence Coordinating Agency).[53] Initially, as head of Special Operations (Operasi Khusus, Opsus) in the early years of the New Order regime, Moertopo, together with army officers of the Siliwangi division, called on DI veterans to aid in the suppression of communists in West Java.[54] In the early 1970s, he apparently used his ties with the Darul Islam elements not only "to target the regime's enemies" but also as a way to "engineer a Golkar victory in the general elections of July 3, 1971."[55] In October 1970 a number of DI leaders had signed a pledge, in which they

---

[51] A good concise analysis of the development of this movement appears in John Sidel, *Riots, Pogroms, Jihad: Religious Violence in Indonesia* (Ithaca: Cornell University Press, 2006), pp. 201–10. See also the International Crisis Group (ICG)'s briefings.

[52] ICG Indonesia Briefing, *Al-Qaeda in Southeast Asia: The Case of the 'Ngruki Network' in Indonesia*, August 8, 2002, p. 5.

[53] Other DI leaders attempting to revive the movement retained their independence.

[54] Quinton Temby, "Imagining an Islamic State in Indonesia: From Darul Islam to Jemaah Islamiyah," *Indonesia* 89 (April 2010): 6–7; Noorhaidi, *Laskar Jihad*, p. 34; Solahudin, *NII Sampai JI*, p. 87.

[55] Temby, "Imagining an Islamic State," p. 8. Some of the best information on the role of Ali Moertopo and ties of the Darul Islam with *Komando Jihad* and the later *Jemaah Islamiyah* appears in Temby's article and in Solahudin's book, as well as in the International Crisis Group (ICG)'s briefings, especially the one of August 8, 2002. See also Martin van Bruinessen's articles previously cited; Jenkins, *Suharto and his Generals*, pp. 57ff; and Sidel, *Riots, Pogroms, Jihad*, pp. 207–9. These sources, however, are by no means totally in agreement regarding the nature of the relationship between these organizations nor the influence of Ali Moertopo on them.

stated they would not support any political party, implicitly backing Golkar in the forthcoming election.[56]

Following the 1971 elections some DI leaders maintained contact with Moertopo and he was at least aware of their plans for mounting terrorist attacks, but he only moved to arrest their leaders shortly before the 1977 elections, using their activities to discredit Muslim politicians.[57] In the lead-up to these elections, Moertopo reportedly once more contacted former members of the Darul Islam and encouraged them to renew their bonds with their former DI comrades in Sumatra, Sulawesi and Java.

It remains obscure whether Moertopo's activities were in line with official government policy or whether he undertook some of them on his own initiative. It is clear, however, that the radical movement was not purely a tool of the intelligence agency, for many of the DI members who joined the organization, frequently now known as the *Komando Jihad*,[58] saw it as providing an opportunity to mount resistance against the Jakarta government, which they increasingly viewed as an enemy of Islam. In other words it was difficult to assess who was using whom, and some later researchers believe that by the late 1970s the actions of groups associated with the *Komando Jihad* were outside the control of Moertopo and his intelligence agency.[59]

At that time Natsir was convinced that one influential *Komando Jihad* leader, H. Ismail Pranoto (Hispran), who was primarily involved in recruiting Muslim activists, was "an *agent provocateur* run by Ali Murtopo."[60] In recruiting these activists Hispran laid particular emphasis on the dangers of communism, and it was he who enrolled such DDII members as Abdullah Sungkar and Abu Bakar Ba'asyir into the Darul Islam.

Abdullah Sungkar and Abu Bakar Ba'asyir, both of Yemeni descent, had been actively involved in the *da'wah* movement since the early years of the

---

[56] Solahudin, *NII Sampai JI*, p. 87.

[57] Ibid., p. 103.

[58] According to Solahudin, it was the Jakarta government that gave the name *Komando Jihad* to the Darul Islam movement in Java and Sumatra in 1976. Ibid., p. 102.

[59] Temby explores in detail the allegations that the *Komando Jihad* was a sting operation masterminded by Moertopo and Kopkamtib, and concludes that these charges are unsupported. See his "Imagining an Islamic State," p. 23 and pp. 13–27 passim.

[60] He stated this in an interview with David Jenkins, on December 12, 1978. See Jenkins, *Suharto and his Generals*, p. 57. According to Jenkins, Natsir argued that because people were dissatisfied with conditions in Indonesia, they were easily led, and Moertopo's agents "planted rumors about the Communist comeback and had promised former Darul Islam activists weapons to fight the leftist 'threat.' The leaders of the Komando Jihad … were former Darul Islam leaders who were 'now in the control of Ali Murtopo and his group…'"

New Order.[61] They had been leaders of the Gerakan Pemuda Islam Indonesia (GPII, Indonesian Muslim Youth Movement), an independent and activist student group that had close ties to the Masjumi in the 1950s. Sungkar became acquainted with Natsir shortly after Natsir was freed from jail, and Ba'asyir and Sungkar in 1969 founded the Radio Dakwah Islamiyah Surakarta (RADIS). In 1970 Natsir appointed Sungkar to head the DDII in Solo (Surakarta) and encouraged him to establish a *pesantren* there. Together with Abu Bakar Ba'asyir, who was a graduate of the famous Gontor *pesantren* in Central Java, Sungkar founded the *pesantren* Al-Mukmin (al-Mu'min) in the village of Ngruki in central Java, just outside Solo. This *pesantren*, more generally known as Pondok Ngruki, aimed to combine the best aspects of two models — the Gontor *pesantren* for the teaching of Arabic, and the Persis *pesantren* in Bangil[62] for the teaching of *shari`a*.

According to Van Bruinessen, "Sungkar, Ba'asyir and their colleagues were fiercely opposed to the Suharto regime, which they perceived as anti-Islamic, and they were strongly influenced by Muslim Brotherhood thought."[63] The two men actively mobilized outside the *pesantren*, using the organizational model of the Brotherhood. They reportedly planned to develop an organization under the name of *Jema'ah Islamiyah*, based on the Muslim Brotherhood's cell system, which they saw as the most fitting means for working toward an Islamic state. Haji Ismail Pranoto, however, persuaded them that, rather than building their own community it would be better to join with an existing community, namely the Darul Islam, and he appointed Sungkar head of the DI community in the Solo area, with Abu Bakar Ba'asyir as his deputy.[64] Sungkar had already been attracted to the Darul Islam because of its militant opposition to the Suharto government.

According to Solahudin, when, in 1976, Natsir heard that Sungkar had joined with the Darul Islam, he told him he had to choose between the DI and

---

[61] On Sungkar's background, see Solahudin, *NII Sampai JI*, pp. 140–1.

[62] Founded by Natsir's old mentor, Ahmad Hassan. On these *pesantren*, see also Sidel, *Riots, Pogroms, Jihad*, pp. 202–4.

[63] Martin van Bruinessen, "Divergent paths from Gontor: Muslim educational reform and the travails of pluralism in Indonesia," *On the edge of many worlds*, ed. Freek L. Bakker and Jan Sihar Aritonang [Festschrift Karel A. Steenbrink], (Zoetermeer: Uitgeverij Meinema, 2006), pp. 197–9. Most of the description of the ties between Ba'asyir, Sungkar and the Jemaah Islamiyah are drawn from this article of Van Bruinessen and from Solahudin's *NII Sampai JI*. The account also relies on another of Van Bruinessen's articles, "Genealogies of Islamic Radicalism," on reports of the International Crisis Group and on Temby, "Imagining an Islamic State in Indonesia."

[64] Solahudin, *NII Sampai DI*, p. 143.

the Dewan Da'wah. Sungkar then chose the DI and resigned his position with the Solo DDII.[65] It seems likely that Natsir's suspicions of Haji Ismail Pranoto might well have influenced his demand that Sungkar make this choice, and they seemed to be borne out a few months later, when Sungkar and Ba'asyir were arrested as a result of meetings they had had with Hispran.[66] On November 10, 1978 both were sentenced to four years in jail. As they were brought to trial, the court documents began to use the term *Jemaah Islamiyah* (Islamic Community) to describe the organization responsible, and it appears that the *Komando Jihad* provided the foundation for this shadowy and loosely knit association. At their trial, "the government made an explicit link between *Komando Jihad* and *Jemaah Islamiyah*." But, as the ICG researcher wrote:

> At the end of 1979, it remained unclear whether Jemaah Islamiyah was a construct of the government, a revival of Darul Islam, an amorphous gathering of like-minded Muslims, or a structured organisation led by Sungkar and Ba'asyir. To some extent it was all of the above, and the name seems to have meant different things to different people.[67]

Regime-Muslim Hostility

As the Suharto regime and the Muslim community became increasingly confrontative, President Suharto gave a speech to an Armed Forces Commanders' meeting in Pekanbaru in March 1980, hitting out against his political opponents. Listing "religion" along with "communism" as a discredited philosophy, the president seemed to be singling out the Muslim Partai Persatuan Pembangunan (PPP) for criticism. The president threatened to "make a total

---

[65] Ibid.

[66] Hispran, who had been a commander in the DI under Kartosuwirjo, was arrested himself in 1977 and the following September was charged with having tried to revive the Darul Islam organization. According to the ICG report "His lawyers tried unsuccessfully to have Ali Moertopo called as a witness." ICG Indonesia Briefing, August 8, 2002, p. 5.

[67] ICG Indonesia Briefing, August 8, 2002, p. 8. Part of the confusion regarding the organization stems from the imprecision of the name, Jemaah Islamiyah, i.e. Islamic Community. It was apparently considered by Sungkar and Ba'asyir as the name for a community they wished to found before being persuaded to join with the Darul Islam; it was used by the government in the trials of the *Komando Jihad* terrorists in the 1980s; and was the name of the organization founded by Sungkar on January 1, 1993, based on the ideology of Salafi Jihadism and the Egyptian organization of the same name. It was the 1993 Jemaah Islamiyah that was apparently responsible for much of the terrorist activity in Indonesia in subsequent years.

correction of deviations from Pancasila and the 1945 constitution," and called on the armed forces to "choose friends" among the political groups.[68]

Suharto's remarks angered not only Muslim groups, but also many former political leaders and members of the Armed Forces, who had believed earlier assurances "that ABRI would … stand above all groups." Some of these retired political and military leaders began to meet to discuss how they should react, and on May 13, they issued a document, which came to be known as the "Petition of Fifty (*Petisi Limapuluh*)." The petition expressed "the heartfelt disappointment" of the Indonesian people with Suharto's speeches, stating that the president had falsely interpreted *pancasila* and had thus used the state ideology "as a tool to attack his political enemies, whereas the founders of the Republic had intended it as a tool to unite the nation."[69] (This statement echoes the objections Natsir was voicing with regard to the introduction of the *pancasila* textbook into the educational system, outlined in the previous chapter.) Included among the signatories of the *Petisi 50* were Generals Nasution, Mokoginta, and Ali Sadikin, as well as former Masjumi leaders Natsir, Burhanuddin Harahap, and Sjafruddin Prawiranegara, together with other "elder statesmen." A delegation from the group, that included Muslims, Catholics, secular nationalists, retired officers and members of both the younger and older generations, met with various parliamentary factions to express their concern at the president's speeches. As spokesman for the delegation, Natsir stated that the president's words were not wise and could endanger national unity.[70]

Angered by this defiance, the government responded immediately. As Jenkins has written: "In the months that followed, the Suharto government was to display a truly Nixonian facility for victimizing its political 'enemies,' hounding them with a meanness of spirit that brought little credit to either the president or those who enforced his will."[71] In Natsir's case, reprisals were to continue for the rest of his life. As before, however, because of his stature and the respect he enjoyed both domestically and internationally, he was never imprisoned or brought to trial, as were some of his colleagues. He was banned from traveling abroad but, other than that, the harassment largely took the form of petty discrimination and exclusion from the type of esteem that his earlier positions in Indonesian political life had earned him.

---

[68] Jenkins, *Suharto and his Generals*, pp. 157–8, citing a transcript of the speech that appeared in *Kompas*, April 8, 1980.

[69] Ibid., p. 162.

[70] Ibid., p. 163.

[71] Ibid., p. 183. On Suharto's reaction to the criticism, see also Elson, *Suharto*, pp. 231–2.

Tensions between the government and its critics were further heightened as the Suharto regime moved to insert its version of the *pancasila* ever more deeply into society. In August 1982 the president declared that "all social-political forces, particularly the political parties, should accept the state ideology as their "*azas tunggal* [sole basis or principle]" and in March of the following year the general session of the People's Consultative Assembly (MPR) passed a resolution that the political parties should conform to this ruling.[72]

Protests against the measure came most strongly from Islamic leaders and associations, though the official Muslim party, the PPP, was the first political party to adhere to the ruling. (This fact only highlighted how far the government had succeeded in cowing party members and installing its loyalists into PPP leadership positions.) In Muslim society generally, however, especially in the mosques, opposition to the ruling was immediate and open. Members of the *Petisi 50* group joined in condemning the government's move.[73] Natsir, together with two other leading members of the group, Sanusi Hardjadinata and General A. H. Nasution, issued papers appealing to Parliament, as well as to other political, legal and religious leaders, not to allow the measures proposed by the president to be implemented. They all called on the government to remain true to the promises it made when first assuming power in 1966.[74] Protests continued for several months.

In Tanjung Priok, the port district of Jakarta, opposition to imposition of the *asas tunggal* sparked a series of small demonstrations and clashes with security forces, during which a non-Muslim soldier entered the local mosque without taking off his shoes and ordered the people to take down anti-government posters on the mosque's walls. The following day he returned and threatened them with a pistol. As Taufik Abdullah has written, the soldiers "had not only shown disregard for the people's feeling, but also, in the eyes of the already provoked Muslims, insulted the house of God."[75] In response to this perceived arrogance, riots broke out on September 12, 1984. As they subdued the protests soldiers and police shot into the crowds, killing dozens, or perhaps

---

[72] Ketetapan MPR No. II/1983 tentang GBHN [Garis-Garis Besar Haluan Negara] Bab IV.

[73] See, for example, the translation of Sjafruddin Prawiranegara's letter to President Suharto of July 7, 1983, protesting the proclamation, *Indonesia* 38 (October 1984): 74–83.

[74] See Moh. S. Hardjadinata, Mohammad Natsir, Jen.TNI (Pir) Dr. A.H. Nasution, *Selamatkan Demokrasi Berdasarkan jiwa Proklamasi dan UUD 1945* (n.p., 1984). Translations of these appeals appeared as M. Natsir, " Indonesia at the Crossroads" (July 25, 1984), Sanusi Hardjadinata, "Growth of Political Life under the New Order" (Bandung, July 4, 1984), and "Pledge by the 1966 'New Order' to Achieve Pure and Consistent Implementation of the National Constitution of 1945" (Jakarta, June 27, 1984) (typescript, in my possession).

[75] Taufik Abdullah, *Indonesia Towards Democracy* (Singapore: ISEAS, 2009), p. 455.

as many as a hundred of the demonstrators.[76] Possibly as a reaction to this brutal suppression, over the following weeks Jakarta was shaken by a series of bomb explosions.

The government quickly moved to crack down on the unrest. As van Bruinessen recounts, "Many suspects were arrested, and in … subsequent trials the authorities attempted to prove the existence of a subversive conspiracy, linking the radical preachers, the riots and the bombings to members of the 'Petition of Fifty' group," who had challenged the government's version of the incident.[77] Three of these critics were arrested and tried along with participants in the riots, and were sentenced to long prison terms. They included Lt. Gen. H.R. Dharsono, former Secretary General of ASEAN, who was accused of heading the alleged conspiracy and sentenced to eight years in jail. From then on members of the *Petisi 50* kept a lower profile, though they continued their meetings and "remained for most of the 1980s the major opposition group to the Soeharto regime."[78]

Violent Opposition to the Regime

This open opposition to the Suharto regime in the political sphere paralleled the militant stream within the Muslim community, the so-called *Komando Jihad*, that embraced more violent methods. During the 1980s further terrorist acts in Indonesia were tied to the network. The first was in January 1985, when a bomb destroyed some of the stupas at the Borobodur temple complex in Central Java and one of those arrested, Abdul Qadir Baraja, in addition to being an itinerant preacher, was a lecturer at the Ngruki *pesantren*.[79]

The second was a bloody shootout at a Muslim school in Way Jepara, Lampung, South Sumatra at the end of 1988 between the regional military command and students at a *pesantren* headed by a radical Muslim preacher. In the army's attack on their compound, many of the *pesantren* students were killed, 27 by the official account, but 200–300 according to local sources.[80]

---

[76] "Jakarta's 'Black September'?" *Impact International*, October 26–November 8, 1984.

[77] Martin van Bruinessen, "Islamic State or State Islam," *Indonesien am Ende des 20. Jahrhunderts*, ed. Ingrid Wessel (Hamburg: Abera-Verl., 1996), pp. 26–7.

[78] Ibid., p. 26.

[79] Ibid., p. 15.

[80] Ibid. See also ICG, "Al Qaeda," pp. 15–6 and Abdullah *Indonesia Towards Democracy*, p. 456, who dates the incident to February 7, 1989. Led by Warsidi the *pesantren* reportedly attracted students from Jakarta and DI members from Aceh and West Java. Col. A.M. Hendropriyono, as commander of the Korem 043 regional military battalion, led the attack on the compound.

As we have seen, the *Komando Jihad* network, based at least in part on the earlier Darul Islam movement, had spread through several regions of Sumatra and Java. It had clear ties with some activist members of the Dewan Da'wah, and its major leader, Abdullah Sungkar, was a follower and admirer of Natsir. He and his friend and colleague, Abu Bakar Ba'asyir, had been arrested and imprisoned in November 1978 because of their ties to the Darul Islam.[81] Four years later, in 1982, they received a sentence of nine years in jail.[82] During their interrogations the two had confessed to being inducted into the *Komando Jihad* by Haji Ismail Pranoto (Hispran), but at their trial claimed that the confession had been made under duress.[83] They appealed their sentences, which were reduced to time served, and both men were then released.

During their subsequent three years of freedom, the two men were active in establishing a "network of small cells devoted to the implementation of Islamic teaching,"[84] but, as Natsir had insisted that Sungkar resign from the Dewan Da'wah, it is uncertain whether these efforts were tied in any way to Natsir or the DDII. Clearly, however, Sungkar at least maintained communication with Natsir. In February 1985, the Indonesian Supreme Court ruled to overturn the reduction in Ba'asyir and Sungkar's jail sentences and issued a summons for their re-arrest. According to the account given by Solahudin in his *NII Sampai JI*, on hearing of the summons, Natsir sent a message to Sungkar warning him of the ruling and urging that he and his friends should flee (*hijrah*) abroad, preferably to Saudi Arabia. With Natsir's help the group escaped via Medan to Malaysia, where Natsir again helped arrange for them to find refuge in Kuala Lumpur.[85] Natsir then reportedly also aided them in traveling to Saudi Arabia. Solahudin writes:

> Their journey was much simplified because Muhammad [sic] Natsir had also lobbied the Saudi Arabian embassy in Malaysia to issue a visa for the

---

[81] Solahudin, *NII Sampai JI*, p. 148.

[82] Van Bruinessen notes that activists in the *Komando Jihad* movement, whom he interviewed in 1989, stated: "Sungkar and Ba'asyir were relative newcomers in the movement, whose role may have been exaggerated in the trials in order to incriminate the DDII." See van Bruinessen, "Genealogies of Islamic Radicalism," p. 129.

[83] See Temby, "Imagining an Islamic State in Indonesia," pp. 29–30, for an account of Sungkar's defense statement at their trial. As noted previously, Natsir apparently believed that Hispran was an Ali Moertopo plant.

[84] ICG Briefing, August 8, 2002, p. 10.

[85] Solahudin, *Dari NII Sampai JI*, pp. 199–200. According to this account, they met in Malaysia with an "important official" who had received a letter from Natsir about them, and who told them that the Malaysian prime minister (Mahathir Muhammad) was aware of their presence and would close his eyes to it. Ibid., p. 201.

two men. The embassy then gave them a visa gratis. Meanwhile an official who was a friend of Pak Natsir gave them money for their plane ticket and for their expenses while in Saudi Arabia…. Apart from going to Saudi Arabia, Sungkar and Baasyir also had another important mission to go to Afghanistan to meet mujahidin leaders there to explore the possibility of cooperation, by sending DI cadres in Indonesia to Afghanistan to get military training.[86]

After their visit to the Middle East Sungkar and Abu Bakar Ba'asyir returned to Malaysia, where they spent more than a decade building up their organization.[87] They now adopted a more internationalist approach in their opposition to the Suharto regime, sending recruits to train in Afghanistan and themselves traveling regularly to the Middle East.[88] According to the International Crisis Group's researcher, during these years the exiles in Malaysia also maintained strong links with the "Ngruki network" in Indonesia, which now extended from the original *pesantren* in Central Java to Jakarta, West Java, Sumatra and South Sulawesi. By 1987 "at least six Ngruki followers had left for Pakistan and Afghanistan, and more were to follow."[89] Within Indonesia, however, the ICG researcher notes, while the Ngruki network was adamantly opposed to the Suharto government, and most of its members were committed to the application of Islamic law in Indonesia, it "does not seem to have engaged in any serious discussion, let alone planning, for achieving specific political ends."[90]

The government's brutality against Muslims during the Tanjung Priok and other incidents as well as its imposition of the *pancasila* doctrine were major factors provoking violent reaction in the religious community. But a contributing factor persuading many devout Muslims that pursuit of a political or even a *da'wah* path could yield no favorable results was the government's determined effort to exclude Muslim parties from participation in Indonesia's political life. The government's treatment of Natsir was a prime example of its anti-Muslim policy, and Abdullah Sungkar openly condemned the ban on Natsir's political activity, urging his followers to boycott the 1977 elections, "because the only good Muslim candidates — the former Masyumi politicians Natsir and Roem — were not allowed to participate." This then was one of

---

[86] Ibid., p. 202.
[87] ICG, "Al-Qaeda in Southeast Asia," pp. 11–3.
[88] Temby, "Imagining an Islamic State," p. 31.
[89] ICG, "Al-Qaeda in Southeast Asia," p. 12.
[90] Ibid., p. 13.

the factors that initially pushed Sungkar from teaching and missionary work toward militancy.[91]

On a personal level Natsir remained close to Sungkar and other of his former students who joined or led the militant Islamic movements during the 1980s. Many of these young radicals continued to see him as their spiritual leader. It is, however, unclear as to what extent Natsir was aware of their more militant activities, as they seem to have diligently excluded him from knowledge of any violent actions they were planning. Reportedly when some of them were plotting to assassinate or kidnap Suharto and other members of his government, they asked their leader, Ir. Sanusi, whether such Muslim leaders as Mohammad Natsir had approved the plan. "Sanusi answered that clearly Pak Natsir would not agree to the plan. But if the plan succeeds Pak Natsir will smile and be happy. He added that if they were successful Pak Natsir would be included in the new government."[92]

For twenty years, Natsir had been the prime actor establishing links between institutions in the Middle East and Muslim students in Indonesia, sending many of his students and followers to receive their further education in Saudi Arabia and Egypt rather than in schools and universities in the West. And from there, the Indonesian students were more easily recruited to join mujahidin forces in their struggle against the Soviet Union in Afghanistan.[93] He thus had strengthened international influences on Muslim activists in Indonesia. But although Natsir was strongly opposed to the Soviet invasion of Afghanistan and deeply sympathized with the frustrations of the Muslim community in Palestine, both there and in Indonesia he favored non-violent ways for oppressed Muslims to pursue justice.

In encouraging his followers in their opposition to the policies of the Suharto regime, he never advocated violence, and consistently opposed the methods of the Darul Islam and other militant movements. As we saw earlier,

---

[91] Van Bruinessen, "Divergent Paths," p. 198. Temby, "Imagining an Islamic State in Indonesia," pp. 30–1. At his trial in 1982 Sungkar cited the ban against the participation of Natsir and others in Indonesian politics as the most worrying and disappointing policy of the New Order. He described Natsir as "an honest and simple politician [*politisi bersih dan sederhana*]" and his banning from participation in the political life of the New Order as "seriously disturbing and frustrating [*sungguh sangat meresahkan dan mengecewakan*]." Solahudin, *NII Sampai DI*, pp. 130–1.

[92] Solahudin, *NII Sampai DI*, p. 175, citing the transcript of the trial of Syahirul Alim, Jakarta, March 25, 1985.

[93] According to the ICG researcher, "The DDII-Rabithah link was also instrumental in providing funding for Indonesians who wanted to fight as Mujahidin in Afghanistan..." ICG Asia Report No. 83 (September 13, 2004), pp. 6–7.

he refused to allow Sungkar to remain a member of the Dewan Da'wah after he joined the Darul Islam. Another incident illustrative of Natsir's attitude occurred during the Tanjung Priok riots. At that time the novelist and author Ajip Rosidi was trying to persuade Sjafruddin Prawiranegara to write his memoir or publish a book of essays explaining his philosophical and religious ideas. According to Rosidi, Natsir intervened in their conversation to say:

> "But Pak Sjaf is urgently needed in the field.... For several days the atmosphere in Tanjung Priok has been seething. The *ummat* there can no longer tolerate the army's behavior, which is provoking their anger through actions that are clearly disparaging and even contemptuous of our religion, such as entering the mosque without taking off their shoes. They [i.e. the Muslims] want to fight back, to struggle. Only Pak Syaf can calm them. They wont listen to anyone else. But if they explode into action, it is we who will lose. How can we fight against a fully armed military"?[94]

From personal experience Natsir knew only too well the futility of militant opposition to a determined and well-armed political authority and he would never encourage his followers to pursue such a course.

Final Years

As noted above, in the years leading up to Natsir's death, the Suharto regime ostracized him in numerous ways, serious and petty. As with other members of the *Petisi 50* group he was forbidden from traveling abroad, so he could no longer perform the *haj* or attend international meetings.[95] Even on personal family occasions the government intervened. At the marriage ceremony for his nephew's daughter, Natsir gave the sermon and was subsequently forbidden by the government representative from attending the wedding reception, presumably because the official took umbrage at some of his remarks.[96] Excluded like all signatories from invitations to official functions, he and the other Masjumi leaders were singled out for further discriminatory measures. Noting the Indonesian custom of inviting former prime ministers to Independence Day celebrations, Jenkins wrote that Suharto was "so angered by the actions of the petition's signatories that he ordered aides to see to it that no further August 17 invitations be issued to Natsir, Burhanuddin Harahap,

---

[94] Ajip Rosidi, *Hidup Tanpa Ijazah: Yang Terekam dalam Kenangan* (Jakarta: Pustaka Jaya, 2008), p. 941.

[95] Jenkins notes that in 1981 he was banned from attending an International Commission of Jurists seminar in Kuwait. Jenkins, *Suharto and his Generals*, p. 184.

[96] Interview with the Natsir family, January 20, 2004.

or Sjafruddin Prawiranegara." In talking with Jenkins, Natsir again contrasted Suharto's behavior in this regard with that of Soekarno who had never barred Natsir from palace invitations, however bitter their disagreements had been. For Suharto, however, "We don't exist any more."[97]

Despite being cut from official guest lists, Natsir did continue to attend some ceremonies as an ordinary citizen, and to follow the courteous practice of visiting the Suharto family at the feast of Idul Fitri, at the end of the fasting month, but in general his presence was not acknowledged. Natsir's children recalled that at one reception when he was being thus ignored, Suharto's protégé B.J. Habibie, who was at the time Minister of Research and Technology, approached and embraced Natsir, expressing the admiration he had felt for the elder statesman ever since as a schoolboy, he had first seen him in Gorontalo.[98] It may well have been this incident that made Natsir more indulgent in turning a blind eye toward Habibie's lack of credentials for leading the Association of Indonesian Muslim Intellectuals (ICMI, Ikatan Cendekiawan Muslim Se-Indonesia) when it was formed in 1990, in contrast to some of his Muslim colleagues.[99]

And when two universities in Malaysia wanted to award Natsir honorary degrees, the Indonesian Embassy in Kuala Lumpur pressured them to withdraw the offer.[100] Even when Natsir became sick and authorities in both Tokyo and Ryadh invited him to come for treatment at Islamic clinics in Japan or Saudi Arabia, the government forbade it. His family recalled him making a joke of the situation, saying: "Maybe the government loves me so much they don't want to lose me."[101]

As his health began to fail, Natsir did not relax his efforts to influence Indonesian politics toward the ideals he had held since the struggle for independence. He was quick to see hope in the tentative effort toward greater

---

[97] Jenkins, *Suharto and his Generals*, pp. 184–5, citing an interview with Natsir, November 9, 1981.

[98] Interview with Natsir family, January 20, 2004. In 1998, after he succeeded Suharto as president, Habibie awarded Natsir the Adi Pradana medal posthumously.

[99] These critics included leaders from both the traditionalist NU, notably Abdurrachman Wahid, and from the modernist community, Deliar Noer, for example. On Wahid, see Hefner, *Civil Islam*, pp. 128, 169–70. Deliar Noer was very critical of Habibie heading the ICMI, saying that he could by no means be considered an Islamic leader, and that he was tied to corruption in that his brother was head of Batam and involved in corruption there, while Habibie did nothing about it. Interview, Jakarta, January 10, 2004.

[100] The universities were Universiti Kebangsaan and Universiti Sains Malaysia. See Noer, *Aku*, p. 901.

[101] Interview with Natsir's children, January 20, 2004.

freedom of speech launched by the Suharto regime in 1990 under the slogan of "*keterbukaan*" (openness). When Suharto himself in his independence day (August 17) speech called out for greater public discussion of differences of opinion, Natsir soon responded in an article, entitled "To Keep the Flame Burning" ("*Agar Pelita Tak Padam*"),[102] which appeared in September 1990, a little more than two years before he died. In this article, he welcomed Suharto's apparent change of heart in now inviting open public debate over contentious issues. However, Natsir was outspoken in laying out his criticisms of Indonesia's political order and his prescriptions for a return of democracy. He showed clearly how little he felt Indonesia's government represented its people:

Who can be chosen as a member of parliament? Not everyone can put themselves forward as candidates. Candidates have to be *screened* first by the government. In other words, they have to receive the government's blessing to be chosen, to become members....

Apart from that, once chosen, the government can augment the body with parliamentary members whom it appoints. So, the entire DPR is made up of representatives that have been *screened* by the government first, and then augmented by members that have been appointed by the government itself. If we look at it, according to the election regulations: the DPR consists of 500 members, 400 elected and 100 appointed. While the MPR has a membership of 1,000, 400 from the DPR and 600 appointed. So the MPR as the highest body — in theory even higher than the president — has 600 of its members appointed and 400 elected. That is the balance. We ask: is this representative of the people or representative of the government?[103]

Later in the article he gave evidence that he still looked to the West to provide an example of democracy in action, citing specifically the United States:

In the West ideas have been developed concerning democracy. In a democratic state there are three institutions: executive, judicial and legislative. But gradually in countries where democracy has proceeded well, there is a fourth institution that is not official but plays a role in the society. That is the mass media. If economic, political and other problems are discussed in the DPR [lower house of Parliament] and the government, the press has a large role. In Indonesia, we hope that the press can also grow as a shaper of

---

[102] Mohammad Natsir, "Agar Pelita tak Padam," *Editor* 2, 4 (September 22, 1990): 94–5.
[103] Ibid., p. 94. Emphasis in the original. He went on to welcome the fact that Minister Sudomo had said that courageous (*berani*) writings should not be banned, but criticized the provision that representatives could be recalled if they said something the government didn't like.

public opinion. If the press shapes public opinion, this will cause the DPR
to absorb it and the DPR will press this on the government. So *formation of
public opinion* rests in the hands of the mass media.

This means that, though the press is not an official institution, in reality
its influence is very strong. An example can be drawn from the Vietnam War.
It was the press that shaped public opinion before the government acted.
That is the strength of the press.[104]

He closed the article by referring to Alexander Solzhenitsyn, who continued
to write even though the people could not read what he wrote. When asked
why, in this situation he was still writing, Solzhenitsyn answered: "*To keep the
flame burning.*"

In his discussions with a journalist from *Editor* during the following
two years, Natsir was even more detailed in his prescriptions for returning
democracy to Indonesia, advocating that presidents should be limited to
two five-year terms, a proposal that he said should be discussed in the upper
house of Parliament, the Majelis Permusyawaratan Rakyat (MPR). Expressing
outrage that the MPR, as the highest legislative body in the land, met only
once every five years "and discusses nothing," he argued that the body should
be reconvened immediately and should play an active role in working out
constitutional changes to ensure that a president could serve no more than
two terms.[105]

As his life drew to an end, rather than becoming narrower in his view
of politics, he became even more outspoken in advocating a return to real
democracy and criticizing the authoritarianism and oppressiveness of the
governing regime in Indonesia. He seemed to fear that this repression was
leading to basic changes in the character of Indonesian society. As my husband,
George Kahin, noted, when he met with Natsir for the last time in January
1991:

> He was clearly keenly disappointed and saddened by the condition of his
> country. This was not only because he saw the Suharto government as
> showing a stiflingly repressive authoritarianism. ("Sukarno," he said, "was a
> gentleman in comparison to Suharto.") It was also because of his perception
> of the state of Indonesian society itself. For he saw most of its upper strata as

---

[104] Ibid., pp. 94–5. The words in italics appear in English.

[105] *Pemimpin Pulang*, pp. 243–4. He contrasted the current situation to that during the
Revolution, when Soekarno and Hatta were the transcendent leaders, and the politicians
"lacked time to ponder such matters of detail and principle." But he stressed that at the
time of the Independence Proclamation the Constitution was considered temporary and
provisional.

having become grossly materialistic, selfish, and shorn of social conscience; with this development being accompanied by a widening gap between rich and poor.[106]

The year before he died Natsir openly called on his followers to support the PPP, the one political party in Indonesia whose values he still did to some extent share, because of his fears that the country was becoming even more authoritarian. In 1992 he issued a "fatwa" that Indonesian Muslims should support the PPP, explaining in an interview his opinion that it was necessary to revive political awareness because, despite the hopeful signs two years earlier, politics in Indonesia were again inclining in the direction of a one-party system, a situation that could not be allowed.[107] He continued:

> Among the three parties, I am closer with PPP. Because of that, in the current election I decided to support PPP. This is on my own initiative; no one approached me. And I have made my choice known to the organizers of the DDII throughout Indonesia.[108]
>
> In the previous election, I indeed chose to be silent. But now I see there is some use [in speaking out]. There is more opportunity. I don't know whether this will succeed or not. But raising political awareness among the citizens [*warga masyarakat*] is indeed important. So that they do not fear participating in politics.[109]

He expressed his hope that in this way he could combat the sense of apathy within the society, especially among the young people. He challenged his readers to participate in political activity, by posing the question that, when students ask the meaning of politics "Should we just stand at the side of the road and watch others act"?

During the final decade of his life, Natsir's health became more precarious and he was frequently hospitalized. At the age of 80 he underwent surgery for an aortic aneurysm and it was at this time that he was invited to both Japan and Saudi Arabia for treatment, but the government forbade him to leave the country. He and his wife Ummi were able to make a final visit to West Sumatra in 1990 to inaugurate an Islamic Center in Padang. But he was too weak to travel to Solok to visit the town where he had received his early schooling and

---

[106] George McT. Kahin, "In Memoriam: Mohammad Natsir (1907–1993)" *Indonesia* 56 (October 1993): 165.

[107] *Pemimpin Pulang*, pp. 246–7.

[108] Many members of the DDII opposed this stand, as they had earlier argued against Natsir's participation in the *Petisi 50*.

[109] Ibid.

Natsir and Ummi, 1988.

had to be carried to the plane on a stretcher for his flight back to Jakarta. The following year Natsir had to enter hospital again for a prostate operation, but before the surgery could be carried out, Ummi collapsed at home and she too was brought to the hospital. She died two days later without the two being able to see each other again. Natsir, however, was able to attend his wife's funeral before returning to the hospital for his operation. Over the following months, his children recall that Natsir's health continued to decline and in October 1992 he had to return to the hospital, where his lungs failed and he was unable to speak for the last few weeks of his life, being able to communicate with his children only through scrawling remarks and questions on a piece of paper. His condition deteriorated rapidly and he died on February 6, 1993 at the age of 84.

Natsir (with from L, General A.H. Nasution, Hardi and K.H. Masykur) at his 80th birthday celebration, July 17, 1988.

Natsir and Ummi with Sultan Hamengkubuwono IX and his wife, 1988.

Natsir, with a representative of the Afghanistan mujahidin, June 1989.

Natsir at the inauguration of the Islamic Center in Padang, September 16, 1990.

Epilogue

Prior to his fall in 1998, Suharto refused to grant Natsir any recognition for his services to Indonesia in the Revolution and in the early years of independence when he served as prime minister and Masjumi party leader. But since the overthrow of the New Order Natsir's reputation has continued to grow within the country, and his contributions to Indonesian history have been acknowledged and honored. B.J. Habibie, during his short tenure as president, posthumously awarded Natsir the Adi Pradana medal in 1998, and President Susilo Bambang Yudhoyono finally named Natsir a National Hero (Pahlawan Nasional) ten years later, in December 2008, the centennial year of his birth. Seminars focusing on Natsir's life and thought have been held and memorial volumes celebrating the 100th anniversary of his birth appeared in both Indonesia and Malaysia.[1] Many of his earlier writings have been reissued.

More important, perhaps, than the legacy he left through his public achievements was the personal example he set for future politicians. His simple lifestyle and incorruptibility have been held up as a stark contrast to the indulgence and corruption that have characterized many of the most successful politicians under both Suharto and his successors. This was one of the aspects of Natsir's life most frequently recalled by those who knew him. Throughout his career he and his family lived in a small unpretentious house in central Jakarta, which was always open to anyone who wished to talk with him. Many friends recalled the lines of people from all walks of life waiting outside the house or sitting on the veranda, none of whom was ever turned away. The same was true when he was traveling in the jungle during the PRRI rebellion, as his companion, Dt. Tan Kabasaran recalled:

---

[1] *100 Tahun Mohammad Natsir: Berdamai dengan Sejarah* (Jakarta: Republika, 2008); Lukman Hakiem, ed., *M. Natsir di Panggung Sejarah Republik* (Jakarta: Republika, 2008); *Mohammad Natsir: Berdakwah di Jalur Politik Berpolitik di Jalur Dakwah* (Selangor: Wadah Pencerdasan Uma Malaysia/Lembaga Zakat Selangor, 2009).

He was a man who was at home with all levels of society; for example, when
he met with a peasant bringing vegetables to his home he would eat with
this man while talking in a low-key and friendly manner. Until the peasant,
however simple, was not afraid or ashamed to express his thoughts.[2]

Natsir saw to it that his family followed his example. His children still
remember the frugal lifestyle their parents insisted they follow in Jakarta.
Natsir himself would ride a bicycle to and from work when he was minister
of information and when he sat in Parliament; only during his few months as
prime minister did he travel in an official car. When his son wanted to buy a
motorbike Natsir would not allow it but told him to use public transport like
everyone else. Nor did he permit his children to accompany him on the *haj*,
believing they should work to accomplish the pilgrimage on their own. During
the years when their father held high political office none of the children was
known by the name Natsir and so received no special privileges. They only
started to "use the name with pride" after the PRRI rebellion when their father
was in jail and his party outlawed.[3]

Equally important was the example Natsir set of a devout Muslim leader,
who was at the same time a fervent believer in democracy and a sincere patriot.
As he sought to reconcile religion and democracy against the background of
a rapidly changing political scene, some of his stances seemed inconsistent, as
in the 1950s, when he was compelled to confront the electoral strength of the
Communist Party, whose atheism conflicted so glaringly with his own deep
religious faith. Natsir's fear of the influence the PKI was exerting over Soekarno
led to the contradictions evident in his speeches before the Constituent
Assembly in 1957, when he argued for Islam to replace the *pancasila* as the
state ideology, in large part because at that time he identified the *pancasila*
with "secularism." But on the whole during the 1940s and 1950s he accepted
its principles and recognized the need to operate within the field of practical
politics, seeking common ground, consistent with his own deeply held beliefs,
among contending political and religious forces.

Natsir's struggle to reconcile his religious and political beliefs has an echo in
the "Arab spring" that has engulfed the Middle East since early 2011, where in
several countries of the region members of the Muslim Brotherhood have been
among those fighting to replace autocratic rule with a representative political
order. They have faced some of the same basic questions as Natsir did fifty years
earlier. And they have put forward some of the same arguments. Natsir would

---

[2] Moch. Lukman Fatahullah Rais, *et al.*, *Mohammad Natsir Pemandu Ummat* (Jakarta: Bulan
Bintang, 1989), p. 130.
[3] Interview with Natsir's family, January 20, 2004.

surely have agreed with Essam El-Errian, a member of the guidance council of the Muslim Brotherhood in Egypt, who, in attempting to define the goals of the Brotherhood within the emerging political order, wrote:

> As our nation heads toward liberty, however, we disagree with the claims that the only options in Egypt are a purely secular, liberal democracy or an authoritarian theocracy. Secular liberal democracy of the American and European variety, with its firm rejection of religion in public life, is not the exclusive model for a legitimate democracy.
>
> In Egypt, religion continues to be an important part of our culture and heritage. Moving forward, we envision the establishment of a democratic, civil state that draws on universal measures of freedom and justice, which are central Islamic values. We embrace democracy not as a foreign concept that must be reconciled with tradition, but as a set of principles and objectives that are inherently compatible with and reinforce Islamic tenets.[4]

It is not yet clear whether Muslims in Egypt and other countries of the region will be more successful than Indonesian Muslims were in the 20th century in realizing their goals.

In the immediate aftermath of Suharto's fall from power, the rise of Islamic fundamentalism and the violence that shook Indonesia over the turn of the 21st century led several scholars to point to the Dewan Da'wah Islamiyah Indonesia (DDII), which Natsir founded and led for over twenty years, as a breeding ground for the intolerance that motivated several of the figures who headed the Jemaaah Islamiyah — the movement responsible for much of the terrorism that plagued Indonesia during those years. And Natsir's earlier efforts to bring the Darul Islam to compromise sufficiently to participate within Indonesia's political order and his defense of those in the Masjumi party who held to more extreme views than he did led some of his political opponents to insist that his aim was creation of an Islamic state. This viewpoint has frequently influenced Western scholars and led them to bracket Natsir with the fundamentalist stream operating within both the Masjumi and the Dewan Da'wah. Such scholars have portrayed Natsir's opposition to the Suharto regime as stemming from the "political mirage" of an Islamic state that led him, together with the fundamentalist stream of Muslims "away from the struggle to achieve a balanced relationship between state and society."[5] Natsir certainly did not see such a "balanced relationship" existing under the New Order. But by thus characterizing his stance, these Western scholars ignore the crux of Natsir's

---

[4] *New York Times*, February 10, 2011.
[5] Robert W. Hefner, *Civil Islam* (Princeton, NJ: Princeton University Press, 2000), p. 126.

criticisms of the Suharto regime, which focused on its autocratic and repressive nature and his desire for the return to a democratic form of government, not, as they imply, an Islamic theocracy. The state Natsir publicly espoused and envisaged was one that responded and was responsible to the various peoples making up the society it governed, whatever their religion or ethnicity.

In the immediate aftermath of Suharto's overthrow a number of the new political parties vied to proclaim themselves heirs to the former Masjumi,[6] but the party's legacy was too amorphous for it to have any real successor. Bernard Platzdasch has perceived this legacy as:

> a miscellany of values comprising *shari'ah*-implementation and devotion to *umat* affairs, including protecting Muslims from Christian missions, tolerance towards other religious communities, maintaining good relations with non-Muslim political parties, democracy, constitutionalism, anti-communism, anti-militarism, and high standards of integrity and morality.[7]

But although the post-Suharto political order offers no clear evidence of any direct legacy from Natsir and his Masjumi party, many elements in the Indonesian political scene in the early 21st century do accord with the goals they embraced. Out of the turbulent political scene over the turn of the century, Indonesia has emerged as a strong democracy with a decentralized political order where Islam provides the foundation of several of the largest political parties and continues to play an important role in the life of the country.

---

[6] These included the Partai Ummat Islam, Partai Masyumi Baru, Partai Politik Islam Indonesia Masyumi and Partai Bulan Bintang.

[7] Bernhard Platzdasch, *Islamism in Indonesia: Politics in the Emerging Democracy* (Singapore: ISEAS, 2009), p. 71.

Bibliography

Works by Mohammad Natsir

Capita Selecta [I] (Bandung, The Hague: Van Hoeve, 1954).

Capita Selecta II (Jakarta: Pustaka Pendis [1957]; PT Abadi, 2008).

Capita Selecta III (typescript [1961]; Jakarta: PT Abadi, 2008).

Natsir, Mohammad [Is]. 1931. "Koerang tegas jang meragoekan," *Pembela Islam* No. 35, October 1931, pp. 2–7.

__________. 1932. "Kebangsaan Moeslimin, 1–5," *Pembela Islam*, Nos. 41–5, January–April 1932.

Natsir, Mohammad. 1936. "Islam dan Kebudajaan, June 1936," in *Capita Selecta* [I]. Bandung, The Hague: Van Hoeve, [1954], pp. 3–9.

__________ [A. Moechlis]. 1940. "Persatoean Agama dengan Negara, [The Union of Religion and the State]," I–IX in *Pandji Islam* Nos. 27–37, July 8–September 16, 1940.

__________. 1951. "Salah paham dan ragu2 tentang pembentukan Prop. Sumatera Utara tidak ada lagi," in *Suara Penerangan* 5, 2 (January 20, 1951).

__________. 1954a. "Sikap 'Islam' terhadap 'Kemerdekaan-Berfikir'," in *Capita Selecta* [I]. Bandung, The Hague: Van Hoeve, pp. 206–29.

__________. 1954b. "Some Observations concerning the Role of Islam in National and International Affairs." Ithaca: SEAP Data Paper, no. 16.

__________. 1956. "Kemampuan Mengendalikan diri sjarat mutlak bagi Kemerdekaan," November 7, 1956. In *Capita Selecta III*. Typescript dated 15 April 1960, p. 8.

__________. 1957a. "Reaksi pertama terhadap 'Konsepsi Presiden'," February 19, 1957. In *Capita Selecta III*, pp. 25–7.

__________. 1957b. "Itu bukan obat tetapi penjakit baru," February 28, 1957. In *Capita Selecta III*, pp. 28–9.

Kumpulan Surat-Surat Pribadi. 1958. Typescript, July–September 1958.

M. Natsir. 1968. *Mempersatukan Ummat*. Bandung: Bulan Sabit.

__________. 1969. *Islam dan Kristen di Indonesia*. Bandung: Peladjar dan Bulan Sabit.

__________. [1970a]. *Beberapa Aspek dari Ajaran Islam Berkenaan dengan Pembangunan*. [Jakarta]: Institut Pendidikan Pekerdjaan Umum dan Tenaga Listrik.

__________. 1970b. *Hidupkan Kembali Idealisme dan Semangat Pengorbanan*. Jakarta: Bulan Bintang.

__________. 1971. *Dibawah Naungan Risalah*. Jakarta: Sinar Hudaya & Documenta.

__________. 1974, 1975. *Dari Masa ke Masa, 1, 2, 3*. Jakarta: Fajar Shadiq.

__________. 1976. Talk to Diplomatic Club Lunch, Jakarta, October 26, 1976 (typescript).

__________. 1978. "Insya Allah: Roem tetap Roem," in *Mohamad Roem 70 Tahun: Pejuang Perunding*. Jakarta: Bulan Bintang.

__________. 1982. *Dunia Islam dari Masa ke Masa*. Jakarta: Panji Masyarakat.

Asas Keyakinan Agama Kami [1984]. Jakarta: DDII.

Indonesia at the Crossroads. 1984a. Jakarta: typescript.

"*Asas Keyakinan Agama Kami....*" [1984b]. Jakarta: Dewan Dakwah Islamiyah Indonesia.

Muhammad Natsir. 1998. "The Indonesian Revolution" [1955], in *Liberal Islam: a Source Book*, ed. Charles Kurzman. New York: Oxford University Press, p. 65.

M. Natsir. 2000. *Islam sebagai Dasar Negara* (foreword by Deliar Noer). Jakarta: Abadi.

__________. 2001. *Agama dan Negara dalam Perspektif Islam*. Jakarta: Media Da'wah.

__________. 2008. "Politik melalui Jalur Dakwah," based on interview with Agus Basri, appearing in *Tempo*, December 2, 1989. Republished as *Politik Melalui Jalur Dakwah*. Jakarta: Media Da'wah.

General Bibliography

Abdul, Mohd. Asri, *et al.*, eds. 2009. *Mohammad Natsir, Berdakwah di Jalur Politik Berpolitik di Jalur Dakwah*. Selangor: Lembaga Zakat Selangor.

Abdullah, Taufik. 1971. *Schools and Politics: The Kaum Muda Movement in West Sumatra (1927–1933)*. Ithaca: Cornell Modern Indonesia Project.

__________. 2001. "Natsir, Seorang Guru yang Perfeksionis Filosofis," in *Pemikiran dan Perjuangan Mohammad Natsir*, ed. Anwar Haryono, *et al.* Jakarta: Firdaus.

__________. 2009. *Indonesia: Toward Democracy*. Singapore: ISEAS.

Abidin, H. Mas'oed. 2001. *Taushiyah Dr. Mohamad Natsir: Pesan Dakwah Pemandu Umat*. Unpublished manuscript.

Alamsjah, St. Rais. 1952. *10 Orang Indonesia terbesar Sekarang*. Bukittinggi & Jakarta: Mutiara.

Alfian, 1989. *Muhammadiyah: The Political Behavior of a Muslim Modernist Organization under Dutch Colonialism*. Yogyakarta: Gadjah Mada University Press.

Anderson, Benedict R. O'G. 1972. *Java in a Time of Revolution*. Ithaca: Cornell University Press.

Aziz, M.A. 1955. *Japan's Colonialism and Indonesia*. The Hague: Martinus Nijhoff.

Barton, Greg and Greg Fealy, eds. 1996. *Nahdlatul Ulama, Traditional Islam and Modernity in Indonesia*. Clayton, Vic.: Monash Asia Institute.

Bastoni, Hepi Andi, dkk. 2008. *M. Natsir Sang Maestro Dakwah*. Jakarta: Mujtama Press.

Benda, Harry J. 1958. *The Crescent and the Rising Sun: Indonesian Islam under the Japanese Occupation 1942–1945*. The Hague and Bandung: Van Heuve.

Benda, Harry J. and Ruth T. McVey, eds. 1960. *The Communist Uprisings of 1926–1927 in Indonesia: Key Documents*. Ithaca: Cornell Modern Indonesia Project.

Boland, B.J. 1971. *The Struggle of Islam in Modern Indonesia*. The Hague: Martinus Nijhoff.

Boroumand, Ladan and Roya Boroumand. 2003. "Terror, Islam, and Democracy," in *Islam and Democracy in the Middle East*, ed. Larry Diamond, Marc F. Plattner, and Daniel Brumberg. Baltimore: John Hopkins University Press.

Brackman, Arnold C. 1963. *Indonesian Communism: A History*. New York: Praeger.

Burns, Peter. 1981. *Revelation and Revolution: Natsir and the Panca Sila* 1981. Townsville: Southeast Asian Monograph Series no. 9, James Cook University of North Queensland.

Cammack, Mark. 1997. "Indonesia's 1989 Religious Judicature Act: Islamization of Indonesia or Indonesianization of Islam?" *Indonesia* 63 (April 1997): 143–68.

Chauvel, Richard. 1985. "Ambon: not a revolution but a counterrevolution," in *Regional Dynamics of the Indonesian Revolution*, ed. Audrey Kahin. Honolulu: University of Hawaii Press, pp. 237–64.

Coast, John. 1952. *Recruit to Revolution*. London: Christophers.

Crouch, Harold. 1988. *The Army and Politics in Indonesia*, rev. ed. Ithaca: Cornell University Press.

Dahm, Bernhard. 1969. *Sukarno and the Struggle for Indonesian Independence*. Ithaca: Cornell University Press.

__________. 1971. *History of Indonesia in the Twentieth Century*. NewYork: Praeger.

Danandjaja, Utomo, ed. 1970. *Pembaharuan Pemikiran Islam*. Jakarta: Islamic Research Centre.

Dengel, Holk H. 1995. *Darul Islam-NII dan Kartosuwirjo: Langkah Perwujudan Angan-Angan yang Gagal*. Jakarta: Pustaka Sinar Harapan.

Dewan Da'wah Islamiyah Indonesia, n.d. *Shibghah Da'wah: Warna, Strategi & Aktivitas Da'wah*. Jakarta: Media Da'wah.

Dhume, Sadanand. 2005. "Radicals March on Indonesia's Future," *Far Eastern Economic Review* 168, 5 (May 2005): 11–26.

Djaja, Tamar. 1980. *Riwayat Hidup A. Hassan*. Jakarta: Mutiara.

Diamond, Larry, Marc F. Plattner and Daniel Brumberg, eds. 2003. *Islam and Democracy in the Middle East*. Baltimore: Johns Hopkins University Press.

Diederich, Mathias. 2002. "A Closer Look at *Dakwah* and Politics in Indonesia: The Partai Keadilan," *Archipel* 64: 101–15.

Dobbin, Christine. 1983. *Islamic Revivalism in a Changing Peasant Economy: Central Sumatra, 1784–1847*. London and Malmo: Curzon Press.

Effendi, Bahtiar. 2003. *Islam and the State in Indonesia*. Singapore: ISEAS.

Elson, R.E. 2001. *Suharto: A Political Biography*. Cambridge: Cambridge University Press.

__________. 2008. *The Idea of Indonesia: A History*. Cambridge: Cambridge University Press.

__________. 2009. "Another Look at the Jakarta Charter Controversy of 1945," *Indonesia* 88 (October 2009): 105–30.

Esposito, John L. and John O. Voll. 1996. *Islam and Democracy*. New York: OUP.

Fealy, Greg. 1996. "Wahab Chasbullah, Traditionalism and the Political Development of Nahdlatul Ulama," in *Nahdlatul Ulama, Traditional Islam and Modernity in Indonesia*, ed. Greg Barton and Greg Fealy. Clayton, Vic.: Monash Asia Institute, pp. 1–41.

Fealy, Greg and Virginia Hooker, eds. 2006. *Voices of Islam in Southeast Asia: A Contemporary Sourcebook*. Singapore: ISEAS.

Federspiel, Howard M. 1970. *Persatuan Islam: Islamic Reform in Twentieth Century Indonesia*. Ithaca: CMIP.

Feith, Herbert. 1962. *The Decline of Constitutional Democracy in Indonesia*. Ithaca: Cornell University Press.

Feith, Herbert and Daniel S. Lev. 1963. "The End of the Indonesian Rebellion," *Pacific Affairs* 36, 1 (Spring): 32–46.

Feith, Herbert and Lance Castles, eds. 1970. *Indonesian Political Thinking, 1945–1965*. Ithaca: Cornell University Press.

Finch, Susan and Daniel S. Lev. 1965. *Republic of Indonesia Cabinets 1945–1965*. Ithaca: Cornell Modern Indonesia Project.

Formichi, Chiara. 2010. "Pan-Islam and Religious Nationalism: The Case of Kartosuwiryo and Negara Islam Indonesia," *Indonesia* 90 (October 2010): 125–46

Furkon, Aay Muhamad. 2004. *Partai Keadilan Sejahtera Ideologi Praksis Polititik Kaum Muda Muslim Indonesia Kontemporer*. Jakarta: Teraju Publishers.

Gibb, H.A.R. 1947. *Modern Trends in Islam*. Chicago: University of Chicago Press.

Gibb, H.A.R. and J.H Kramers. 1953. *Shorter Encyclopaedia of Islam*. Ithaca: Cornell University Press.

Gunawan, Hendra. 2000. *M. Natsir & Darul Islam*. Jakarta: Media Da'wah.

Hakiem, Lukman. 1992. *70 tahun H. Buchari Tamam: Menjawab Panggilan Risalah*. Jakarta: Media Da'wah.

Hakiem, Lukman, ed. 1993. *Pemimpin Pulang: Rekaman Peristiwa Wafatnya M. Natsir*. Jakarta: Yayasan Piranti Ilmu.

Hamka. 1967. *Ajahku*, 3rd printing. Jakarta: Penerbit Djajamurni.

__________. 1978. "Persahabatan 47 Tahun," in *Muhammad Natsir 70 tahun: Kenang-kenangan Kehidupan dan Perjuangan*. Jakarta: Pustaka Antara.

Harjono, Anwar, dkk. 1995. *M. Natsir: Sumbangan dan Pemikiran untuk Indonesia*. Jakarta: Media Da'wah.

__________, et al. 2001. *Pemikiran dan Perjuangan Mohammad Natsir*. Jakarta: Pustaka Firdaus.

Harvey, Barbara. 1974. "Tradition, Islam and Rebellion: South Sulawesi, 1950–1965," PhD dissertation, Cornell University.

__________. 1977. *Permesta: Half a Rebellion*. Ithaca: Cornell Modern Indonesia Project.

Hassan, Muhammad Kamal. 1980. *Muslim Intellectual Responses to "New Order" Modernization in Indonesia*. Kuala Lumpur: Dewan Bahasa dan Pustaka.

__________. 1987. "The Response of Muslim Youth Organizations to Political Change: HMI in Indonesia and ABIM in Malaysia," in *Islam and the Political Economy of Meaning*, ed. William R. Roff. Berkeley: University of California Press.

Hatta, Mohammad. 1970. *Sekitar Proklamasi*. Jakarta: Tintamas.

Hefner, Robert W. 2000. *Civil Islam: Muslims and Democratization in Indonesia*. Princeton: Princeton University Press.

Hindley, Donald. 1964. *The Communist Party of Indonesia 1951–1963*. Berkeley: University of California Press.

Hosen, Nadirsyah. 2007. *Shari'a & Constitutional Reform in Indonesia*. Singapore: ISEAS.

International Crisis Group. 2002. ICG Indonesia Briefing, *Al-Qaeda in Southeast Asia: The Case of the "Ngruki Network" in Indonesia*, August 8.

________. 2003. ICG Asia Report No. 63, *Jemaah Islamiyah in South East Asia: Damaged but Still Dangerous*, August 26.

________. 2004. ICG Asia Report No. 83 "What is Salafism?" September 13.

Ingleson, John. 1979. *Road to Exile: The Indonesian Nationalist Movement 1927–1934*. Singapore: Heinemann.

Jackson, Karl D. and Lucian W. Pye. 1978. *Political Power and Communications in Indonesia*. Berkeley: University of California Press.

Jenkins, David. 1984. *Suharto and His Generals: Indonesian Military Politics 1975–1983*. Ithaca: Cornell Modern Indonesia Project.

________. 2009. "Soeharto and the Japanese Occupation," *Indonesia* 88 (October): 1–103.

Jones, Sidney. 2005. "The Changing Nature of Jemaah Islamiyah," *Australian Journal of International Affairs* 59, 2 (June): 169–78.

Kahin, Audrey R., ed. 1985. *Regional Dynamics of the Indonesian Revolution*. Honolulu: University of Hawaii Press.

Kahin, Audrey. 1999. *Rebellion to Integration: West Sumatra and the Indonesian Polity*. Amsterdam: Amsterdam University Press.

Kahin, Audrey R. and George McT. 1995. *Subversion as Foreign Policy: The Secret Eisenhower and Dulles Debacle in Indonesia*. New York: New Press.

Kahin, George McT. 1951. *Nationalism and Revolution in Indonesia*. Ithaca: Cornell University Press.

________. 1953. "Indonesian Politics and Nationalism," in *Asian Nationalism and the West*, ed. William L. Holland. New York: Macmillan, pp. 65–196.

________. 1956, *The Asian-African Conference, Bandung, Indonesia*. Ithaca: Cornell University Press.

________. 1993. "In Memoriam: Mohammad Natsir, 1907–1993," *Indonesia* 56 (October 1993): 158–65.

Kanahele, George. 1967. "The Japanese Occupation of Indonesia: Prelude to Independence," PhD. Dissertation, Cornell University.

Karim, Shofwan. n.d. *Bio-intelektual dan Perjuangan Mohammad Natsir*, pts. 1–IV. Padang: Singgalang.

Kelsay, John. 2007. *Arguing the Just War in Islam*. Cambridge: Harvard University Press.

Kementerian Penerangan. n.d. [1951?]. *Kami Perkenalkan…!* Jakarta, Kementerian Penerangan Rep. Indonesia.

Kepel, Gilles. 2002. *Jihad: The Trail of Political Islam*, tr. Anthony F. Roberts. Cambridge, MA: Harvard University Press.

Laffan, Michael Francis. 2003. *Islamic Nationhood and Colonial Indonesia: The* umma *below the winds*. London/New York: RoutledgeCurzon.

Laffan, Michael. 2004. "An Indonesian Community in Cairo: Continuity and Change in a Cosmopolitan Islamic Milieu," *Indonesia* 77 (April): 1–26.

__________. 2007. "'Another Andalusia': Images of Colonial Southeast Asia in Arabic Newspapers," *JAS* 66, 3 (August): 689–722.

Legge, J.D. 2003. *Sukarno: A Political Biography* [1972]. Singapore: Archipelago Press, 2003.

Liddle, R. William. 1996. "*Media Dakwah* Scripturalism: One Form of Islamic Political Thought and Action in New Order Indonesia," in *Toward a New Paradigm: Recent Developments in Indonesian Islamic Thought*, ed. Mark R. Woodward. Tempe AZ: Arizona State University, pp. 323–56.

Magenda, Burhan Djabir. 2008. "*Peranan Bapak M. Natsir sebagai Politisi dan Negarawan.*" Typescript prepared for Seminar Nasional Satu Abad M. Natsir, Jakarta, July 15, 2008.

Mahendra, Yusril Ihza. 2001. "Mohammad Natsir dan Sayyid Abul A'la Maududi," in *Pemikiran dan Perjuangan Mohammad Natsir*, ed. Anwar Harjono *et al.* Jakarta: Firdaus, pp. 98–113.

Malim, Drs., H. Misbach. 2008. *Shibghah Da'wah: Warna, Strategi & Aktivitas Da'wah*. Jakarta: Media Da'wah.

McDonald, Hamish. 1980. *Suharto's Indonesia*. Victoria, Australia: Fontana/Collins.

McVey, Ruth T. 1983. "Faith as the Outsider: Islam in Indonesian Politics," in *Islam in the Political Process*, ed. James P. Piscatori. London: Cambridge University Press, pp. 199–225.

Mohamad Roem 70 Tahun, Pejuang-Perunding, 1978. Jakarta: Bulan Bintang.

Morris, Eric. 1985. "Aceh: Social Revolution and the Islamic Vision," in *Regional Dynamics*, ed. A. Kahin, pp. 83–110.

Mossman, James. 1961. *Rebels in Paradise: Indonesia's Civil War*. London: Cape.

Mrazek, Rudolf. 1994. *Sjahrir: Politics and Exile in Indonesia*. Ithaca: Cornell Southeast Asia Program.

Mughni, Syafiq A. 1994. *Hassan Bandung: Pemikir Islam Radikal*. Surabaya: PT Bina Ilmu, 1994.

Nakamura, Mitsuo. 1976. "The Crescent Arises over the Banyan Tree: A Study of the Muhammadijah Movement in a Central Javanese Town," PhD dissertation, Cornell University.

Nasution, Adnan Buyung. 1992. *The Aspiration for Constitutional Government in Indonesia*. Jakarta: Pustaka Sinar Harapan.

Nishihara, Masashi. 1975. *The Japanese and Sukarno's Indonesia*. Honolulu: East West Center.

Noer, Deliar. 1973. *The Modernist Muslim Movement in Indonesia 1900–1942*. Singapore: Oxford University Press.

__________. 1987. *Partai Islam di Pentas Nasional 1945–1965*. Jakarta: Grafiti.

__________. 1990. *Mohammad Hatta: Biografi Politik*. Jakarta: LP3ES.

__________. 1991. "Kedudukan Natsir Masa Kini," *Panji Masyarakat*, August 1–10, pp. 25–9.

________. 1993. "The Confrontational Natsir? A Commemorative Essay." Jakarta: typescript, February 15.

________. 1996. *Aku Bagian Ummat Aku Bagian Bangsa: Otobiografi*. Bandung: Penerbit Mizan.

Noorhaidi. 2005. "Laskar Jihad: Islam, Militancy and the Quest for Identity in Post–New Order Indonesia," PhD. Dissertation, University of Utrecht.

Pembela Islam. 1931. No. 36, October, cited in "Persatuan Islam" (typescript, n.d.), p. 48.

________. 1931–32. Nos. 35, 37, 39–47. October 1931–June 1932.

Piscatori, James P. 1983. *Islam in the Political Process*. London: Cambridge University Press.

Platzdasch, Bernhard. 2009. *Islamism in Indonesia: Politics in the Emerging Democracy*. Singapore: ISEAS.

Pringle, Robert. 2010. *Understanding Islam in Indonesia: Politics and Diversity*. Honolulu: University of Hawaii.

Puar, Yusuf Abdullah, ed. 1978. *Muhammad Natsir: 70 tahun Kenang-kenangan Kehidupan dan Perjuangan*. Jakarta: Pustaka Antara.

Purwoko, Dwi. 2001. "Islam, Nasionalisme dan Negara: Percikan Pemikiran M. Natsir," in *Negara Islam*, ed. Dwi Purwoko, *et al*. Depok: Permata Artistika Kreasi.

H. Rahmah el Yunusiyyah dan Zainuddin Labay el Yunusy: Dua Bersaudara Tokoh Pembaharu Sistem Pendidikan di Indonesia. Jakarta: Pengurus Perguruan Diniyyah Puteri Padang Panjang, 1991.

Raja Juli Antoni, ed. 2008. *Aba: M. Natsir sebagai Cahaya Keluarga*. Jakarta: Yayasan Capita Selecta.

Rais, Moch. Lukman Fatahullah, *et al*. 1989. *Mohammad Natsir Pemandu Ummat: Pesan dan Kesan Tasyakkur 80 Tahun Mohammad Natsir*. Jakarta: Bulan Bintang.

Rasyidi. 1972. *Koreksi terhadap Dr. Nurcholis Madjid tentang Sekularisasi*. Jakarta: Bulan Bintang.

Roem, Mohamad. 1959. "The P.R.R.I. Rebellion and its Background: I–IV." Typescript, January–February.

________. 1977. *Bunga Rampai dari Sejarah II*. Jakarta: Bulan Bintang.

________. 1983. *Bunga Rampai dari Sejarah 3*. Jakarta: Djaya Pirusa.

________. 1988. *Bunga Rampai dari Sejarah Buku Keempat*. Jakarta: Bulan Bintang.

Roff, William. 1967. *The Origins of Malay Nationalism*. New Haven: Yale University Press.

Rose, Mavis. 1987. *Indonesia Free: A Political Biography of Mohammad Hatta*. Ithaca: Cornell Modern Indonesia Project.

Rosidi, Ajip. 1986. *Sjafruddin Prawiranegara: Lebih Takut kepada Allah SWT*. Jakarta: Inti Idayu Press.

________. 1990. *M. Natsir: Sebuah Biografi 1*. Jakarta: PTGirimukti Pasaka.

________. 2008. *Hidup Tanpa Ijazah: Yang Terekam dalam Kenangan*. Jakarta: Pustaka Jaya.

Salim, Leon. 1966. *Bung Sjahrir: Pahlawan Nasional*. Medan: Masadepan.

Samson, Allan. 1968. "Islam in Indonesian Politics," *Asian Survey* 8, 13 (December).

Samson, Allan A. 1971–72. "Army and Islam in Indonesia," *Pacific Affairs* 44, 4 (Winter): 545–65.

__________. 1973. "Religious Belief and Political Action in Indonesian Islamic Modernism," in *Political Participation in Modern Indonesia*, ed. R. William Liddle. New Haven, CT: Yale University Southeast Asia Studies, pp. 116–42.

__________. 1974. *Concepts of Politics, Power, and Ideology in Contemporary Indonesian Islam*. Cambridge, MA. MIT Center for International Studies.

__________. 1978. "Conceptions of Politics, Power, and Ideology in Contemporary Indonesian Islam," in *Political Power and Communications in Indonesia*, ed. Karl D. Jackson and Lucian W. Pye. Berkeley: University of California Press, pp. 198–226.

Schwarz, Adam. 1994. *A Nation in Waiting: Indonesia in the 1990s*. Boulder: Westview Press.

Shiraishi, Takashi. 1990. *An Age in Motion: Popular Radicalism in Java, 1912–1926*. Ithaca: Cornell University Press.

Sidel, John T. 2006. *Riots, Pogroms, Jihad: Religious Violence in Indonesia*. Ithaca: Cornell University Press.

Solahudin. 2011. *NII Sampai JI: Salafy Jihadisme di Indonesia*. Jakarta: Komunitas Bambu.

Sukarno. 1959. *Dibawah Bendera Revolusi*. Jakarta: Panitiya Penerbit Dibawah Bendera Revolusi.

Soekarno. 1969. *Nationalism, Islam and Marxism*. Trans. Karel H. Warouw and Peter D. Weldon, with an introduction by Ruth T. McVey. Ithaca: Cornell University Modern Indonesia Project.

Suhelmi, Ahmad. 2002. *Polemik Negara Islam: Soekarno versus Natsir*. Jakarta: Teraju.

Sundhaussen, Ulf. 1982. *The Road to Power: Indonesian Military Politics 1945–1967*. Kuala Lumpur: Oxford University Press.

Surjo Sediono, C.K.H.R. 1958. *Peristiwa Tjikini*. Jakarta: Soeroengan.

Syah, Djalinus. 2002. *Mohammad Natsir dalam Kenangan*. n.p: Aulia Foundation.

Taylor, Alistair M. 1960. *Indonesian Independence and the United Nations*. Ithaca: Cornell University Press.

Temby, Quinton. 2010. "Imagining an Islamic State in Indonesia: From Darul Islam to Jemaah Islamiyah," *Indonesia* 89 (April 2010): 1–36.

Tentang Dasar Negara Republik Indonesia dalam Konstituante, 3 vols. Jakarta: Percetakan Negara, n.d.

Tjiptoning. 1951. *Apa dan Siapa*. Jogjakarta: Kedaulatan Rakjat, pp. 33–41.

Van Bruinessen, Martin. 1996. "Islamic State or State Islam," in *Indonesien am Ende des 20. Jahrhunderts*, ed. Ingrid Wessel. Hamburg: Abera-Verl., pp. 19–34.

__________. 2002. "Genealogies of Islamic Radicalism in post–Suharto Indonesia," *South East Asia Research* 10, 2 (July): 117–54.

__________. 2006. "Divergent paths from Gontor: Muslim educational reform and the travails of pluralism in Indonesia," in *On the Edge of many worlds*, ed. Freek L. Bakker & Jan Sihar Aritonang [Festschrift Karel A. Steenbrink], Zoetermeer: Uitgeverij Meinema, pp. 152–62.

_________. 2009. "Modernism and anti-modernism in Indonesian Muslim responses to globalization." Paper presented at the Workshop "Islam and Development in Southeast Asia: Southeast Asian Muslim Responses to Globalization", organized by JICA (Japan International Cooperation Agency) Research Institute, Singapore, November 21–22.

Van Dijk, C. 1981. *Rebellion under the Banner of Islam: The Darul Islam in Indonesia.* The Hague: Martinus Nijhoff.

Van Nieuwenhuijze, C.A.O. 1950. "The Dar Ul-Islam Movement in Western Java, *Pacific Affairs* 23, 2 (June): 169–83.

Ward, K.E. 1970. *The Foundation of the Partai Muslimin Indonesia.* Ithaca: Cornell Modern Indonesia Project.

Ward, Ken. 1974. *The 1971 Election in Indonesia: An East Java Case Study.* Monash, Vic.: Monash Papers on Southeast Asia No 2.

Weinstein, Franklin B. 1976. *Indonesian Foreign Policy and the Dilemma of Dependence.* Ithaca: Cornell University Press.

Westerling, Raymond "Turk." 1952. *Challenge to Terror.* London: William Kimber.

Wright, Lawrence. 2006. *The Looming Tower.* New York: Knopf.

Yamin, Muhammad. 1959. *Naskah-Persiapan Undang-Undang Dasar 1945* Jilid Pertama. Jakarta: Jajasan Prapantja.

Young, Ken. 1994. *Islamic Peasants and the State: The 1908 Anti-tax Rebellion in West Sumatra.* New Haven: Yale Southeast Asia Studies.

Zakaria, Gamal Abdul Nasir. 2003. *Mohammad Natsir: Pendidik Ummah.* Bangi: UKM.

Index

Printed and bound by CPI Group (UK) Ltd, Croydon, CR0 4YY

07/07/2026

14916229-0002